John Adair

Also by Peter Case

THE SPEED OF ORGANIZATION (*with S. Lilley and T. Owens, editors*)

Also by Jonathan Gosling

NELSON'S WAY: Leadership Lessons from the Great Commander (*with S. Jones*)

Also by Morgen Witzel

ROBBER BARONS AND MUCK RAKERS: The Birth of American Corporate Culture

BUSINESS IN SOUTH-EAST ASIA (*with Ian Rae*)

THE TEUTONIC KNIGHTS

ENCYCLOPEDIA OF THE HISTORY OF AMERICAN MANAGEMENT

SINGULAR AND DIFFERENT: Business in China Past, Present and Future (*with Ian Rae*)

MANAGEMENT: The Basics

THE ROAD TO CRÉCY: The English Invasion of France, 1346 (*with Marilyn Livingstone*)

MANAGING IN VIRTUAL ORGANISATIONS (*with Malcolm Warner*)

DOING BUSINESS IN CHINA

FIFTY KEY FIGURES IN MANAGEMENT

THE CORPORATE GOVERNANCE DEBATE, 1878–1914 (*editor*)

THE EMERGENCE OF BUSINESS ETHICS (*editor*)

THE DEVELOPMENT OF MODERN ADVERTISING (*editor*)

BIOGRAPHICAL DICTIONARY OF MANAGEMENT (*editor*)

BUILDERS AND DREAMERS: The Making and Meaning of Management

ORGANIZATION BEHAVIOUR (*editor*)

FINANCIAL MANAGEMENT (*editor*)

HOW TO GET AN MBA

HUMAN RESOURCE MANAGEMENT (*editor*)

KEY TEXTS IN MARKETING (*editor*)

DICTIONARY OF BUSINESS AND MANAGEMENT (*editor*)

John Adair

Fundamentals of Leadership

Edited by Jonathan Gosling, Peter Case and Morgen Witzel

First published 2007 by
PALGRAVE MACMILLAN
Houndmills, Basingstoke, Hampshire RG21 6XS and
175 Fifth Avenue, New York, N.Y. 10010
Companies and representatives throughout the world

PALGRAVE MACMILLAN is the global academic imprint of the Palgrave
Macmillan division of St. Martin's Press, LLC and of Palgrave Macmillan Ltd.
Macmillan® is a registered trademark in the United States, United Kingdom
and other countries. Palgrave is a registered trademark in the European
Union and other countries.

ISBN 13: 978–0–230–00205–0   hardback
ISBN 10: 0–230–00205–6   hardback

This book is printed on paper suitable for recycling and made from fully
managed and sustained forest sources.

A catalogue record for this book is available from the British Library.

Library of Congress Cataloging-in-Publication Data

John Adair : fundamentals of leadership / edited by Jonathan Gosling,
Peter Case and Morgen Witzel.
    p. cm.
Includes bibliographical references and index.
ISBN-13: 978–0–230–00205–0
ISBN-10: 0–230–00205–6
    1. Adair, John Eric, 1934– 2. Leadership. I. Gosling, Jonathan. II. Case,
Peter, 1959– III. Witzel, Morgen.

HD57.7.A28J66 2007
658.4'092–dc22   2006051221

10   9   8   7   6   5   4   3   2   1
16   15   14   13   12   11   10   09   08   07

Printed and bound in Great Britain by
Antony Rowe Ltd, Chippenham and Eastbourne

We dedicate this book to John Adair. His passion for the subject is matched only by his determination to have an impact: in both respects he is an inspiration to all three of us.

Contents

List of Tables

List of Figures

Foreword

On the day this foreword was written (28 June 2006), there were over 20,000 books on leadership available on the Amazon.co.uk site. Reading these from cover to cover would take more than a lifetime and there is precious little advice on which ones to start with. However, a persistent presence in the top 50 most popular purchases, and often in the top 10, is the work of John Adair. How might we explain this? On the one hand Adair's Action-Centred Leadership, and the now trademark three circles, appear disarmingly simple. On the other hand, beneath this simple model lies a pragmatic utility that has served many existing leaders well, and over a considerable period of time. For example, there are many military leaders today – at all ranks and in all three armed services – who will know, and will have used, his principles both in the classroom and in the field. Furthermore, as this volume demonstrates unequivocally, John's influence in the leadership worlds has been huge. Indeed, it remains a self-evident truth that however much more traditional academics wallow endlessly in their evermore arcane reconstructions of leadership, many actual leaders prefer the clean lines of Adair's Action-Centred Leadership (ACL) to the hazy adumbrations of alternative leadership theorists. Perhaps this is one of the key themes of Adair's own work – a strong dose of humility is a major asset to all leaders.

As this collection of chapters suggests, John Adair has led the British 'rush' to leadership for longer than anyone can care to remember; indeed, if it was not for John perhaps none of the writers and readers of this volume would be in the positions they are in today. However, this is not a hagiography and nor would John want one: his approach has always been to debate ideas robustly rather than subordinate his ideas to a culture of quiescence. After all, if leadership is to mean anything, it means taking risks, mobilising opinions and accepting that not everyone will be with you.

It may be that we will never agree on the way forward for leadership, despite John's best efforts to corral the community of leadership scholars along an agreed path, but such a conclusion does not mark a failure on his part but rather a critical and constructive step on the road to a wider understanding of leadership and a greater sharing of responsibility. Ultimately few of us can ask for more from our work than to say with justification that – like John Adair – we made a difference.

Keith Grint
Professor of Defence Leadership and Deputy Principal (Management and Leadership) Defence College of Management and Technology Cranfield University
June 2006

Notes on the Contributors

Sir Brian Burridge is the Senior Strategic Adviser to a multinational aerospace company. He spent almost 39 years as an RAF pilot, finally becoming Commander-in-Chief Strike Command, responsible for the entire front-line of the RAF. In 2003, he was the UK's National Commander in the Iraq War. He also spent a number of years in Ministry of Defence policy posts. An alumni of the Cabinet Office Top Management Programme, he has an MBA from the Open University Business School and is also an Honorary Doctor of the Open University. He was previously a Defence Fellow at King's College London. He writes and lectures on strategic leadership and military command both in the UK and internationally. Recent publications include 'The Rollercoaster Ride of Strategic Leadership'.

Peter Case, Professor of Leadership and Organization Studies at the Centre for Leadership Studies, University of Exeter, 2003–05, is now Professor of Organization Studies, Bristol Business School, University of the West of England, UK. He serves as chairperson of the Standing Conference on Organizational Symbolism and is a member of the editorial boards of *Leadership, Culture and Organization*, and the *Leadership* and *Organizational Development Journal*. Peter's research encompasses the ethics of leadership, organisation theory and multicultural aspects of management development. He has held visiting scholarships at Helsinki School of Economics and the Royal Institute of Technology of Stockholm. Peter is interested in the social and organisational impact of information and communication technologies and has published in such journals as *Organization, Human Relations, Journal of Management Studies, Management Learning*, and *Culture and Organization*.

Dr David Faraday was formerly a senior lecturer at the University of Surrey, where he was responsible for professional training and skills development in Chemical Engineering. He founded LEADTEAM Ltd in 2000 as a vehicle for bringing his innovative management training and skills development ideas to a wider audience. While at Surrey, David was the leader of the TRANSEND project (HEFCE, FDTL) and the inaugural recipient of the *FRANK MORTON MEDAL* for 'Excellence in Teaching in Chemical Engineering', in addition to being an Esso Teaching Fellow and the recipient of numerous awards and grants in teaching and training. David now runs training courses and programmes through Evolve LEADTEAM Ltd in management skills, interpersonal skills and engineering. His client base is diverse, ranging from the Organisation for the Prohibition of Chemical Weapons to the Royal Collection and includes many commercial organisations, government departments and higher education institutions.

Dr S. Martin Gaskell Dr Martin Gaskell was educated at Downing College Cambridge and the University of Sheffield. He was appointed Director of Studies at St George's House, Windsor Castle in 2002. Prior to his current appointment, Dr Gaskell was Assistant and Deputy Rector of Liverpool John Moores University (1980–86), Deputy and Acting Provost of London Guildhall University (1986–89) and Rector of the University of Northampton (1989–2002). In the 1990s, Dr Gaskell was Chairman of the Standing Conference of Principals, and he was a member of several major higher education bodies. He serves as a governor of several organisations and charities in the field of health and education. He is a Fellow of the Royal Historical Society and holds an Honorary LLD of Leicester University. He is a social historian, specialising in the history of housing and town planning, on which he has written extensively.

Jonathan Gosling is Director of the Centre for Leadership Studies, and Head of Executive Education at the University of Exeter. He has designed and directed development programmes for many companies, especially focusing on international and rapidly changing businesses. His current research looks at how leadership can foster continuity through tough transitions. Jonathan was co-founder of the International Masters in Practicing Management (IMPM), a collaboration of business schools around the world. He is also the joint author of 'Nelson's Way: leadership lessons from the Great Commander' (2005).

Tim Harle's career (From *Yes Minister* to *The Office*), spans Whitehall, FTSE-100 senior executive, a Silicon Fen Board role, and more. Variety and deep engagement in cultural change brought experience   even wisdom. So he moved to consultancy and now works in the private, public and non-profit sectors. Tim is passionate about customer service and addressing injustice. He has spoken at both business schools and theological colleges; his recent articles include a critique of leadership competencies.

Alan Hooper is the Founder and first Director of the Centre for Leadership Studies, University of Exeter. He is also a Visiting Professor at Bristol Business School. Formerly a Colonel in the Royal Marines, Alan has broad leadership experience at the strategic level and consults widely on leadership and change-management with a particular focus on helping people realise their leadership potential. He is the author of four books.

Tom Kennie is Director of the Ranmore Consulting Group (www.ranmore.co.uk). Ranmore specialize in leadership and management development in both the professional service and higher education sectors. In the latter context Tom has, for the past five years, been co-director (with Professor Robin Middlehurst) of the national Top Management Programme for Higher Education offered by the Leadership Foundation for Higher Education. Before founding Ranmore in 1995 he spent six years with DTZ, an international firm of property advisors latterly as Director of Human Resources. Immediately prior to this he was responsible for training and development at Balfour Beatty. He has also been a full-time academic at both the University of Surrey and the University of Technology in Kingston, Jamaica. He holds Visiting Professor posts at Sheffield Hallam University and Nottingham Business School and is an Adjunct Professor at the University of Technology, Sydney.

Greg McMahon's experience started with civil engineering design and construction, and now includes fields such as personnel and administration, international marketing, training establishments, research and development, consultancy and regulatory services, industrial relations, defence services, corporate support functions, and information services. Greg has managed change processes in the computerisation and super-computerisation of professional offices, commercialisation and privatisation of government services and in the implementation of structural efficiency principles and enterprise bargaining. He has masters degrees in engineering and in economics, is a Master Project Director, and a Fellow of the Australian Institute of Management. He has been published internationally and nationally. Greg has developed an instrument for assessing leadership needs within an organisation and his work in his technical speciality, flood estimation, is now recommended practice for his profession.

Wai-ming Mak gained his MA in management learning at Lancaster University and DBA in organisational learning at the University of Hull. He teaches leadership skills to undergraduates and MBA students, and conducts leadership workshops for public, private and non-profit organisations, both in Hong Kong and the Chinese mainland. His current research focuses on applying Chinese philosophy in leadership development. As a volunteer, he is Leader Trainer and Deputy Training Commissioner of the Scout Association of Hong Kong. He is elected Vice Chairman, Adult Resources Sub-Committee of the Asia Pacific Region of the World Scout Bureau.

Robin Middlehurst is Professor of Higher Education at the University of Surrey. She started her higher education career as a researcher with John Adair at the University of Surrey and has since led research projects in a range of territories including leadership, governance, quality enhancement and 'borderless' higher education. Between her early years at Surrey from 1986–90 and her present role at the university from 1998, Robin held an academic post at the Institute of Education, University of London and was Director of the Quality Enhancement Group in the UK's national Quality Agency (HEQC/QAA) from 1993–98. Robin has been a member of the Governing Board of two universities and is a consultant to many UK institutions and national and international agencies on higher education policy and practice. She was lead consultant to Universities UK for the establishment of the Leadership Foundation.

Dr John Potter is a Chartered Psychologist with a PhD in Leadership. His current work is in management development with a particular interest in leadership, corporate culture and teamwork. John specialises in training and development programmes to involve the whole workforce and promote their commitment to the corporate vision and mission. He is joint author with Alan Hooper of 'Intelligent Leadership' (2000).

Morgen Witzel is Honorary Senior Fellow of the School of Business and Economics, University of Exeter. He has written widely on management practices, management history and leadership, and is the author of numerous articles in journals including the *Financial Times, European Business Forum* and *The Smart Manager*, as well as academic journals including the *Journal of General Management* and *Human Systems Management*. He has written or co-authored 11 books including 'Builders and Dreamers: The Making and Meaning of Management', 'Robber Barons and Muck-Rakers: The Birth of American Corporate Culture', 'Doing Business in China', 'Singular and Different: Business in China Past, Present and Future', the 'Biographical Dictionary of Management' and 'Fifty Key Figures in Management'.

Ewart Wooldridge took up his appointment as Chief Executive of the Leadership Foundation for Higher Education in January 2004. Previously he was the Chief Executive and Director of the Civil Service College, now known as the CMPS, the Government's Centre for Management and Policy Studies. He was also a director within the corporate development group of the Cabinet Office actively working on civil service reform and the modernisation of public services. He was also the Cabinet Office champion for relations with the voluntary sector. His previous career spanned HR and line director positions in the private and public sector in engineering, printing and the media. From 1992–96 he was Director of Operations at London's South Bank Arts Centre. He was awarded the CBE in the Queen's Birthday Honours in 2004.

1

Introduction and Acknowledgements

Jonathan Gosling, Morgen Witzel and Peter Case

Adair: some fundamentals

John Adair occupies a somewhat unique place in the topography of leadership studies. He is the closest so far to a UK-based leadership 'guru'; he held the first Chair in Leadership (in 1979), has tirelessly promoted the field at universities in the UK and beyond, and contributed over 30 books to the topic. But he has largely eschewed scholarly journals, concentrating instead on having an impact on practising managers. He locates his own work in a tradition that he traces back to Xenophon, through a canon of mainly Western philosophers and social scientists, but unconnected to his contemporaries. Although his books and courses are aimed at practitioners, and much of his instructional approach is based on 'the careful analysis of leaders' actions', his three-circle model of 'action-centred leadership' demonstrates a keen appreciation for the systemic complexity of the contexts in which an individual struggles to fulfil a leadership role.

Anyone who has taught leadership studies will attest to the popularity of Adair's approach. Over a million people have been through his courses on 'action-centred leadership', and the chapters collected in this volume examine some of the wider ramifications in a number of important fields. The basic construct of his model is disarmingly simple – and therein, perhaps lies the secret of both its popular appeal and, correspondingly, a surprising lack of scholarly interest. The theory does two things very clearly: first, it *describes* the sphere of leadership action, and second it *prescribes* a leader's work – what Adair calls 'the generic role of leader'.

These three terms – task, team and individual – refer to the material with which a leader works, see Figure 1.1. They are the fundamental units of concern, but none are necessarily 'given', and Adair makes no assumptions about their essential characteristics. A task might be clearly defined and agreed; but it might equally well be highly contested, constructed in the discursive community of actors. Similarly, teams might be structural units of a formal organisation, or equally a group defined only by a common

1

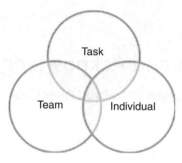

Figure 1.1 Action-centred leadership
Source: Adair 1973.

interest in one issue – their *de facto* task. The team is made up of individuals, but the characteristics and requirements of team and individual are quite distinct.

Each of the three circles require a leader's attention but not always in equal measure or at the same time. In order to provide for the needs of the task, the team and the individuals a leader must ensure various functions are performed:

- Defining the task
- Planning
- Briefing
- Controlling
- Evaluating
- Motivating
- Organising
- Setting an example

This list of functions can be drawn up in various ways; what is perhaps more important for an appreciation of Adair's model is that it requires the leader to pay attention to the needs of these three categories. Anyone finding themselves in a leadership role should figure out for themselves what the task needs, what the team needs and what each individual needs. The leaders are thus called to do some quite specific things. Only then, finding themselves in the work of leading, can he or she begin to think seriously about the skills and characteristics he or she may want to develop.

This is a very important and often overlooked point. Many other writers start with a list of traits, competencies or virtues required of a leader, and never quite get around to dealing with what one is supposed to be doing. Adair teaches three approaches together: qualities (what you are), situational (what you know) and functional (what you do). Many other approaches (think of transformational leadership) emphasise the supposed results of the work of leaders, and hint at the kinds of rhetoric that leaders might employ to these ends. Others emphasise the virtues or competencies one should practice, dissociated from the specific context and, crucially, the person. But very few give such clear, practical and sensitive advice to leaders about what to do.

Adair's broadly systemic view of the leadership function is refined in his many books – he has published 43 books to date, 36 on leadership or other aspects of effective organisation (innovation, communication, decision-making), seven on military history, mostly about the English Civil War. Some of the leadership books address particular sectors, for example two on leadership of the Churches. Most deal with leadership as a generic aspect of any organised effort. But Adair's efforts and influence extend beyond this impressive corpus of published works. He has been instrumental in establishing leadership studies in the universities of Surrey and Exeter (he held the UK's first Chair of Leadership Studies at Surrey from 1979); in the leadership development offered by St. George's House and the Windsor Leadership Trust; and in the recent burgeoning of public sector leadership centres. In the 1970s he became Associate Director of the Industrial Society in order to promote a leadership course based on action-centred leadership. This became known as the Runge Programme, and over a million people took this or related courses. Between 1981 and 1986 Adair worked with Sir John Harvey-Jones at ICI introducing a leadership development strategy that helped to change the loss-making, bureaucratic giant into the first British company to make a billion pounds profit.

From St Paul's School he won a state scholarship and Open Exhibition to Cambridge University. He holds the higher degrees of Master of Letters from Oxford University and Doctor of Philosophy from King's College London, and he is also a Fellow of the Royal Historical Society. Recently the People's Republic of China awarded him the title of Honorary Professor in recognition of his 'outstanding research and contribution in the field of Leadership', and in 2006 he was appointed to the UNESCO Chair in Leadership Studies which is linked to the United Nations University International Leadership Institute in Jordan. In 2004 the Centre for Leadership Studies at the University of Exeter made him the first recipient of their Award for Lifetime Contribution to Leadership Studies.

Although clearly a doyen of leadership studies and of leadership development, Adair remains critical of what he sees as the confused and overly eclectic approach to the subject. He is adamant that we have enough knowledge to be able to say unequivocally how to make leadership more effective in most situations, so researchers should concentrate on contextual and cultural adaptations of this knowledge. He sees his own contribution – identifying the three circles of a leader's work towards Task, Team and Individual – as fundamental, even axiomatic.

Those who study leadership (some of whom also practice it) approach the task in varying ways. Some do so as if this is a natural science, seeking underlying and perennial principles that allow us to both explain and predict how individuals and systems will behave under given circumstances. From this perspective, progress is achieved through occasional breakthroughs and long periods of testing and elaboration of theories until they become acceptable as 'laws'. But as in the Social Sciences more generally, many scholars do not accept the natural science analogy. Bent Flyvbjerg (2001) argues that those aiming for practical wisdom must be concerned with 'what matters' to individuals and communities. Deciding on what matters is inevitably a political process, in which the results of scientific study are used by all sides as part of their rhetoric. In so doing, they change the collective understanding of 'what matters', and what should be studied; social science is a part of social debate and conversation, not something apart. This is not to say that social sciences can be any less rigorous or methodical: they must provide a qualitatively distinct tenor informed largely by well-intentioned critical thinking, undertaken in the company of others, aiming overall to contribute to making judgements about what matters. The criterion, in this paradigm of social science, is not so much 'truth' as 'wisdom'. While Adair makes unabashed claims for the truth of his three-circle model, we suspect that the power of his work is actually derived from the discursive wisdom and good sense expressed in his fine prose.

Adair in historical context

Before considering the raison d'être of the present volume and introducing the various contributions, it seems appropriate to place John Adair within a wider historical landscape of leadership literature and thought, especially given his own passionate interest in historical scholarship. As Adair himself frequently notes, discussion about the nature and practice of leadership go back many centuries. In the classical world, Plato's 'philosopher-king' and the Confucian 'sage-king' are both examples of constructed archetypes of the ideal leader – as indeed is the Daoist 'servant-leader' (Adair 1989). Several years after these examples, the Indian writer and statesman Kautilya constructed a model that partakes a little of both concepts. Classical writers on leadership spoke of the need for the leader to possess a mixture of wisdom, virtue and authority, though how these concepts were defined and exercised differed between schools of thought.

The medieval period saw Eastern writers turning to the importance of self-mastery for leaders, for example in the Japanese classics the *Hagakure* (In the Shadow of Leaves) and the famous *Book of Five Rings*. The central idea was that it was first necessary to master oneself before one could lead others effectively. Western medieval culture also considered this idea of 'self-improvement' and produced a number of what became known as 'mirrors for princes', handbooks which instructed young leaders on their duties and were read by merchants as well as nobles; John of Salisbury's 12th-century *Policraticus* was particularly influential. In these Western works, the emphasis was not so much on self-mastery as on duty and obligation to God and to society – the two being seen, particularly by John of Salisbury, as inextricably linked.

As Adair (1989) notes, in the 16th century Machiavelli broke the link between Christian morality and successful leadership, and in the new humanistic age, the emphasis turned away from archetypes of leaders to leaders themselves. To understand what makes a great leader, it was thought necessary to study previous great leaders and emulate them. Thus Maurice of Nassau, Gustavus Adolphus and Frederick the Great were studied by aspiring generals, while later generations of politicians pored over the careers of Colbert, Walpole and Pitt the Younger. This 'great man' approach to leadership persisted into the early 20th century and lingers to this day, and indeed it has been suggested that in books like *Great Leaders* (1989), Adair is helping to perpetuate it.

In the aftermath of the First World War and Russian Revolution, however, searching questions began to be asked about leadership in the Western world. Mary Parker Follett's *Creative Experience* (1924) is significant in that it poured cold water on the theory that so-called 'great leaders' were necessarily possessed of a higher form of knowledge or had greater access to truth; her views were introduced into the British milieu by Lyndall Urwick, among others. The Second World War brought still more searching questions. Though the Allied forces had of course won, there were many notable failures of leadership during the conflict. In the immediate aftermath of the war, analysing the Allied successes and failures, Luther Gulick, long-time chairman of the Institute of Public Administration in New York, criticised those who confused 'leadership' with 'command'. Being put in a position of authority, argued Gulick, did not make one a leader; the critical function of the leader was to 'translate purpose into programme' (Gulick 1948: 78), and Gulick left the door open for a number of ways in which this could be done. This did not mean that 'great leader' theory was necessarily dead and buried, but alternative theories were opening up.

The second half of the 20th century saw a rapid growth in interest in leadership, and 'psychological' theories of leadership, especially those coming out of American academia, began to make an impact on the intellectual understanding of leadership. As early as the 1930s, the German-American psychologist Kurt Lewin had conducted experiments suggesting that leaders who operated in a democratic, consensual manner were more likely to stimulate their followers to be more productive and independent – though importantly, Lewin also found that under *laissez-faire* leadership, in which people were expected to lead themselves, work levels and efficiency declined (Lewin *et al.* 1939; Morrow 1969).

Lewin's work led to a rapid growth in research into the psychological and behavioural factors affecting leadership, for example, by Elliott Jaques and others at the Tavistock institute, which also began to influence concepts about how we grow and develop leaders. For example, it had long been recognised that it was possible to train leaders, perhaps not from scratch, but to improve on existing potential; now, theorists began to develop new and – supposedly – better ways of doing so. Later still, Warren Bennis would develop his trait theory of leadership. Lewin's work, among others, also led to an interest in leadership in group situations, with theorists such as Rensis Likert arguing that leadership was best exercised by participative, consensual groups rather than dynamic individuals.

At the same time, ideas of situational leadership and contingent leadership were gaining ground. The work of Fred Fiedler in developing the contingency model of leadership showed that external as well as internal success factors were present; that is, leaders were successful, or otherwise, partly as a result of conditions in their environment (see for example Fiedler 1967). Douglas McGregor's contingency theory of leadership, published around the same time, similarly suggests that leaders are not successful solely because of who they are and what they do, but are affected by time and place (McGregor 1967).

All of the above efforts added a great deal to our stock of knowledge *about* leadership, but they did not, collectively, bring us much closer to an understanding of what leadership is. In the mid-1990s, the respected leadership writer Frank Heller of the Tavistock Institute concluded glumly:

> It is clear that no paradigm [of leadership] has emerged in the diverse constituencies of social science. This could mean that the jury is still out, but with more time and effort, an acceptable evidence-based role for organizational leadership will emerge. Alternatively, it is possible that organizational behaviour and, in particular, changes in organizations over time, require a broader explanation in which personal leadership will remain a molecular component in a molar concept that has yet to evolve (Heller 1996: 2549).

What – if anything – does John Adair owe to the evolution of leadership theory over the past centuries? As noted above, his passion for history and his frequent reference to famous – and not-so-famous – historical examples of the past might suggest that he still belongs in the 'great leaders' mode. But a closer examination of books such as *Great Leaders* quickly shows that this is not so. He writes persuasively on the 'servant-leader' and his inclusion of figures such as Lao Tzu and Jesus and Gandhi as exemplars. Elsewhere, in *Not Bosses But Leaders*, he speaks of 'leadership as a form of service, with humility as its hidden badge' (Adair 1987: 146).

There is one critical distinction that must be made. Adair asserts the importance of the leader, but does not assert the leader's primacy. A leader is an essential ingredient in the mix, but that does not give leaders supreme power over others; he would agree with Gulick's (and Xenophon's) view that leaders and commanders are two different things. His view of leadership as 'the ability to influence others to achieve a common goal' (Adair 1987: 5) is roughly in line with the findings of Lewin, whose experiments showed that where groups had active, participating leaders, work levels and efficiency increased. In that sense, then, it is not so hard to reconcile Adair's view of the role of the leader with many of the modern theories of leadership.

The Tavistock approach to studying group dynamics was, as Adair acknowledges, a formative influence. The typical Tavistock working conference is convened as a temporary organisation with the primary task of studying the exercise of authority within the conference organisation itself (Rice 1965). Conference members observe and study their own behaviour and that of other members, and are able to draw on their emotional experience of these relationships. Crucially, they can observe and interpret their own willingness to follow others, their sense of authority and confidence, the collusive or counter-dependent behaviour of groups and the crowd dynamics of the collective membership. All this happens in real time, with people who share a common task in revealing and understanding these processes 'in the here and now'. The 'primary task' is a key concept, clearly defined and agreed, but often subverted by unconscious responses to the difficulties it poses. For example, although everyone in the conference might agree that the task is to study intergroup relations, one group might become envious of the insights apparently generated in another group, and develop an isolationist stance in order to defend its members against feelings of inadequacy. This anti-task behaviour is a social reality, and expresses a felt need that is probably not consciously known or articulated. Task leadership in this context might be exercised by someone who reignites curiosity and openness towards the learning opportunity in these dynamics, perhaps by leading a delegation to observe the other group(s). This brief example illustrates the kind of experience which, one can easily see, might have provided Adair with the raw material for a model emphasising the interrelated needs of task, team and individual.

There remains, however, the concern as to whether Adair focuses too much on the individual and not enough on the group. Part of the problem may be a presentational one. In many of his books, such as *Not Bosses But Leaders* and the later *The John Adair Handbook of Management and Leadership* (1998), Adair speaks directly to the leader or aspiring leader. Indeed, his style is frequently reminiscent of those medieval mirrors for princes, or Castiglione's *Book of the Courtier* from the 16th century. He is speaking to the leader as an individual: suggesting, guiding, coaching. He is not so much questioning other theories of leadership – although he casts doubt on some of them, such as situational leadership, but he is hardly alone in that – as seeking to explain and define leadership in terms that an individual leader can understand and use. This means, however, that although the three elements of task, individual and team are given equal weight, it is easy for readers to develop a bias, even if subconsciously, towards the individual.

Thus it may be that one of the greatest strengths of Adair's body of work is also one of its greatest weaknesses. In developing a powerful and simple model of practical leadership which can be easily understood and used by leaders, he has inadvertently downplayed the role of the team. In *The Inspirational Leader* (2003), Adair speaks frequently about the role of leaders in inspiring others to create and to achieve, and there is a stronger sense of the linkage between leader and group than in some of his other works. Is this because in trying to create a universal philosophy of leadership, Adair is consciously disassociating himself from highly consensual models such as Likert's 'System 4'? Certainly many of the leaders he profiles in *Great Leaders* would not fit the definition of System 4, yet they were successful leaders nonetheless. One can see Adair wishing to avoid being tied to any particular theory about 'good' leadership, but there is still arguably a lack of appreciation of the role of group dynamics and 'followership'.

Adair, of course, would refute this charge vigorously; in his view, the team is of critical importance, and one of the inferences of the three-circles model is that the task, individual and team should be given equal weight. But the impression persists that the 'individual' somehow is *primus inter pares*. Does the fault lie then with the interpreters? By trying to shoehorn Adair's philosophy into leadership into existing academic leadership theory, are we somehow doing him a disservice? The contributions in this volume suggest that we need to spend more time looking at what Adair's philosophy is, and less at what it is not.

One question that can be answered quickly is Adair's relevance beyond the Western intellectual milieu. Two pieces of evidence can be offered. First, Adair consciously sets out to create a universal approach to leadership, and he draws his intellectual support from Eastern as well as Western culture; there are few philosophical concepts in his books that would be unfamiliar to an educated Chinese or Japanese. Second, as Wai-ming Mak shows in this volume, action-centred leadership can be transferred very successfully to Asian settings.

Adair's contribution to the literature and the conceptualisation of leadership is significant – but will it be lasting? How robust is his assertion of a clear distinction between team, operational and strategic leadership? With the benefit of over 30 years of continuous practice, how do we evaluate the impact of Action-Centred Leadership (ACL)? Is his model crucially dependent on a robustly individualistic leader acting *'ex machina'* on task, team and other individuals? Can we really understand the functioning of organisations, and the place of leadership within them, without a theory of unconscious tasks and group process? These are amongst the questions one might ask of any strongly asserted theory; it is especially important that we ask them of this immensely influential and temporally extended body of work.

In one sense, his contribution to the history of leadership is already assured, through those million people who have been through his leadership course, and the others who will follow. His work at Sandhurst, and the institutions he helped to create at the University of Surrey and the University of Exeter, not to mention St George's House (see Chapter 7, this volume), will survive long after him. But will his contribution to our broader understanding of leadership survive?

In the dissemination of his ideas, Adair has faced several obstacles. The first of these is that he is British, which has made it harder for his ideas to become accepted in America. Part of the reason for this may be simply commercial; Adair has published many of his books with small British publishers, which have lacked the distribution and marketing clout to turn his books into American bestsellers, a necessary condition to be noticed by the American academic world.

At home, too, despite his achievements at Surrey and Exeter, he has been confronted by the peculiarly British view that leaders are 'born and not made', an idea that was long prevalent in the culture, and still lingers in parts of the business community. As recently as 1937, Sir Charles Renold, chairman of the Federation of British Industry, ancestor to the modern CBI, resigned in protest when the Federation adopted a motion advocating that it should support training programmes for managers and business leaders. It is significant that Adair's ideas were developed through practice with the British army rather than in the British business community, and found their first acceptance there.

A third barrier has been his own method of presentation. As noted above, he often takes a very personal approach in his writing; alternatively, as in *Great Leaders*, his tone is literary rather than scholarly. He is writing, quite unashamedly, for a popular audience; his work shows this. However, this approach was never going to win the sympathy or support of the academic community on either side of the Atlantic. It was once said of the great popular American historian Francis Parkman that 'his work would have been regarded with less suspicion by his fellow historians had his writing been less fluent'. Adair may have suffered from something of the same prejudice.

It will be interesting to see how Adair's ideas continue to be received, especially as the generations trained in action-centred leadership go on to train succeeding generations. How will Adair's concepts be adapted or evolve? Will the three-circles and the rainbow model continue to be taught, or will they give way to new action-centred leadership concepts? It is of course far too soon to tell. But the contributions in this book suggest that, despite the demands of situation and contingency, there is an enduring aspect to many of Adair's ideas. It is not just that concepts such as the three circles are easily remembered and learned; as the chapters that follow show, there is strong evidence that the concept is truly effective. And if that is the case, then there is an equally strong argument for saying that Adair's ideas will survive the test of time. Something about these simple and effective models touches a chord, with both leaders and trainers of leaders. One of the contributions this book makes is to allow those who use action-centred leadership to explain in their own words why this is so.

Contributions to this volume

The current volume brings together contributions from across a number of sectors, and various perspectives. In order to help the reader navigate this diverse set of reflections on John Adair's oeuvre and teaching, the book is organised into three parts: Part I presents four theoretical perspectives on Adair's work; Part II is dedicated to Adair's influence on certain institutions – the military, civil service, higher education and the Church; and Part III offers two examples of ACL in international contexts. Finally, in Part IV John Adair contributes his own comment in the form of a direction-setting polemic. In a unique and specially written essay he sets out his agenda for leadership studies and development over the next 40 years.

Part I opens with an essay of powerful advocacy. Alan Hooper was the Founder Director of the Centre for Leadership Studies at Exeter University, under the guidance of John Adair, and he remains a fervent admirer of Adair's work. The Greek origin of Hooper's chapter title, *strategos*, appropriately captures the classical underpinnings of Adair's writing and reflects the strategic perspective that Hooper adopts with respect to his oeuvre. Beginning with a detailed review of two books, *Great Leaders* and *Effective Strategic Leadership*, Hooper is principally concerned with the manner in which Adair's writing speaks to those in senior organisational roles. As part of a personal evaluation and critique of the current state of leadership in the UK, Hooper laments the fact that not many people in top positions are familiar with Adair's work. This is an issue that is explored with reference to an interview Hooper recently conducted with Adair. The classical theme emerges again when Hooper considers Adair's role as a teacher and 'influencer'. Adair's teaching style might best be understood as Socratic and, as an instigator of 'seriously grown-up debate', Adair's appeal is more pragmatic than theoretical. Rather than an 'academic's academic', according to Hooper, Adair should be viewed as a 'practitioner's academic', which epithet is not to downplay the serious historical scholarship that informs his work. As a teacher and confidant, Adair has influenced a huge number of practitioners and educationalists, some of them very senior indeed; Sir John Harvey Jones (ICI), Rupert Hambro (Hambro Bank), Sir Geoffrey Maddrell (Total Group), and Sir Bob Reid (British Rail) are amongst those mentioned as leaders who have sought John Adair's advice and guidance. As a *strategos* through both his writing and teaching, Adair has acted as a 'conscience' for those acting in a strategic capacity in the UK and beyond. John Potter's chapter seeks to situate John Adair's contribution theoretically within the wider context of leadership studies. As with other contributors to this volume, Potter sets the scene by locating the genesis of Adair's thinking in the innovative training he initiated at the Royal Military Academy, Sandhurst. Potter, who was one of Adair's successors as a lecturer at Sandhurst, argues that the Functional Model of leadership deserves to be treated as a core part of the canon of theory in the field. The chapter discusses the relationship of ACL to other models of leadership, such as trait and situational theory, arguing that in each case Adair's approach compares favourably with these alternatives and often possesses certain advantages in terms of its practical applicability. Along with other authors in this collection, Potter is of the view that, in its elegant simplicity, ACL embodies a universality that enables it to withstand the many and varied tests of time. ACL, he contends is as apposite to the virtual worlds of the internet and challenges of distributed leadership as it was to the specific rigours of military training in the 1960s. The chapter concludes with three cases which exemplify the way that the ACL framework can be utilised to address differing leadership problems.

Fittingly enough for a book dedicated to the work of a leadership innovator, the next chapter provides some original reflections on the current state of leadership theory and practice. As a business historian, Morgen Witzel's novel perspective on leadership enables him to reexamine critically some of the common sense assumptions prevalent in the field. Challenging the idea that leadership is solely in the gift of talented leaders – an idea that has dogged the subject for centuries, if not millennia – Witzel proposes, instead, that leadership is exercised and becomes effective through the interaction *between* leaders and their followers. Leadership, he claims is fundamentally dyadic and *relational*. Insofar as ACL gives emphasis to the key part played by the individual in the leadership process, some critics might view Adair's work as falling foul of the kind of egocentrism and phallogocentrism that characterises all so-called 'great man' theories. Witzel disabuses us of such misconceptions. He points out that a relational conception of leadership is inherent and explicit within the 'three circles' model of leadership, with its tripartite interrelationship between individual, team and task. Furthermore, Witzel is able to deploy Adair's 'rainbow model', with its seven generic functions, to analyse the effectiveness of a dyadic conception of relational leadership. He begins his exploration with a consideration of action theory both in terms of philosophical origins and application within the fields of leadership and organisation studies. Leaders are certainly responsible for initiating action *volitionally* but their followers' actions also feed back into the leader's own volitional equation. It is not just a one-way street. Drawing on his considerable knowledge of history, Witzel then treats the reader to a fascinating array of illustrations, ranging from the premodern to the contemporary – from Lao Tzu and Machiavelli to Cadbury and Semler. As he reminds us, 'leaders on their own can do nothing; no leader can do everything'. What is required in dyadic leadership are the three factors of consent, convergence and communication. Witzel concludes his contribution with a *cri de coeur* for a cultural shift in the way that leadership is conceptualised in the western world; one which downplays the role of the 'heroic' or narcissistic individual and brings to the fore interactive and relational processes.

In the next chapter Tim Harle presents a thought provoking set of comparisons between two unlikely bedfellows. He contrasts two lists, each comprising five elements: the 'Five Minds of the Manager' proposed by Gosling and Mintzberg (2003) in their *Harvard Business Review* article, and the five models that describe the Anglican priest's vocational calling as represented in The Declaration read out during ordination services. Beginning with an outline of Adair's influence on leadership development within the Church of England (reaffirming and adumbrating observations made by Gaskell in his contribution), Harle sets out to reflect critically on three key questions. Firstly, despite Adair's espoused emphasis on 'serving to lead', can the ACL model be accused of promoting the notion of the 'heroic individual' which has come under such criticism in recent leadership literature? Second, is ACL premised on an unhelpful Cartesian worldview? Third, has Adair's hierarchical modelling of team, operational and strategic leadership stood the test of time, particularly in the light of recent research developments in the areas of chaos and complexity modelling? Ever sensitive to the etymological roots of the terms he employs and careful to capture nuance, Harle treats the reader to a rich exploration of these questions – juxtaposing sources from academic organisation and leadership sources, popular management literature, biblical references and concepts drawn from comparative religion. While the argument is subtle, Harle concludes that readers of *The Ordinal* and the *Harvard Business Review* have much to learn from one another concerning the meaning and practice of leadership. Furthermore, because of his explicit interest in Church leadership, Adair's work offers a useful synthesis of elements that span this ostensive but ultimately illusory divide.

In the first of four chapters on Adair and institutions, Air Chief Marshal Sir Brian Burridge reflects on the historical and contemporary influence of the ACL framework on leadership training in military contexts, particularly the RAF. Burridge outlines the manner in which Functional leadership initially took root at military academies such as Sandhurst and Cranwell during the 1960s and gradually became a standard feature of officer training. He documents how notions of leadership as a 'given' attribute of certain elite classes, prevalent in the pre- and immediately post-WWII period, gradually gave way to Adair's (then radical) idea of leadership as a set of skills and qualities that could be developed within military recruits. The chapter goes on to evaluate whether ACL has stood the test of time. Burridge alerts us to the fact that military contexts have changed. We have moved from the relative stasis of Cold War symmetrical warfare to a far more complex and unpredictable world in which enemies no longer take the form of nation states who abide by the traditional conventions of engagement. Leaders within the armed forces have to be able to manage a variety of roles: one day warriors in combat with terrorists, the next peace keepers trying to maintain stability in war torn regions or distributing aid to communities ravaged by natural disaster. Burridge asks whether the ACL model of leadership training is suitable preparation for these new demands and whether it can accommodate such innovations as Mission Command and Constructive Dissent. The chapter is very upbeat on all counts. Comparing ACL with more recent advances in military doctrine based on the value systems of the Strength Deployment Inventory, Burridge concludes that Adair's work is as applicable to officer training today as it ever was.

In the next chapter Ewart Wooldridge, CBE, presents a reflective evaluation of the current state of leadership development within the UK public sector. While acknowledging a debt to Adair's ACL model, Wooldridge is concerned primarily to scrutinise recent Government initiatives, such as the Cabinet Office inspired 'Leaders UK' project, aimed at producing joined up leadership provision across the various public sector services – NHS, police, civil service, higher education and defence. Drawing from a wealth of experience of working on leadership development in various institutions, Wooldridge admits to having a sense of déjà vu with respect to recent political initiatives and is candid about the difficulties of sharing leadership learning and knowledge between the various centres that are now proliferating across the sector. The political aspirations are worthy but there are practical difficulties in resolving tensions that result from trying to derive (and disseminate) generic leadership lessons from institutions which operate in individually complex and specific contexts. Wooldridge provides an insightful critique of various civil service espousals and Government research reports, yet remains optimistic that progress is being made towards the goal of 'joining up' public sector leadership development. He finds value in selected academic research and believes that more could usefully be commissioned to inform decision-making and practice. It is vital, he contends, to shift emphasis away from the developers and onto actual frontline leaders.

Continuing the public sector theme and broadening it somewhat, Robin Middlehurst, Tom Kennie and Dave Faraday provide a rich account of the impact Adair's ideas have had on leadership in higher education, civil engineering and the legal profession. Their chapter begins with an overview of

Adair's influence at the University of Surrey following his appointment there as the world's first every designated professor of leadership studies in 1979. Dave Faraday and Tom Kennie offer brief case studies of Adair's legacy with respect to leadership development in engineering at Surrey and the surveying profession respectively. Following from these cases and in a related professional vein, Robin Middlehurst takes a historical view of how Adair's ideas have fed into leadership debates in universities and colleges in the UK. Having set out a valuable summary of Adair's contribution in tabular form, the chapter concludes with a critical comparison of ACL with a range of alternative perspectives on leadership.

In the fourth of the chapters on institutional context, S. Martin Gaskell charts the significant influence that John Adair has had on the provision of leadership training and development within the Church of England. Gaskell, who is currently Director of Studies at St George's House, Windsor Castle, draws on his intimate knowledge of the St George's House archive to produce a comprehensive historical account of the way in which Adair's work has shaped Church leadership debate and practice for more than 40 years. The story begins in 1962 with the publication of an article in *Theology* in which Adair promotes the idea of staff training for Church leaders that would parallel the kind of provision he innovated in the military. These suggestions came to fruition when, under the Deanship of Robin Woods, St George's House launched a four-week 'Clergy Long Course' which Adair oversaw as Director of Studies during a period of secondment from the Royal Military Academy, Sandhurst, between 1968 and 1969. Following these early initiatives, Adair's impact on Church leadership has been continual and persistent. He has written several reports in which his theory of overlapping needs have been applied to the context of the Church and the Diocese and in which the role of bishop is characterised as crucial to visionary and administrative leadership. His books, *The Becoming Church* (1977) and *Creative Church Leadership* (Adair and Nelson 2004), have also informed continuing debates concerning how the Church might best meet the challenges of a radically changing constituency and social context. Adair played a central part in the founding of the Windsor Leadership Trust at Windsor Castle in the mid-1990s, a body whose work in bringing together and promoting leadership learning across sectors he has contributed to ever since. As to whether this has resulted in a 'better' Church, whatever that might mean, Gaskell is more circumspect. Although Adair's ideas and innovations have met with a mixed reception from a clergy that is sometimes suspicious of outside ideas, there is no doubt, Gaskell concludes, that the Church owes a great debt to John Adair for the part he has played in facing up to its various leadership challenges.

In the first of two chapters that engage with Adair's international influence, Greg McMahon charts the history and course of Functional Leadership (FL) in Australia. In a parallel to the earlier chapter by Burridge,

McMahon notes how FL initially gained a foothold in Australia because of its successful uptake by the military in the mid-1960s, notably the Australian Army and Royal Australian Air Force. The Army leadership doctrine published in 1973, for example, was based explicitly on the FL framework. From its military inception, FL has been disseminated into private sector industry and commerce, universities and other parts of the public sector. Adair himself has visited Australia to help promote and propagate his model of leadership development. McMahon suggests that FL's progress corresponds to phases in the development of management knowledge and philosophy, ranging from 'Management By Objectives' of the 1960s, through 'TQM' in the 1980s and, most recently, on to 'Management For Outcomes'. In his assessment of FL's influence, McMahon makes strong claims regarding FL's universal applicability and ability to adapt to waves of change in management fashion and practice. Inspired by Adair's work on strategic leadership, McMahon draws on his own published research to illustrate how FL – a 'first principles' technique – can be elaborated and move from a consideration of micro leadership issues to organisational or community level concerns. The chapter concludes with two case studies, one based on the restructuring of an engineering office and the other focusing on a corporate takeover, to illustrate the analytical and practical fecundity of Adair's FL model.

In similar international vein, Wai-ming Mak offers a detailed and informative account of the introduction of ACL training and development in the Chinese speaking world. Something of an evangelist for John Adair's ideas and methods, Mak has been instrumental in educating students at Hong Kong Polytechnic University using ACL and, through his consultancy work, has introduced the model to organisations operating in a range of sectors in the region. He provides outlines of his courses and explains how he has adapted materials for use in the Chinese context. Mak's chapter also documents Adair's influence on the scouting movement worldwide and provides specific information about the impact of ACL on scout training in the Asia-Pacific region. Being critical of the ego-centrism of certain Western styles of leadership, Mak believes that Adair's approach – insofar as it gives emphasis to collaboration – is commensurate with classical Chinese conceptions of the leadership role, particularly that of Lao Tzu. This helps explain its appeal to the Chinese and Mak is hopeful that ACL will continue to flourish in the region.

John Adair's concluding chapter sets a different tone. He takes only a brief look back at the impact of his work over the past 40 years; instead he faces forward to the next half-century, setting out his assessment of the task facing leadership scholars and developers. True to form, he advocates a clear-cut and unabashed focus on helping leaders to be more effective – with a special emphasis on the wisdom and foresight so necessary for 'good leadership and leadership for good'.

These chapters are part of a series of events celebrating the work of John Adair; but taken as a whole they provide a fascinating overview of ideas and activities in the large but relatively uncharted territory between leadership studies and leadership practice. Somewhere in that zone, leaders and their advisors wonder what to do and how to do it. This 'wondering' is the real work of leadership development. The chapters collected here give us a glimpse of this work in contemporary Britain, extending beyond immediate references to Adair and Action-Centred Leadership. Although John Adair is still far too active and inventive to allow us to talk of a legacy quite yet, the vigour and excitement communicated by these chapters is, we hope, a fitting tribute to his contribution thus far.

References

Adair, J. (1973) *Action Centred Leadership*, London: McGraw-Hill.

Adair, J. (1977) *The Becoming Church*, London: SPCK.

Adair, J. (1987) *Not Bosses But Leaders*, Guildford: Talbot Adair Press.

Adair, J. (1989) *Great Leaders*, Guildford: Talbot Adair Press.

Adair, J. (1998) *The John Adair Handbook of Management and Leadership*, London: Thoroghgood.

Adair, J. (2003) *The Inspirational Leader*, London: Kogan Page.

Adair, J. and Nelson, J. (eds) (2004) *Creative Church Leadership*, Norwich: Canterbury Press.

Fiedler, F.E. (1967) *A Theory of Leadership Effectiveness*, New York: McGraw-Hill.

Flyvbjerg, B. (2001) *Making Social Science Matter*, Cambridge: Cambridge University Press.

Gosling, J. and Mintzberg, H. (2003) 'The Five Minds of a Manager', *Harvard Business Review*, November, pp.54–63.

Gulick, L.H. (1948) *Administrative Reflections from World War II*, University, AL: University of Alabama Press.

Heller, F. (1996) 'Leadership', in M. Warner (ed.) *International Encyclopedia of Business and Management*, London: Routledge.

Lewin, K., Lippitt, R. and White, R.K. (1939) 'Patterns of Aggressive Behavior in Experimentally Created Social Climates', *Journal of Social Psychology*, vol. 10, pp.271–301.

McGregor, D. (1967) *The Professional Manager*, New York: McGraw-Hill.

Morrow, A.J. (1969) *Practical Theorist: The Life and Work of Kurt Lewin*, New York: Teachers' College Press.

Parker-Follet, M. (1924) *Creative Experiences*, London: Longmans [merged with Penguin Books 1970].

Rice, A.K. (1965) *Learning for Leadership: interpersonal and intergroup relations*, London: Tavistock.

Acknowledgements

We would like to express our gratitude to Ken Keir and Pauline Wiseman of Honda for their persistent support of open-minded enquiry into leadership; and to colleagues at the HR consultancy Hewitt, who hosted an Award ceremony in 2005 that honoured Adair's contribution to leadership studies, instigating the work that led to this publication. We are especially appreciative of the serious and thoughtful work undertaken by independent reviewers of all the chapters published here. Finally, we extend our special thanks to Tricia Doherty and Ian Sutherland for organising and progressing most of the work on all three: the award ceremony, the colloquium and this book.

This volume is the outcome of a specially convened colloquium at St George's House, Windsor, in the summer of 2005. Sponsored by Honda, the colloquium invited papers assessing the contribution of Adair's ideas. We have not been able to include all these papers in this collection: others are available from the Centre for Leadership Studies, Exeter University, on www.leadership-studies.com

Part I
Perspectives on Adair's Work

2
Strategos: An Exploration of John Adair's Influence on Strategic Leadership

Alan Hooper

Introduction

The purpose of this chapter is to explore John Adair's tireless effort to influence strategic leadership, especially in the UK. Drawing on his background as an historian and commencing with his time as a lecturer at Sandhurst, Adair has spent his working life teaching and writing about leadership. For the most part, it has been a lonely journey, and often a frustrating one.

The chapter will focus on his contribution to strategic leadership, as a writer, as a teacher and as an influencer. It will consider 'Adair the author' by reviewing two of his most acclaimed books: *Great Leaders* (1989) and *Effective Strategic Leadership* (2002). The 13 years separated by these publications represent, arguably, the most fruitful period of Adair's work. It was during the 1990s that, having been the sole flag-bearer for so long, he was at last joined by others prepared to write about leadership, especially from the Centre of Leadership Studies at the University of Exeter. Just as they were inspired by his earlier work (such as *Great Leaders*) so he drew on the writings of others in his own influential *Effective Strategic Leadership*.

The chapter will then consider Adair's role as 'teacher and influencer'. He has influenced a vast cross-section of people by his thinking on leadership as a 'teacher' in such varied institutions as the Royal Military Academy, Sandhurst (senior lecturer), the Industrial Society (Associate Director), St George's House, Windsor (Director of Studies) and the Universities of Surrey (Professor) and Exeter (Visiting Professor). He has also influenced an even wider audience through his public lectures and also on in-house programmes. To this can be added his less-publicised coaching role to chairmen and chief executives, and to senior management teams.

His efforts to promote leadership and influence thinking, especially at the strategic level, have been tireless. He has often been a lone voice, and a provocative one. So the chapter will conclude by considering what may be his 'strategos' legacy.

Adair the author

It has been said that those who write about ideas, especially those which shape our lives, have as much, if not more, influence as those who provide the practical leadership. There are some who do both (such as Churchill) and their impact can be profound, but most have the talent to do only one or the other to a high level. If it is true that the pen is mightier than the sword, then John Adair has had a significant impact on the thinking about strategic leadership, particularly over the past 15 years.

He has been a prolific writer and indeed, continues to be, with seven books published in the last four years. His influence on the whole topic of leadership has been considerable and in particular the 'three-circles model' has been adopted by numerous organisations and a multitude of people around the world. For a long time he was virtually the only person writing about leadership in UK (Meredith Belbin, a contemporary, focused more on the team). This reticence is in stark contrast to the United States where there has long been a strong tradition of writing about leadership embracing the work at Ohio State University and the University of Michigan, and including a proliferation of authors such as Bennis, Kotter, Stogdill, Fiedler, Peters, Rosabeth Moss Kanter, Hersey and Blanchard.

The reluctance of the British to write on this topic up until the last decade is puzzling, especially as there have been numerous examples of individuals who have exercised leadership at the highest level, many of whom had been particularly successful in very challenging circumstances. It was almost as though the British were more comfortable about exercising leadership than writing about it. It is even more puzzling when a number of them were happy to share their experiences via public lectures or 'Chatham House Rules' talks thus providing evidence that they had thought about their leadership challenges in depth. It may have something to do with the 'British reserve', or maybe it is to do with our nation's fondness for the laid-back attitude of the gifted amateur when a professed professional approach is often met with sarcastic comments. Whatever the reason, it left Adair as virtually the only person in the country writing about leadership during the 1970s and 80s. As a result, his influence on strategic leadership has been profound and there are numerous individuals who have operated at the top level whose thinking and subsequent action have been grounded in the words of John Adair.

I have chosen to concentrate particularly on *Great Leaders* (1989) and *Effective Strategic Leadership* (2002): the first is because they were written in different decades and thus reflect Adair's thinking at those particular periods of his life; and the second because they were both written for the audience of that moment – or so it would appear. On closer inspection, the format is similar (i.e., both books are divided into three parts each addressing a topic matter which is then explored in depth). At first sight,

Great Leaders appears to be a weighty historical tome whilst the second book is written for today's public who claim they have less time to read and study. And yet, the messages conveyed by both books have very similar themes. So, does the second publication represent a development in Adair's thinking, or it is an illusion? Let us examine each in turn.

Great Leaders

Great Leaders was published in 1989 and its purpose is made clear in the very brief Introduction: 'to review some of the great leaders in history, and to identify the main facets of leadership' (Adair 1989: 9). What emerges is a concept of leadership that resonates with the environment of today's world. The book is divided into three parts (none of which are titled) each of which contains groups of loosely associated aspects of leadership, with one exception (to which I will return later). Part One starts with knowledge and, appropriately, with the idea of Socrates and the Ancient Greeks. It embraces other areas, such as Leadership Skills, Direction Setting, Decision-making and Inspiration using examples ranging from Xenophon to Slim and Montgomery.

The second part of the book starts by looking at the Roots of the British Tradition and includes chapters on Polar Explorers and Leadership in a Changing World. It is in this part that the exception appears; one chapter devoted to just a single leader. Given the range of talent of leaders across history it is intriguing that the person on whom Adair has focused his attention is Nelson. For those of us with a knowledge of the Royal Navy this is no surprise. His style, example and influence still impact on today's Navy 200 years after his death. Nelson was a leader way ahead of his time, acknowledged as a military genius by his peers and superiors, loved by his men and also rated a national hero – no mean achievement. The genuine outpouring of grief at his funeral (which even Admiral Villeneuve, the defeated French Commander at Trafalgar attended) was on the scale of the funeral of Diana, Princess of Wales in 1997.

Part Three embraces Charisma and Women Leaders, looks at different styles of leadership and ends by peering into the future.

So, what is the overall impression from this book? Underpinning everything is the historical perspective. Adair studied history at Cambridge and this education has left a deep impression on his thinking. It is almost as though the quote at the beginning of the book 'visit the past in order to know the present' (*ibid.*: 9) has been his handrail throughout his life as he has sought a deep understanding of leadership. His examples range across the broad canvas of world events from Ancient Greece to modern political leaders (such as Margaret Thatcher). Cases are selected to illustrate a point, regardless of the century from which they originated. For example, the chapter on Making the Right Decisions (*ibid.*: 73–98) includes reference to Tacitus, Hannibal, General Robert E. Lee, Eisenhower and Golda Meir. This range of examples drawn from history requires significant scholarship and a deep knowledge of individuals' leadership. It is one thing to write an in-depth appraisal of an individual great leader's style and achievements; it is quite another to weave several examples into a tapestry. Significantly, it is this ability to draw from such a rich vein of knowledge that impresses those who attend Adair's seminars.

So, first, Adair is an historian. What else do we draw from this book? Although the various sections of each chapter are clearly laid out in both the Contents and the book itself, there does not appear to be a logical link between them. For instance, Leadership Skills (*ibid.*: 29–38) starts with The Case of Nicomachides and includes a section entitled 'A Leader in Estate Management'! The apparent haphazard selection of sub-headings in some of the chapters can make it difficult for the reader to follow the trend of thought via a perusal of the Contents but, when one starts to read the content, it is a different matter. The connections in the thought process flow naturally and are easy to follow (*viz* from 'phrone-sis' on page 74 through 'persuasion' (*ibid.*: 76) to being a 'progress-chaser' (*ibid.*: 79)). The linkage is aided by a number of practical examples and specific case studies (an Adair trademark) to illustrate a particular point. For example, in the chapter entitled 'The Art of Inspiring while Informing' he includes two case studies: one about Slim's leadership of the Forgotten Army in the Burma Campaign of 1943; and the other of Montgomery's famous speech on 13 August 1942 on assuming command of the Eighth Army. Both cases provide appropriate evidence to underpin this particular aspect of leadership.

As Adair guides us through these classic examples from history he takes us with him on his discovery of leadership. It is almost as though we are partners on the journey. We travel with him, discussing key issues of leadership such as humility, intuition, coolness under pressure, listening, the dangers of self-perception – and fun. And all the while he illustrates these aspects with choice examples of practical leaders. The educational process is one of two important aspects of this impressive book. There are nuggets about strategic leadership scattered throughout the book. The reader has to do quite a lot of mining to uncover the veins – but they are there! This is the educational value of the publication; readers have to do their part to get the most from it by applying themselves and reflecting on Adair's ideas.

The other important aspect of the book is the way the author explores what these great leaders actually did when faced with real challenges. Whether we be scholars or practitioners, we can all learn from Alexander's behaviour lost in the Gedrosian desert at the head of 30,000 thirsty men (*ibid.*: 66–7) or Nelson's absolute trust in his men, especially his officers (*ibid.*: 177, 183). Indeed, the Commander of the Royal Navy Task Force during the Falklands War in 1982, Admiral Sir Sandy Woodward, referred to his ships' captains as 'a band of brothers', echoing Nelson's relationship with his sea captains at Trafalgar some 180 years previously (Woodward and Robinson 1992) – and today's armed forces principle of mission command can be traced, in part, back to Nelson's style of leadership.

A number of leadership styles are explored with perceptive insight to draw out the key learning. Thus, under one cover, we are able to examine such diverse leaders as Shackelton, Abraham Lincoln, Hitler and Gandhi. Rich pickings indeed! However, perhaps the most impressive part of Adair's thesis is reserved for the final chapter entitled 'Leaders of Tomorrow'. His conclusion from this sweep across history is that 'greatness now is more a matter of quality rather than degree' and that it is possible to be 'a great leader' as a supervisor, a hospital sister or a teacher (*ibid.*: 297) and that 'real excellence goes hand-in-hand with humility' (*ibid.*: 300). Lord Hunt (the leader of the first British expedition to climb Everest in 1953) is quoted as saying that a leader has been well described as a 'first companion' (*ibid.*: 295).

It is Adair's ability to draw lessons from some of the great leaders in history, reflect on them, identify the key characteristics and then relate them thoughtfully to today's world that is the lasting memory of this book – and that is also the connection with the other book that I now want to review.

Effective Strategic Leadership

Effective Strategic Leadership is the first book to focus specifically on the strategic level of leadership and is one of several titles written by Adair in the 'Effective Leadership and Management' series published by Pan Macmillan. Essentially, these are books written for the practitioner, as the titles imply. And yet Adair's historical foundations come to the fore in the opening pages when he refers to Socrates and Xenophon. There is also a clear acknowledgment to the military roots of strategic leadership with Chapter 2 being devoted to that topic. These foundations provide key components to Part One (entitled: Understanding Strategic Leadership) whose last chapter explores the role of the strategic leader and includes some interesting sections on imagination, humility and the anatomy of wisdom.

This leads neatly into Part Two (Leading the Way), which provides excellent pragmatic guidelines. To me, this is the real value of the book. There are probably more practical tips on strategic leadership than in any other publication, with the possible exception of Warren Bennis' *Managing People is Like Herding Cats* (1998). If more leaders at the top of organisations had read this section we would have a much higher level of strategic leadership in UK today. Chapter 5 is about the first hundred days, which is a critical period for any top leader. It is at the beginning of their tenure that leaders establish their style and priorities, and this chapter provides good guidelines. No less important is the next chapter on 'building the top team'. This commences with '... we did this ourselves' quote from Lao Tzu (Adair 2002: 140) and contains excellent advice on choosing the right team as well as discussing the problems with top team leadership, including a perceptive comment on 'the necessity for disagreement' by Peter Drucker (*ibid*.: 155–6). The chapter concludes with the hallmarks of team excellence – both practical and helpful.

The other three chapters in this section are all in a similar vein. The aspects that caught my eye included 'unfreezing your strategic thinking' (*ibid*.: 170–1), the principle of thinking one level up (*ibid*.: 180), the importance of flexibility (*ibid*.: 191–5), vision and values (*ibid*.: 207–10) pacing change (*ibid*.: 219–22) and Chapter 9 on finding time for individuals. There are case studies woven into the whole of this section, but no more so than this last chapter, including a typically useful piece about Slim.

Part Three is entitled 'I am myself my own Commander'. This is itself an interesting title; it will resonate with those in the military, but not necessarily so with those who are not. Chapter 10 concentrates on what is required to be an effective strategic leader (thinking, planning – but also vocation and creativity). The next chapter considers five strategies that work with people. These are worth spelling out because here lies the key to effective behaviour:

Trust
Love All
Integrity
Be Courteous
Be Generous

When one reflects on these characteristics, it becomes very evident why some individuals are effective at the top level, and others are not. Courtesy is a case in point.

The final chapter is a treat. It is entitled 'Discovering Wells of Inspiration' and it reflects Goffee and Jones' work examining the ingredients of inspirational leaders (Goffee and Jones 2000). Adair not only explores the nobility of spirit in adversity which enables ordinary people to inspire those around them (*ibid*.: 308), but he also dissects its meaning, primarily by quoting Slim's (1956) thought process when considering how to beat the Japanese Army in Burma (*ibid*.: 309–12). The chapter combines the exploration of inspiration (notoriously difficult to explain) with some pragmatic advice on strategic leadership, particularly the value of mentors. Although short, this chapter contains gems of advice.

So, we have in this publication valuable lessons for both current and future strategic leaders. It is a book which provides an excellent aide-memoire for the reader to return to (such as when trying to cope with difficult colleagues on the board). It is perhaps best summed up by the explanation on the front cover: 'an essential path to success guided by the world's great leaders'. The path is indeed laid by chosen extracts of successful leaders but Adair also guides the reader expertly.

Adair the teacher and influencer

Having looked at Adair's authorship of these two influential books, let us now move on to his role as a teacher and influencer.

Alongside his colleagues and friends, Charles Handy and Warren Bennis, he has influenced literally tens of thousands of people by his thinking on leadership, both as a public speaker and when conducting one of his thoughtful tutorials for university postgraduate students or at business seminars. Indeed, many who have attended the latter consider those sessions to have had the most influence on their own leadership development, particularly at the strategic level. But more than that, he has tirelessly sought to influence people at the top of organisations by engaging them in debate about their own strategic thinking and direction. His influence internationally is significant. For instance, he has twice been listed amongst the 40 people worldwide who have contributed most to management thought and practice.

But this has often been a lonely and frustrating journey, not only because he has for so long been the sole voice of leadership in the UK but also because so many leaders at the top of organisations are reluctant to listen and seek advice. The second part of the chapter will examine Adair's role as a teacher, explore why so few top leaders are learners, will then consider his views and influence on the practical issues of leadership, and compare these with other authors and contemporary leaders. I will also draw on my interview with him at Windsor on 28 April 2005.

Adair the teacher

Adair's style as a teacher is Socratic. Invariably, he will start a seminar by asking questions of the group and will draw from them, their views on leadership (interestingly, Warren Bennis adopts a similar approach). Not only does this enable him to shape the seminar around their interests, it also keeps him abreast of what people are thinking and quickly establishes a rapport with a group. Although he will then present his thesis, it is apparent that he is more interested in the subsequent questions and discussion (this is also true of his public lectures) – and it is during this last phase that he excels. The more searching the questions, the deeper the answers. Indeed, he likes nothing better than to be part of a vigorous debate around a certain aspect of leadership, sharing ideas, arguing (and often disagreeing) with colleagues on an equal footing.

It seems to me that he is more comfortable in this role than as 'the expert' – and yet, he has been forced into the latter position for years because there were not enough people with the knowledge to challenge his views or debate on the same level, that is until Exeter University introduced its Postgraduate Diploma/MA in Leadership Studies in 1993. The first cohort of that groundbreaking programme included a mixture of individuals from both the public and the private sectors, all with a practical interest in Leadership. They learnt the rudiments very quickly and by the time they came to Adair's third lecture they were challenging and pushing him all the way. As a result he became reenergised and guided them further down the path of knowledge. The more questions they asked, the deeper the group explored, with Adair as mentor rather than a teacher. As one of them remarked at the end of a particularly stimulating session: 'that was rather a grown-up discussion!'

It is therefore appropriate in the context of this volume to acknowledge the special relationship between John Adair and Exeter's Centre for Leadership Studies.[1] Together they have furthered the understanding of this fascinating topic and just as John has provided expertise and knowledge he, in turn, has been stimulated by the level of discussion and quality of thinking which has emerged from Exeter.

Adair the influencer

Adair has been very much in demand for some 40 years as a speaker on leadership and continues to be so. Indeed, a trip abroad this year took him to China, where his work has been well received (see the contribution of Mak in Chapter 11). The invitations have come from a variety of sources including corporate organisations, management institutions and senior leaders. Institutes and organisations seeking a good keynote speaker at their conferences, corporates requiring guidance for their senior management team, and senior leaders looking for a good mentor have all sought his extensive knowledge of leadership. Sir John Harvey Jones (ICI), Rupert Hambro (Hambro Bank), Sir Geoffrey Maddrell (Tootal Group), and Sir Bob Reid (British Rail) have all sought his advice and guidance.

He has promoted the same line on leadership to all these individuals and audiences; a practical approach based on sound common sense and founded on his 'three-circles' model. So, if he has been able to reach out to such a large audience for so many years, why are there still so few effective strategic leaders in the UK? I asked him this question during an interview on 28 April 2005. Adair's response was:

> Because of their egos. Their drive to get to the top mitigates their ability to listen and to learn. Most of them have had no leadership training,

and many have got to the top principally through the strength of their personalities.

These observations will strike a chord with many and explain in part why so many individuals at the top of organisations are not effective, especially in our fast-changing world. In the same interview he pointed out that even the military, who are good at identifying strategic leaders, are less successful at developing them – although, it must be added that this gap is now being addressed through courses run by the Defence Academy. Strength of personality is always likely to be part of the DNA of top leaders (de la Billière 1992). One only has to look at the strong personalities operating at the top of the British military command structure in World War Two (Keegan 1991) to realise that only the strongest will survive in the heat of battle – or in the high pressure of business. There are very high stakes involved. That being accepted, the UK in particular is not producing enough effective strategic leaders. Adair has argued (2005) that there is only a small percentage who have the capability to operate at the top level. Whilst accepting this point, others (Hooper and Potter 2000; Hodgson 2004) argue that the small percentage could be increased through appropriate development and more self-awareness. Adair suggests that organisations should focus on key aspects of strategic leadership and use these to identify and develop potential. He believes there are seven such aspects:

- Providing direction
- Strategic thinking and strategic planning
- Making it happen
- Getting the interrelated parts in an organisation properly balanced
- Relationship between the strategic leadership and the outside world
- Releasing the corporate energy
- Identifying today's and tomorrow's leaders

In amplification Adair (2005) believes that so much of this is about priorities. 'Making it happen' is about focus (Sir Terry Leahy is very good at this, which is why Tesco is such a success; conversely, Greg Dyke was less focused when running the BBC – hence his rapid departure in January 2004 in the wake of the Gilligan-Kelly incident). With regard to thinking and planning Adair points out that the urgent tends to over-rule the important – but strategic leaders need to concentrate on the latter, and to do a lot of thinking: 'there are great dividends from deep, continuous thinking'.[2]

In his research into the 'Top Leader's Journey' Hodgson (2004) has also identified the same trait (he calls it 'focus of attention'). He has identified other similar themes such as spotting and developing potential, inspiration and energy, managing upwards and outwards. In addition, Hodgson speaks of 'credibility' which he says 'is like a kind of currency' (Hodgson 2004:

19). This mirrors the view of others (Hooper and Potter 2000) and Adair (2005) who believes:

> Leaders have a 'bank of credit' on which they can draw. For instance, provided their professional reputation is good, their people will accept some personal failings (such as Nelson's mistress, Churchill and drink), but if they 'overdraw' their reputation will be affected. It is their followers who will decide on this.[3]

This leads us to the behaviour and style of top leaders – and their integrity. Only those who have operated at the very top have a realistic idea of the pressures, responsibilities and loneliness of leadership at this level. It is also characterised by experiencing emotions ranging from euphoria to despair (witness Tony Blair having to cope in the full glare of the public eye with such an emotional swing from the announcement on 6 July this year that London had won the Olympic bid for 2012, to the following day's suicide bombings in the capital). No 'training' can prepare a leader for such an emotional high and low, especially when the world's media is dissecting every public statement and monitoring all the body language. In such circumstances, only the toughest survive.

Strategic leaders develop their style over time and hone their skills through experience. All are different and individual (thank goodness); some are grown by their organisations (Lord Browne at BP and Sir Terry Leahy at Tesco) and others start along one journey and then switch course to make their name in another field (e.g., Lord Paddy Ashdown – from the Royal Marines via the Foreign Office and politics to become the UN High Representative for Bosnia and Herzegovina; and Sir Stuart Hampson – from the Foreign Office to becoming Chairman of John Lewis Partnerships). Whatever their journey, by the time they have reached their pinnacle they have developed considerable self-confidence and courage for, without these two ingredients, they would not be able to do their job properly. For instance, during his time running Bosnia, Ashdown has forced out two presidents and sacked 60 officials. He has been accused of being aggressive but he has countered this by pointing out that: 'This is a big job. Take three recently warring peoples, full of enmity and mistrust and bring about reforms. So you make enemies. You can't possibly not' (quoted in Swain 2005: 6).

The point here is that when they set out on life's journey, people like Tony Blair and Paddy Ashdown did not know where they would end up. They may well have been filled with ambition, energy and drive, but they did not know that this would lead to them having to take difficult and often courageous high-level decisions on a regular basis. This is much more about leaders being able to relate to people and judging when is the right moment to take a decision, than it is about pure competence. This is what separates potential strategic leaders from the rest. It also embraces what Goffee and Jones (2000) call 'tough empathy': leaders who demonstrate that they care passionately about the work their people do will, in turn, get their backing. As Greg Dyke remarked (Goffee and Jones 2000: 68) 'Once you have the people with you, you can make the difficult decisions that need to be made.'

The ingredients for success at the strategic level are different from those required at the operational level. It is true that they are forged in the same foundation – but they are different. It therefore follows that individuals who are successful at the operational level will not necessarily succeed at the top. The reverse is also true (Mountbatten did not shine as a ship's captain). The key is to identify, develop and groom individuals for senior positions so that they become leaders with 'a noble purpose' (Adair 2005) rather than displaying some of the worst characteristics of narcissism (Maccoby 2000).

On the whole the public sector is better at this development than the private. In particular, the Armed Services and the Civil Service are good at identifying individuals of high potential and then providing them with the sort of career path which gives them the necessary breadth and experience to enable them to operate effectively when they reach the top. The companies in the private sector who do this well include BP, an organisation which is currently grooming individuals for the top jobs, one of whom will eventually succeed Lord Browne. Barclays Bank have also introduced a development programme for their senior leaders following an initiative from Matt Barratt who, when he became CEO in 1999, was the third chief executive in 12 months.

So, where is Adair's hand in all this? We have seen evidence of his influence on the thinking about strategic leadership through his identification of the seven key aspects. However, he was conscious that this was not sufficient if the percentage of effective leadership was to be increased. What was required was an appropriate programme for individuals at the right moment in their careers. He has long been a Fellow of the Windsor Leadership Trust, which runs its programme at St George's House, Windsor (most appropriate as he was the Director of Studies there in 1968/69 at the beginning of its life). He was the instigator of a new initiative for the Trust in 2001: 'Consultation for Newly Appointed Strategic Leaders'. This consists of a four-day programme for those who have just moved into strategic leadership roles (for example, bishops, chief constables, vice-chancellors, generals and chief executives of charities, businesses and companies). The dynamic discussions amongst the 20 participants on the programme, expertly guided by experienced facilitators and stimulated by a few carefully chosen outside speakers, provides just what is needed to prepare individuals for the responsibilities of their next appointments. Above all, this format enables senior leaders to share difficult and often personal issues with peers in a safe and confidential environment. It thus tackles the 'loneliness at the top' issue very effectively by providing a means for each cohort to provide support to each other after they have completed the programme.

Of course this programme is not catching enough people – but it is a start. And it is being mirrored by similar senior leadership programmes such as Exeter University's 4 × 4 Group (for those operating at the strategic level) and another run for the Armed Services by the Defence Leadership Centre under the auspices of the UK Defence Academy. This one-week course was piloted in November 2002 and is now mandatory for all newly-appointed one star rank (brigadier equivalent) of the three Armed Services. It is reckoned that this programme will therefore have sufficient impact on the culture of all three services within three years through such mechanisms as a mandatory 360° appraisal for all delegates. If only other organisations could arrange their leadership development programmes so efficiently we would soon improve the UK strategic leadership effectiveness!

Conclusion

This chapter has investigated John Adair's influence on strategic leadership over a long period by considering the impact of two of his books *Great Leaders* and *Effective Strategic Leadership* and also his role as a teacher and influencer.

As a writer he has drawn on his background as an historian and developed ideas founded on the past but also related to the present. Above all, his writing has been for the practitioner and we have seen how his ideas have developed as he has learnt, in turn, from those he has 'taught'. This Socratic approach lies at the heart of his work and it is why his ideas are still developing – and still relevant.

Being a writer has enabled Adair to give himself time to reflect. However, if he had just stuck to his writing he could not have had the same influence as he has achieved as a public speaker and agitator (the speed with which Sir Richard Greenbury responded to Adair's public criticism of Marks and Spencer in 1994 is a case in point). His affable personality and innocent questions hide a sharp mind and many a chief executive has been surprised by his rapier-like analysis of what is wrong and, more importantly, what needs to be done to improve the situation. Not many individuals who have not had the responsibility of running a large organisation have that ability – and that is why Adair has been in demand. Crucial has been his ability to appreciate sympathetically the pressures to which top leaders are subjected. The reason he is so effective is because he has had an ambition to be a strategic leader since the age of 20 and has therefore been thinking at that level since he was a young man – it therefore comes naturally to him. Although he may not have succeeded in that initial aim he has achieved far more by his ability to influence thousands of people, helping them to think better and operate more effectively at the strategic level.

Adair is not so much an academic's academic as a practitioner's academic. He focuses on the practical; constantly seeking to understand the realities of situations, offering advice based on extensive study of leadership for over 45 years. Above all his role has been that of an intelligent, curious and critical sounding board. It is for consideration that his 'strategos' legacy will be that of being the 'conscience' of those exercising power at the strategic level, constantly holding a mirror to their integrity, both through his writing and via face to face discussion.

Notes

1   The author was appointed Programme Director of the first Postgraduate Diploma/ MA in Leadership at Exeter University in 1992, and subsequently the Founding Director of the Centre of Leadership Studies in 1997. John Adair was appointed the first Visiting Professor of Leadership Studies at Exeter University. The successful development of the study of leadership at Exeter during this period was largely due to the close working relationship between these two individuals and Sir Geoffrey Holland, the then Vice-Chancellor of the University.
2   Interview with Adair, 28/04/05.
3   Interview with Adair, 28/04/05.

References

Adair, J. (1989) *Great Leaders*, Guildford: Talbot Adair.
Adair, J. (2002) *Effective Strategic Leadership*, London: Macmillan.
Adair, J. (2005) Personal Interview, Windsor, April 28, 2005.
Bennis, W. (1998) *Managing People is like Herding Cats*, London: Kogan Page.
de la Billière, P. (1992) *Storm Command*, London: Harper Collins.
Goffee, R. and Jones, G. (2000) 'Why Should Anyone be Led by You?', *Harvard Business Review*, Sep–Oct, pp.63–70.
Hodgson, P. (2004) 'Working Where the Buck Stops', *The Ashridge Journal*, Autumn.
Hooper, A. and Potter, J. (2000) *Intelligent Leadership*, London: Random House.
Keegan, J. (1991) *Churchill's Generals*, London:Weidenfeld & Nicholson.
Maccoby, M. (2000) 'Narcissistic Leaders: the Incredible Pros, the Inevitable Cons', *Harvard Business Review*, 78(1), pp.69–77.
Slim, W. (1956) *Defeat into Victory*, London: Cassell.
Swain, J. (2005) 'King Paddy reigns supreme', *Sunday Times News Review*, London: 17 July, p.6.
Woodward, S. and Robinson, P. (1992) *One Hundred Days*, London: HarperCollins.

3
Bridging the Gap: A Perspective on the Contribution of John Adair

John Potter

Setting the scene

This chapter addresses three areas where John Adair has, in the author's view, made a major contribution to the world of understanding leadership. Firstly the position of John Adair as a major thinker on leadership is established from his roots in the military world which then expanded to impact on a wide range of organisations from the Church to organisations highly focused on creating profit. Secondly Adair's ideas on the needs of task, team and individual are related to a number of other approaches to leadership, namely the American bipolar task-relationship behavioural approach and then the more psychoanalytic approach which acknowledges the unconscious aspects of leadership processes. Thirdly three short case studies are presented which the author would like to suggest show how Adair's Functional Leadership Approach was successfully applied to address some problem situations in terms of leadership. These three case studies emphasise, in the author's view, that Adair's approach really does 'bridge a gap' between academic and practical approaches to leadership in a number of organisational settings. The first case study relates to the academic world of leadership research and the study suggested that there was considerable evidence that followers really do perceive leadership as being related to the satisfaction of the three sets of needs of task, team and individual. The second case is an informal, virtual setting with a number of individual followers having a common interest who were drawn together to take action on a shared problem as a group. The task, team and individual needs approach was used to provide structure to focus the efforts of this group and provide social support in a very ambiguous situation. The third example was in the area of culture change where the Adair approach was used on the surface level with the intention of causing change at the deeper level of underlying assumptions.

John Adair's varied career has enabled him to experience a wide range of human activities and organisations and in particular it has enabled him to gain a unique perspective on leadership and its various aspects at all organisation levels. Perhaps the most significant catalyst in terms of formulating the Functional or Action Centred approach to leadership development was the time he spent on the staff of the Royal Military Academy Sandhurst. The present author followed in Adair's footsteps in terms of developing the theoretical and conceptual input to the leadership development process of the Royal Military Academy Sandhurst between 1979 and 1987 and that work was greatly facilitated by the groundwork which John Adair had put in place in the mid-1960s.

The main aim of this chapter is to look at the way the work of John Adair has been translated into practical leadership development tools and processes since its inception in the 1960s. Readers of a great deal of academic material are often left with the feeling that the concepts presented are good ideas, but what do you actually do on Monday morning when you try to apply them to the real world? John Adair's approach has a great strength in that from the earliest exposure the reader has with his material, it becomes rapidly apparent that there are straightforward ways to apply the principles of functional or action-centred leadership. This forms a powerful bridge between academic and practical worlds where it is so often said that there is a need for effective leadership. Although much of Adair's early work had its roots in the world of the military, he has successfully taken his ideas and gained acceptance over a wide range of organisations in both the public and private sectors.

Leadership inherently features a considerable amount of ambiguity and this tends to be challenging in terms of translating concepts into practical applications in the organisational setting. John Adair investigated a number of approaches to gaining an understanding of the psychological processes which exist within small group situations and eventually turned to group theory, which was a relatively new subject in the 1960s. Coupled with his desk research, John Adair observed groups of young army officers training on the Barossa Training area attached to the Royal Military Academy and started to notice the difference between those leaders who achieved the task, built a team and took account of the needs and abilities of the individual members of their team compared to those that did not satisfy these three sets of needs. This was explained very well in group theory by the three issues of needs encountered when a group develops and works together – the needs of the task, the needs of the team and the needs of individuals within the team. John Adair then set about looking at what the successful leaders actually did and what behaviours they displayed in order to carry out those functions and meet the three sets of needs of the group. And so the concept of functional leadership was formed based on what functions the leader needs to perform in order to meet the three sets of needs, in contrast to a previous focus, which had been on the qualities of the leader and how these matched certain situations.

The historian turned behaviourist

Much of the contemporary writing about leadership has a significant psychological component, largely due to the methodologies and research approaches on which it is based. However, this may be a dangerously narrow approach, because leadership should be viewed as an inherently complex human phenomenon to be approached through multi-disciplinary means. We should draw on sociology, anthropology, ethics, philosophy and history as well as psychology and behavioural science. John Adair's approach, whilst grounded in various issues of human behaviour, is essentially multi-disciplinary, and looks for causal relationships between leaders carrying out behaviours within a certain framework and the output that those behaviours produce in terms of task, team development and individual contributions (Adair 1983). Adair argues that it enables a spectral shift to be made towards creating more effective leadership processes for any individual, particularly in team situations and those with clear resource and time constraints. But the model is also applicable in situations where a longer timescale is involved and where there is more ambiguity than in a simple command task. In these more complex situations there is more scope for variation of the emphasis placed on the three aspects of satisfying task, team and individual needs particularly as time progresses.

John Adair entered the world of leadership study from the perspective of an historian. His first researches focused around great leaders of the past and his book *Great Leaders* (Adair 1989) details many outstanding examples throughout history. The basic emotions such as fear, anger, excitement, passion and love have probably not changed a great deal over many centuries, although our tolerance of how we display those emotions and accept displays from others has shifted. Thus it is worth considering what writers and commentators have said about leadership in the past and John Adair has provided excellent evidence for this assertion in his book *Effective Strategic Leadership* (Adair 2002). The words of Socrates on what makes a good leader still ring true even in today's society of electronic communication, mass international travel, resource limitations, international terrorism and suicide bombers. Adair (2002: 16) quotes Socrates pointing out that leaders in both business and military situations need to perform much the same functions:

> selecting the right man [sic] for the job
> punishing the bad and rewarding the good
> winning the goodwill of those under them
> attracting allies and helpers
> keeping what they have gained
> being strenuous and industrious in their own work

In some respects the six basic issues above form the foundations for Adair's functional approach to leadership. More specific than the early approaches of Socrates and his followers, they can lead to the development of specific skills through training. One of Adair's clearest expositions of the functions of leadership was created in *Effective Leadership* (Adair 1983) where they appear as follows: Defining the task, planning, briefing, controlling, evaluating, motivating, organising, and setting an example.

In his published work, Adair varies both the number and descriptions of functions, but all provide a framework for addressing the three needs of task, team and individual.

These essential leadership functions were not however created without substance.

Adair draws on the pronouncements of key figures in history and his own observations of how significant individuals such as Alexander the Great, Napoleon and Nelson operated. However, like most researchers, writers and commentators on leadership, John Adair developed a degree of frustration that leadership seemed to be a concept which was esoteric, formless and ill defined and at the same time, subject to personal interpretation and bias. The present author subsequently shared that frustration when he tried, as part of his contribution to leadership development in the courses run at the Royal Military Academy, to create working definitions of leadership and leadership processes. Such frustration was not reduced by a reading of Stogdill (1974) which presents over 160 definitions of leadership. The present author found it convenient to consider leadership as operating on three levels. Initially these were labelled as the strategic or 'big picture' level, the ambient or 'day-to-day' level and the episodic or 'small group' level where a specific task was being undertaken within well-defined boundaries. The episodic level of leadership activity often forms the basis for leadership training and development exercises as it is often relatively straightforward to give a small group of individuals a task to perform, and to study formal and informal processes of leadership. This idea of 'episodic' leadership emerged from a study of the work of Forgas (1979) on social episodes. Essentially social episodes are relatively short-term events with specific boundaries and well-defined outcomes, a situation often created in leadership development programmes. The concept of episodic, frontline or team leadership was explored by Hooper and Potter (1997) and used to identify specific competence requirements of leaders in episodic leadership situations. These competence areas were somewhat different to the leadership functions identified by Adair in that they focused specifically on leadership, whereas Adair's leadership functions include various aspects of management such as planning. The concept of 'leadership competence' was then extended to the operational level, which requires creating an environment in which episodes can take place effectively; and the strategic level, which involves creating the overall direction in which the organisation was moving.

His life experience shaped his views

In his early days, John Adair had a varied set of experiences as both leader and follower, which undoubtedly helped shape his views on leadership both as a subject of interest and a capability which could be developed within a wide range of individuals. He was adjutant of a Bedouin regiment in the Arab Region at the age of 20 and subsequently spent time as a deckhand on an Arctic trawler. After these two very different experiences he studied history at Cambridge University and then taught at the Royal Military Academy Sandhurst, which gave him an opportunity to study leadership development in a controlled environment. He became the world's first Professor of Leadership Studies at the University of Surrey in 1979 linked to the Department of Psychology and then set about a process of endeavouring to persuade other academic departments to embrace leadership in their academic curriculum. This was especially successful in the engineering area which was particularly amenable to Adair's 'command task' approach because of the close link between group project work and leadership.

John Adair was, however, almost alone in his efforts to establish leadership as an academic subject in the UK. In the 1980s, leadership was not viewed as a genuine academic subject by most universities; in fact many claimed that we knew all we needed to know about leadership and that there was no real point in exploring the issue. Adhering to the Great Man Theory, they focused on the possession of leadership qualities, regardless of the difficulty in defining those qualities in specific terms and in developing them other than through arduous experience or in training situations. The same could not, however be said of thought in the university world of the USA. In particular, the American Department of Defense thought that leadership was a subject worthy of rigorous research and during the 1960s and 1970s several American writers such as Ralph Stogdill (Stogdill 1974), Jane Mouton and Robert Blake (Blake and Mouton 1964), Paul Hersey and Ken Blanchard (Hersey and Blanchard 1969) investigated leadership thoroughly and created a number of interesting and useful models. Although some of this research was funded by the Department of Defense, it appears that the research started to attract a range of individual researchers who wanted to examine leadership beyond the military world.

The development of the subject

Adair, like many others, has offered a structured account of the development of thought on leadership during the 20ᵗʰ century. Firstly, there was the so-called Qualities Approach based on the Great Man Theories of the early part of the 20ᵗʰ century. In spite of growing interest in a more psychological approach than simply the 'born leader' argument, there appears to be relatively little in-depth research done on leadership in the 1900–30 period. Due to the difficulties in defining leadership qualities, how they might be identified in a specific individual and then how specific qualities might be developed it was necessary to take a different view on leadership. Theoretical interest shifted towards what the situation needed rather than focus on what qualities were or were not possessed by the leader. The Situational Approach, however, could not avoid the need to identify people to take the lead, and gave rise to leader selection systems based on group interaction and exercises. A number of these were employed during World War Two in the UK by the War Office Selection Boards (WOSBs) and more recently by the British Army in the Regular Commissions Board (RCB) process used to select potential officers. In the 1960s the Americans developed a behavioural approach mainly based on factor analysis of the characteristics of leaders and how they operate in specific situations. Stogdill (1974) gives a comprehensive explanation of both the work of the University of Ohio and the University of Michigan in this respect. In essence the research suggested that leaders operate with two types of behaviour: that directed towards achieving the task and that towards creating, developing and maintaining relationships. This was the essence of the Managerial Grid defined by Blake and Mouton (1964), which suggested five key leadership styles:

High Task and Low Relationship Style
High Task and High Relationship Style
Low Task and High Relationship Style
Low Task and Low Relationship Style
Medium Task and Medium Relationship Style

WHAT GRID?

The argument focused on the idea that leaders should nominally occupy the centre of the space with a medium level of emphasis on both task and relationship behaviour. It is then relatively easy to move to one of the four corners as necessary to achieve a specific outcome. This approach to leadership refers to one of the laws of cybernetics and expert Systems, namely Ashby's Law of Requisite Variety which states that the element in a system with the greatest number of options tends to control the system (Ashby 1956).

A related approach to the Managerial Grid was the Life Cycle Theory proposed by Hersey and Blanchard (1969). In basic terms, this involved the identification of four spaces of leadership behavioural style obtained by using the task and relationship axes to create a two-by-two, four cell matrix. In modern terms the analogy would be to imagine a Windows type environment with the two dimensional grid of task behaviour on the ordinate axis and relationship behaviour on the abscissa and then click on each corner of the grid bringing the 'corner' to the centre of the grid in a 'click and drag' process. Whilst this obviously removes the option of the 'medium task/medium relationship' behaviour, it creates a wider range of behavioural style mixes than the basic four corners. Specifically it matches the mix of task and relationship behaviour to the needs of the group being led. The argument is that groups, which are newly formed and hence 'immature', need direction and some psychological distance between the group and the leader. This group state is identified by high commitment but low competence. As the group develops under the direction of the leader, their competence will increase but their commitment may falter. Hersey and Blanchard argue that the mix of behaviour needs to be directed to both task and relationship issues in this situation. As group competence increases, then so too the commitment should increase somewhat, reducing the need for direction but increasing the dependency on social support and peer relationships, and hence a tendency for high competence but variable commitment. Once the commitment has been increased by the encouragement, social support and relationship-oriented behaviour of the leader then the group will be in a position to display high competence and high commitment, requiring a hands off, low task and low relationship behavioural style by the leader.

This appears at first sight to be fundamentally different to the Adair Functional Approach, which seems to suggest that the leader always should be seen to 'be leading' and in control of the situation. The Blake-Mouton approach also tends to suggest that the low task/low relationship is something to be avoided and the style has been described as 'departure lounge' leadership, often displayed by an individual in the final stages of their leadership career when they see little point in creating new tasks or in developing work relationships. But in the language of the 1990s and onwards this low task and low relationship style does find some support. The essence of empowerment and enablement is a reduction in command and control directive tendencies and the promotion of a 'hands off' approach in which the group is encouraged to 'lead itself' rather than rely on the leader for direction. This is the basis of such activity as Focus Groups and Quality Circles where the leader often chooses to submerge herself or himself within the group instead of dominating the proceedings. To take Ashby's Law of Requisite Variety seriously, leaders need a wide range of styles. But while they need flexibility in the way they deal with situations, they must at the same time retain consistency over a number of aspects including consistency to a set of values. Adair's Functional approach, in the present author's view, provides a model for ambiguous situations where uncertainty may prevail. In particular, crisis situations require direction and a focus of activity. This is where the Functional Approach can make a major contribution. As an example one deals very differently with the management of a road traffic accident in terms of making the situation safe, gaining control and dealing with casualties compared to running a creative marketing session. In the former situation, direction is required whereas in the second situation facilitation is more appropriate. Two major differences are the timescale and the level of urgency. The contribution that the task, team and individual approach can make is to focus the attention of the followers on producing outcomes in short timescales and this is a major benefit of Adair's approach.

This aspect of leadership was addressed in a classic article in the *Harvard Business Review* 'How to adopt a leadership pattern' by Tannenbaum and Schmidt (1973). These writers relate leadership style to the communication and decision-making patterns adopted by the leader. At one extreme they identify the leader who communicates on a one-way basis by telling the followers what to do. We might label this style the 'autocratic' approach. In some respects it is reflected in Adair's leadership function of defining the task and briefing the group. The middle of the Tannenbaum-Schmidt scale describes the leader being more democratic in that although still the centre of attention, they listen to inputs from the group while retaining the authority to make the final decision. In terms of the Functional Approach this could be interpreted as representing the functions of planning involving the group, controlling with varying degrees of intervention, motivating through interaction, organising and even setting an example in terms of being decisive in an appropriate way.

The third style identified by Tannenbaum and Schmidt relates once again to the 'subordinate-centred approach' to leadership which could be labelled '*laissez-faire*' leadership. This is perhaps a misnomer in that some people might interpret '*laissez-faire*' as lacking precision, being indecisive and not outcome focused. Indeed it was the present author's experience that when he attempted to introduce this style to the military leadership programme at the Royal Military Academy Sandhurst it was rejected on the perception that the leader was 'sloppy'! This was a complete misinterpretation of the nature of *laissez-faire* leadership which is really about the leader immersing themselves in the group and steering its direction from within rather than from a position of psychological distance. Thus the present author renamed the style 'covert' leadership and this found acceptance by the military community, particularly as certain Special Forces groups used the style extensively in their four-person operational cells.

John Adair's model does relate well to the Tannenbaum-Schmidt approach in that the emphasis on the functions can vary in intensity and delivery. He reports that in his work at the Royal Military Academy Sandhurst he used only three visual aids, one which related to the three overlapping circles of task, team and individual needs and the other two relating to decision-making along the lines of the ideas presented in the Tannenbaum-Schmidt paper.[1] Once again we find that the Functional Approach relates well to other leadership models and indeed often combines the attributes of several models. It does so in a way that avoids the need to explain much in the way of theoretical background and, as such, bridges the gap most effectively between thought on leadership and its practical application.

It is argued that the period of the 1980s termed by the present author 'the black hole of leadership' reflected on one hand the behavioural approach of the American researchers and writers and on the other hand the qualities and situational approach of the British and European writers. It was in this environment that John Adair shifted thinking in the United Kingdom from the characteristics of the leader as a person and the situations in which they displayed effectiveness to a generic approach of what the leaders actually 'did' in terms of satisfying the needs of the leadership situation. At the risk of over-generalising, it is here that there is a considerable difference between the American and the British approaches to leadership both in terms of selection and development processes. The American approach seems to be primarily related to the behaviours shown by the leader in terms of two clusters; task behaviours and relationship behaviours. This was certainly reflected by the work of Mouton and Blake, Ralph Stogdill and a number of studies including those undertaken at Ohio State University. As such, the approach was primarily leader-centred, albeit requiring considerable sensitivity to a limited range of situational factors. The British approach pro-moted by John Adair was less scientific and more direct. The major differ-ence was that Adair's three-part model focused on the leader's attention on the task needs, the needs of the team involved and the needs of individuals within that team rather than the characteristics of the leader *per se*. It is focused on actions rather than characteristics. The suggestion was that if the leader performed certain functions as outlined above, those three needs would be satisfied, albeit that the emphasis would shift between the three sets of needs according to the situation. The beauty of this action-centred approach was that the functions of defining the task, planning, briefing, controlling, evaluating, motivating, organising and setting an example lent themselves to the training process. The American approach on the other hand described multiple sets of leader behaviours and it was difficult to define a set of both task behaviours and relationship behaviours that would be applicable in all leadership situations, which was the claim of the Functional Approach.

Furthermore, the Functional Approach tends fundamentally to focus on people issues rather than task issues. Two-thirds of the model relate to human needs (team and individual) whilst one-third relates to the task needs. American models seemed to place equal emphasis on the needs of the task and the needs of the people. In the final analysis tasks need are achieved through the efforts of people and this is one of the fundamental aspects of Functional Leadership which the present author feels has led to the longevity of John Adair's work.

We can thus draw a map of the development of thought on leadership during the 20th century. It is Management Science which is the relatively new subject of the past 100 years, brought into existence by the need to control mass production. Essentially the management theorists and practitioners such as Henri Fayol, Alfred P. Sloan, and F.W. Taylor focused on the need to control complex human work activity by work division and essentially these approaches tended to be task focused. However, leadership, identified as far back as the time of Socrates, Xenophon and Plato has been a feature of human activity throughout history.

Whilst some might contest the detail of this model, Figure 3.1 does draw our attention to a number of issues relating to how thought on leadership has shifted from basically the Great Man Approach to a wider acknowledgement

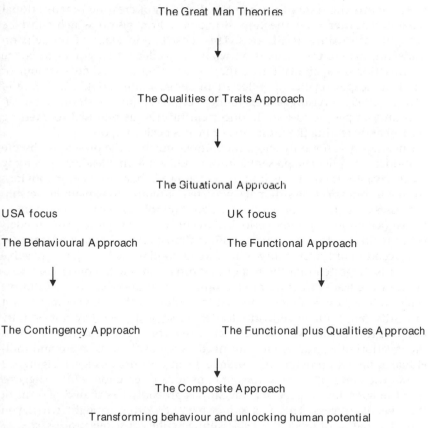

The Great Man Theories

↓

The Qualities or Traits Approach

↓

The Situational Approach

USA focus	UK focus
The Behavioural Approach	The Functional Approach
↓	↓
The Contingency Approach	The Functional plus Qualities Approach

↓

The Composite Approach

Transforming behaviour and unlocking human potential

Figure 3.1 Development of thought on leadership throughout the 20th-century
Source: Hooper and Potter 1997, 2001.

that there is no one approach to understanding leadership which meets the needs of all situations. In addition, this map suggests that there is a distinct flow from leadership being viewed as a command and control phenomenon to one where command and control is just one style, relevant only to certain situations, namely those typified by ambiguity or crisis.

This fundamental trend was identified by Senge (1990a) in his *Sloan Management Review* article 'The Leader's New Work'. Although this was essentially about leaders creating the Learning Organisation through developing five key aspects of the organisation (systems thinking, personal mastery, mental models, shared vision and team learning) it has considerable relevance to the role of the leader. In essence leadership, according to Senge is about unlocking human potential through the promotion of learning at the corporate, departmental, team and individual levels. In *The Fifth Discipline* (Senge 1990b) and *The Fifth Discipline Fieldbook* (Senge *et al.* 1994) Senge points the leader firmly in the direction of creating organisational capability rather than the imposition of a firm vision which must be brought into reality at all costs. This 'post heroic' stage of thought on leadership where the focus is on what the leader actually does to create organisational capability rather than attempting to become a saviour or charismatic personality is reflected in Senge's later book *The Dance of Change* (1999), advising leaders to focus on developing both the organisation and its people to handle uncertain futures, as opposed to exerting control and creating the future she or he has decided upon.

Uncertainty is not only about the future – much of the present is obscure or hidden from us. The present author would argue that leadership activity must have an unconscious impact on followers, beyond its more obvious conscious ones. Yet we still make persistent attempts to explain leadership processes on a purely conscious level. For example the importance of nonverbal behaviour is often overlooked in conscious level leadership models yet in reality, as in the animal world, it almost certainly plays a large part in perception of leader ability. When we respond to leadership in a positive way, it is suggested that the response is often not due to conscious assessment of the leader's ability or credibility but an unconscious or intuitive reaction based on confidence in that individual. Although we can attempt to justify our confidence in the leader consciously, we may not be fully aware of the reasons why we experience the 'confidence' reaction. Perhaps the creation of a structure for our needs, such as the task, team and individual approach, provides reassurance on an unconscious level. Figure 3.2 shows the concept of conscious-unconscious interaction which suggests that the conscious aspect of leadership is probably less than 5 percent of the overall process. This is a somewhat interesting thought when you consider that most models of leadership describe conscious processes.

This conscious-unconscious split is seldom referred to in the mainstream leadership literature. Among the few writers to do so are Andrew and Nada

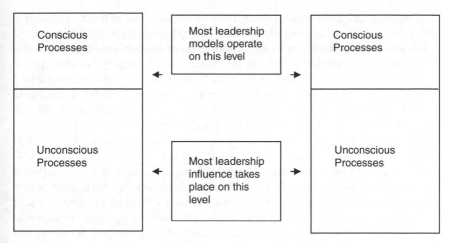

Figure 3.2   The conscious-unconscious aspects of leadership impact

Kakabadse (1998). In their book *Essence of Leadership* they acknowledge the relevance to the leadership process of the Freudian recognition of an unconscious mind. For example, they relate leader development to child-hood experience and the extent to which an individual develops the tendency towards being narcissistic. There is no 'one size fits all' theory of personality development; however, the major contribution made by the Kakabadse team is the acknowledgement that there is an unconscious aspect to leadership. So how does this relate to the John Adair model? In the main, Adair simply ignores these concerns. But another interpretation might be that the simplicity of the Functional Approach provides a rational pathway through situations beset by unconscious reactions. The eight basic functions can be learnt and internalised by the leader so that she or he automatically tends to perform them in leadership situations.

The present author has been exposed to leadership theory for well over 30 years. When a situation arises such as a road traffic accident or other crisis situation, the coping behaviour he displays is automatic and the basic functions are performed without any real conscious thought. The display of these behaviours tends to influence others in the situation who may be confused and needing direction and more positive outcomes tend to be produced than would be the case without the basic functions being addressed. Thus John Adair's model has the virtue of being easily inter-nalised by individuals and as such provides a 'click whirr' response to situations which require leadership behaviour. Cialdini (2001) claims in his book *Influence, Science and Practice* that both animals and humans have automatic responses to certain trigger stimuli, responses he calls 'click whirr'. For example it has been shown in many experimental situations that individuals will be compliant if the word 'because' is used to qualify a request. Real life bears out this assertion that we are all hard-wired with 'click whirr' responses. For example the present author was in a queue at a major European airport when an individual walked briskly past the queue to the immigration desk saying 'do you mind if I jump the queue *because* I have a bus to catch?' We all had buses, trains and taxis to catch yet became compliant due to the use of the word 'because' as a qualifier. Even the present author who was aware of the mechanism did not feel inclined to challenge the individual. 'Click-whirr' responses are very powerful in eliciting compliant behaviour and perhaps this is one of the reasons why relatively well-defined approaches to leader operation such as the functional approach are so powerful. Perhaps the functions produce click-whirr responses in the followers which reduce their feelings of uncertainty and promote a sense of comfort in situations which are ambiguous. Perhaps it is the simplicity of Adair's Functional Approach that allows it to be so readily internalised once the leader has been involved in a number of training exercises where the functions are examined and the success of the leadership activity assessed. With practice it seems to be the case that the functions become 'click-whirr' responses which happen almost without the leader giving them conscious thought, and which promote complementary 'click whirr' responses in others, who thus become 'followers'.

The leadership-management debate

One topic somewhat bypassed by the Adair Functional Approach is the leadership-management debate. In fact it does this by integrating leadership and management rather than differentiating between the two processes. A number of writers including Bennis (1998) and Kotter (1990) attempted to separate leadership and management. Whilst of interest from an academic perspective, the present author believes this can be problematic in practice. Bennis focuses on comparing a list of characteristics such as leaders being innovative whilst managers are simply administrators and that leaders inspire trust whilst managers rely on control. The way the lists differentiate between the 'leader' and the 'manager' are loaded in terms of the 'leader' characteristics column appearing more desirable than the column relating to the characteristics of the 'manager'. In Kotter's approach, the emphasis is on leadership processes compared to management processes. Management processes tend to focus on planning, organising, controlling, problem solving and creating predicable outcomes whilst leadership processes tend to focus on establishing direction, aligning people in emotional terms, motivating, inspiring and producing change. Again there seems to be an implied assertion that 'leadership' is somehow better and more desirable than 'management'. In the real world, of course, this is an assertion fraught with problems. For organisations to survive and prosper it is vital that management issues are addressed and handled in a competent way. Arie de Geus (1997) in his book *The Living Company* points out that most corporate bodies such as companies tend to have a limited life span in the order of less than 50 years. De Geus studied those corporates which did achieve longevity and found that they displayed several characteristics in common: they were sensitive to their environment, they were cohesive with a strong sense of identity, they were 'tolerant' rather than over controlled from the centre and they were conservative in financial terms. It does seem that taking all four factors into consideration they reflect both leadership and management issues in an integrated way. If we return to the eight functions proposed by Adair in his Functional Leadership Model we find both leadership and management: it is somewhat interesting to attempt the separation. The present author has attempted to do this but not without some difficulty.

Defining the task	– primarily management
Planning	– primarily management
Briefing	– management and leadership
Controlling	– management and leadership
Evaluating	– primarily management
Motivating	– primarily leadership
Organising	– primarily management
Setting an example	– primarily leadership

The fact that Adair's Functional Leadership contained a significant amount of management orientated behaviour is in the present author's view one of the reasons why the model has achieved such longevity.

The artificial separation of leadership and management by authors such as Bennis and Kotter was simply a passing phase. Common sense prevailed and most leadership development programmes seem at the present time to contain a significant amount of management focus, thus creating a more integrated approach to leadership development in both the worlds of business and the public sector. It is interesting that for nearly 40 years the Adair model has been retained by an enormous range of organisations including the armed forces, the police service, the church, government departments and some of the private sector. That surely points to the wisdom of the basic focus on the leader performing certain functions to meet the needs of the task, the team and the individuals within it.

Is the functional approach simply about team or frontline level leadership?

Because the three-circle model is readily addressed in teaching situations and then practised with 'command task' exercises there is a tendency to think it relates primarily to the team or frontline level of leadership. This has already been addressed earlier in this chapter in terms of identifying the episodic level of leadership activity. So what about the operational and strategic levels? Adair would argue that the three circles and the satisfaction of the three sets of needs through the leader performing certain functions is highly relevant. In particular in recent times he has turned his attention almost entirely to the strategic level and this is addressed in his book *Effective Strategic Leadership* (Adair 2002).

At the strategic level, seven leadership functions are proposed:

Providing direction for the organisation as a whole
Getting strategy and policy right
Making it happen
Organising or reorganising
Releasing the corporate spirit
Relating the organisation to other organisations and to society as a whole
Developing tomorrow's leaders

It is interesting that his approach now includes a much greater acknowledgement of the emotional and even spiritual nature of leadership, something that seemed to be lacking in the earlier basic functional approach. Such expressions as releasing the corporate spirit certainly reflect an emotional aspect and the phrase 'making it happen' has a motivational bias. This higher-level perspective describes the work of people who have already proven their leadership ability. Nonetheless, we recognise a basic strength of Adair's work in that it points us in the direction of specific areas of leadership operation which are capable of development through the right experiences, training and education.

Whilst Adair has focused on the team or frontline aspects of leadership and more recently on the strategic level, he does not seem to have explored the operational level to the same extent. This is not an implied criticism because inherently satisfaction of the task, team and individual needs will impact on the organisation at the operational level, indirectly if not directly. The issue at the operational level is concerned both with the culture of the organisation and with the more transient issue of climate, or 'atmosphere'. The operational level is influenced by a number of issues: whether managers are seen as bosses or coaches, where human energy is deployed in terms of constructive, defensive or aggressive behaviour and what it feels like to be part of that organisation, the elusive aspect of climate or 'atmosphere'. Goleman (2000) has made an interesting contribution in his article 'Leadership That Gets Results' in that he relates leadership style to the impact each style produces on climate. The most significant finding from the research carried out to explore these styles was that the traditional approaches of coercive and pace-setting leadership seem to produce a negative impact on the climate of the organisation compared to the other styles he labels at democratic, authoritative based on a vision, coaching and the promotion of effective working relationships throughout the organisation. In some respects the Adair approach based on the application of the leadership functions would seem to promote coercive leadership and leadership by example which could be seen as pace-setting leadership. However, if we focus instead on the satisfaction of the needs of the task, the team and individuals within the team, then Adair's Functional Leadership Model seems to relate well to Goleman's research in that it would: (1) take account of individual input (individual needs); (2) promote relationships (affiliative needs); (3) involve coaching (individual and group needs), and (4) promote the idea of a sense of direction (defining the task, briefing and planning). Thus it is the manner in which the Functional Approach would be applied that is the important issue in producing a positive impact on climate at the operational level rather than the individual functions themselves.

So does the Functional Approach work in practice?

In the experience of the present author the answer to this question has to be affirmative. Three mini cases are now presented which outline how the Functional Approach was applied to a number of situations.

Case study one – leadership research

In a doctoral research study carried out between 1979 and 1985 in his role as a military psychologist at the Royal Military Academy Sandhurst, the present author used a multi-dimensional scaling approach to compare the extent to which various leadership models reflected perceptions of the followers in real life situations (Potter 1985). Of all the models investigated, the most consistent in the clustering of the views of the participants was that effective leaders did take care of the needs of the task, the team and the individuals in the team whereas in the case of ineffective leaders this did not happen to the same extent. Simple task-relationship models did not have such descriptive validity.

It is interesting to consider the extent to which unconscious processes may have contributed to the findings of this research. The individual subjects concerned in the investigation were in a somewhat stressful military environment with considerable uncertainty and ambiguity. The leaders who made the task element clear may well have provided some degree of reassurance for their followers that in turn may well have given them a confident feeling, regardless of any real reduction in uncertainty. The investigation simply picked up their confidence, but did not enquire more deeply into its causes. In any case, the leaders who pulled each team together and helped promote a common focus were described in a positive way as were the leaders who took the trouble to maintain contact with each individual. Thus it could be argued that there was an implied unconscious and emotional impact due to the leader operating in a focused way, addressing these three sets of needs proposed by Adair.

Case study two – imposing the functional approach framework on an ambiguous situation

The second practical application of the Functional Approach to leadership was the initiating of an action group following a fraud in which the present author's mother became a victim. Some 500 elderly investors lost approximately £2m between them at the hands of an unscrupulous financial scheme, supposedly underwritten by a major High Street Bank. No individual investor had the resources to tackle this challenge on an individual basis as the costs of litigation against the intermediaries responsible for marketing the produce would have greatly exceeded the probable return to the individual investor. However the present author decided to implement the Functional Approach and set up an action group to focus on the three sets of needs. Firstly each investor was invited to make a modest non-returnable donation to a fighting fund, based on £5.00 per £1,000 invested. As this amount based on the average investment of £4,000 it was a relatively low risk exercise for each investor yet raised a fighting fund of around £10,000 which was more than enough to pilot a test case for negligence through the judicial system. The task needs were to assemble evidence and create a case to show negligence against the various intermediaries concerned to trigger their Professional Indemnity Insurance and thus compensate investors. The second aspect was to take account of the team needs in the situation. The approach taken was to divide the country which included the whole of the United Kingdom into ten geographical areas each containing on average 50 investors. Each area had a local contact person and this person was then contacted by the individual investors in their area. Each area representative would then stay in contact with the coordinator, the present author and in that way, information could be disseminated throughout the network in a very efficient way and each individual investor felt part of a team. In addition to the telephone communications, each area rep was sent a monthly update in writing which then would be forwarded to individual investors. In the early stage global mail shots were sent as updates to all investors but to conserve resources with the passage of time the more limited approach of writing to the area representatives worked well. Finally it was important to realise that each individual investor was a separate case. Some had only £500 invested whilst a number had amounts as high as £15,000 invested. Thus individual needs were catered for as most of the area representatives were the investors with the higher levels of investment in the bonds. The outcome was a success in that the test case brought to court produced a judgement in favour of the investor and against the intermediary who was found to be negligent in recommending the bonds as a secure investment. The Professional Indemnity Insurance situation meant that all investors were compensated due to the legal precedent, which had now been created. The reality is that it is unlikely that any compensation would have taken place without the test case and that case could only be brought to court funded by the whole group of investors. Thus the framework of taking care of the needs of the task, building a team and accommodating individual needs enabled a positive result to take place for the investors, and the present author feels that this was a result which would not have been so readily achieved using another leadership model.

In this situation there was a high level of anxiety on the part of the followers in terms of the risk of pursuing the legal action. However, creating the structure of addressing task, team and individual needs did much to reduce that level of anxiety and thus almost certainly had a strong unconscious emotional impact on the followers in terms of social support.

This case study was interesting in that it was not simply an example of leadership which proved to be effective but a mix of management and leadership, notably with regards to the task issue. Adair's Functional Approach does seem to act as a good reference point to ensure that task needs are addressed and in doing so, it bridges the gap which is a potential danger of the attempt to separate leadership and management.

Case study three – the functional approach applied to culture change

The third example of the application of the Functional Approach took place in a culture change programme in the mid-1990s for a major aerospace company. The company had invested heavily in a Total Quality Programme but was not achieving the desired results. This was a clear case of focus just on satisfying one set of needs, the task needs, without addressing either the team or individual needs. A training and development programme was devised to address the corporate culture and the extent to which certain management and leadership behaviours were rewarded or otherwise. The programme involved developing the participants in terms of the basic functions of leadership already identified, namely defining the task, planning, briefing, controlling, evaluating, motivating, organising and setting an example. As part of developing the participants in terms of their effectiveness in these areas, four key themes of coaching, goal setting, counselling and cross functional relationship promotion were introduced. The programme developed towards a sound awareness of frontline and operational leadership as it was primarily aimed at the first line and middle management levels of the organisation. Some 12 types of management behaviour were identified including the four constructive behaviours above of coaching, goal setting, counselling and cross functional awareness development. The focus was on these four positive behavioural sets rather than the defensive and conflict behaviours which were reducing organisational effectiveness. The culture of the organisation was investigated using an organisational culture instrument called the OCI produced by a company called Synergistics and this data showed that on average the four positive behaviour sets increased by around 15 percent whereas the negative behaviours reduced by a similar amount. This thus provides a third example of how the Functional Approach of widening leadership behaviour from simple task issues to take into account the socio-emotional aspects of team and individual development can produce a highly significant effect in an organisational setting. In one effectiveness assessment of this programme, it was estimated that the improvement in cross functional communication saved the company in excess of £800,000 for an investment in the development programme of less than £100,000. In terms of value added, the Functional Approach made a major contribution to the success of the organisation.

As with the previous two case studies, although the assessment of the culture change process based on the task, team and individual needs of the participants was made on a conscious level which could be presented and articulated in quantified terms, there was anecdotal evidence to suggest that the programme had produced a deeper impact on the culture of the organisation even though many participants did not recognise it at the time. Many participants commented several years after the programme that the exercise had changed the way they thought about themselves and others and that they had created cross functional relationships which had lasted for many years after the development programme had finished. As such the impact of the programme at the underlying assumptions level of the organisation should not be overlooked. Schein (1992) has commented that it is these underlying assumptions of which the members of the organisation are not always consciously aware, that are the real determinants of organisational culture. It could be argued that the programme based on the surface model of addressing task, team and individual needs produced a shift on an unconscious emotional level which shifted the culture of the organisation by creating change at the level of these underlying assumptions.

Summary and conclusions

From all the publications produced and the research carried out in recent decades it is clear that there is no single model of leadership applicable to all situations. Leadership is a highly complex, often emotionally-based process much of which takes place on a level of which we are not aware. However, we are often faced with a real need for leadership and this is where the Adair Model of Functional Leadership has a major role to play in providing a framework to create significant outcomes in a variety of situations. The model is simple to understand and apply and can be used to produce a spectral shift in the leadership effectiveness of almost any individual. It is relevant at the team or frontline levels, the operational level and the strategic level. This last aspect is particularly of note due to the lack of effective ways of developing strategic leadership ability other than by experience. It is argued in this chapter that John Adair has made a substantial contribution to our thinking on the nature of leadership and how it may be developed. His ideas may readily be related to other approaches to leadership and in a number of instances seem to be superior to them. Adair's contribution has stood the test of time and is just as relevant in the current hi-tech, e-based world as it was in the 1960s when it was first proposed. It can act as core framework to which other approaches to leadership can be related and as such has provided a highly effective foundation for our thoughts on leadership both at the present time and for the future.

The case studies were real situations in which there was a need for leadership. The research situation provided a unique opportunity to look at leadership perception in a stress related situation and it was clear that individuals do tend to assess leader performance in the three areas of task, team and individual. This leads us to the idea that if we develop leaders to be aware of these three areas and then provide them with the tools to satisfy the three sets of associated needs, we will be promoting more effective leadership. The virtual, informal action group situation was greatly facilitated by superimposing the task, team and individual model over the work of the group. Successful outcomes were achieved and this was primarily due in the view of the author to having a clear idea of the task needs, developing a social support system for some anxious and very exposed followers and remembering that each follower had different needs and different tolerances in terms of their ability to handle the challenges posed by the situation. In terms of the culture change project, the surface model of Adair's task, team and individual needs led to changes at a much deeper level addressing Schein's concept of deep underlying assumptions. Adair has made a significant contribution to our thought on leadership and how it may be developed in a range of organisational settings both formal and informal.

Notes

1   Personal comment made by John Adair to the present author, 2005.

References

Adair, J. (1983) *Effective Leadership*, London and Sydney: Pan Books.

Adair, J. (1989) *Great Leaders*, Guildford: The Talbot-Adair Press.

Adair, J. (2002) *Effective Strategic Leadership*, London: Macmillan.

Ashby, W.R. (1956) *An Introduction to Cybernetics*, London: Chapman Hall.

Bennis, W. (1998) *On Becoming a Leader*, London: Arrow Books Limited.

Blake, R.R. and Mouton, J.S. (1964) *The Managerial Grid*, Houston: Gulf Publishing.

Cialdini, R.B. (2001) *Influence, Science and Practice*, Needham Heights, MA: Allyn & Bacon.

de Geus, A. (1997) *The Living Company*, Boston: Harvard Business School Press.

Forgas, J.P. (1979) *Social episodes: The study of interaction routines*, London and New York: Academic Press.

Goleman, D. (1996) *Emotional Intelligence*, London: Bloomsbury.

Goleman, D. (1998a) *Working with Emotional Intelligence*, London: Bloomsbury.

Goleman, D. (1998b) 'What Makes a Leader?', *Harvard Business Review*, November–December.

Goleman, D. (2000) 'Leadership That Gets Results', *Harvard Business Review*, March–April.

Hersey, P. and Blanchard, K.H. (1969) *Management of Organizational Behaviour*, Englewood Cliffs, NJ: Prentice Hall.

Hooper, R.A. and Potter, J.R. (1997) *The Business of Leadership*, Aldershot: Ashgate Publishing Company.

Hooper, R.A. and Potter, J.R. (2001) *Intelligent Leadership: Creating a Passion for Change*, London: Random House.

Kadabadse, A. and Kakabadse, N. (1998) *Essence of Leadership*, London: International Thomson Business Press.

Kotter, J.P. (1990) *A Force for Change*, New York: The Free Press.

Potter, J.R. (1985) *Leader role perception*, unpublished PhD Thesis Guildford, University of Surrey.

Schein, E.H. (1992) *Organizational Culture and Leadership* (2nd edn), San Francisco: Jossey-Bass Publishers.

Senge, P.M. (1990a) 'The Leader's New Work', *Sloan Management Review*, Fall.

Senge, P.M. (1990b) *The Fifth Discipline*, London: Century Business.

Senge, P.M. *et al.* (1994) *The Fifth Discipline Fieldbook*, London: Nicholas Brealey Publishing Limited.

Senge, P.M. *et al.* (1999) *The Dance of Change*, London: Nicholas Brealey Publishing Limited.

Stogdill, R.M. (1974) *Handbook of Leadership: A Survey of Theory and Research*, London: Macmillan.

Tannenbaum, R. and Schmidt, W.H. (1973) 'How to Choose a Leadership Pattern', *Harvard Business Review*, May–June.

4

The Leaders and the Led: Dyadic Approaches to Leadership

Morgen Witzel

This chapter is about the exercise of leadership. Specifically, it asks whether leadership is something that is done *by* leaders, or whether instead, leadership is exercised and becomes effective through the interaction *between* leaders and their subordinates. After looking briefly at the nature of action in a more general sense, we will consider alternative approaches to leadership that stress interactivity. The chapter concludes that by seeing leadership effectiveness as a matter of successful interaction between people within an organisation – between 'leaders' and 'subordinates', to use classical leadership terminology – rather than simply a matter of the leader exercising his or her leadership skills, we will come a little closer to understanding how leadership actually works. The 'rainbow model' devised by John Adair, setting out the seven generic functions of leadership, is used to analyse the effectiveness of this concept.

Much of the theory of leadership, in every sphere – business, politics, the military, non-governmental organisations – emphasises the primary role of the leader in leadership. Leadership, good or bad, comes from leaders and is inherent in leaders as individuals. It is assumed in many of the major writings on leadership (e.g., Machiavelli 1532; Clausewitz 1819; Lewin 1948; Fiedler and Garcia 1987; Bennis 1989; Kotter 1990) that leadership is something that is inherent in leaders, a quality or 'vital force' that flows outward from the leader and causes subordinates to follow the direction the leader has set.

This view of leadership is a powerful one, and it is not the purpose of this chapter to challenge the importance of the leader as an individual. It can be argued that terms such as 'leader' and 'follower' or 'subordinate' are loaded ones, and may not be appropriate to the needs of modern leadership. That may true, but it is not the purpose of this chapter to enter into that debate. Neither is it to enter into the discussions about formal and informal leadership (e.g., Argyris 1964), or to comment on studies such as those of Lewin (1948), Fiedler and Garcia (1987) and Sirota *et al.* (2005)

which suggest that participative or democratic leadership is the 'best' model of leadership, superior to autocratic or command-and-control models.

Instead, the central idea of this chapter is that no matter what terms are used, and no matter what model of leadership is followed, from command and control to participative democracy, the effectiveness of *any* leader depends upon the willingness of others to work with them and to share their vision – again, in classical terminology, to be 'led'. Every leader relies on this principle, as Machiavelli (1531) pointed out in cogent fashion. As Manfred Kets de Vries (2004) has shown in his study of Saddam Hussein, even the most brutal tyrant cannot rule without the consent – however obtained – of the governed. One political scientist, Mary Parker Follett (1924), has gone so far as to argue that there is no such thing as control; actions which appear to be *controlling* actions by a leader are in fact actions which *coordinate* the activities of others, and which require their consent – again, however obtained. All control, says Follett, is in fact coordination.

Thus, in tandem with leadership we have also what has been termed 'followership' (Kelley 1992; Goffee and Jones 2006). 'Followers are the other side of the leadership equation. Without them, there is no relationship and no leadership. If leadership is a dynamic relationship … it is logical that followers, too, live in the same dynamic relationship, but see things from a different perspective' (Goffee and Jones 2006: 190).

One of the most powerful metaphors used by John Adair in his description of action-centred leadership is of how leadership can be broken down into seven generic functions, in the same way that refracted light produces the seven colours of the rainbow (most recently in Adair 2002). Summarising briefly, these seven functions are (1) providing direction; (2) setting strategy and policy; (3) execution or 'making it happen'; (4) organising; (5) releasing the corporate spirit; (6) bridge-building between the organisation and society; and (7) developing the next generation of leaders. It is the purpose of this chapter to provide a background against which the seven functions of the rainbow can be – often subtly – reinterpreted to take account of the concept of followership.

We begin with a brief theory of the importance of followers, linking this to the more general philosophical theory of action. While it may be possible to distinguish between leaders and followers in static situations, in action they depend on each other utterly, and are bound in a series of dyadic interactions. The bulk of the chapter is taken up with an examination of existing models of leadership that take this interaction into account. We conclude by applying the concept of interactive leadership to the rainbow model, and suggest that for these seven functions to be carried out effectively, there are three prerequisites: consent, convergence and communications.

Leaders and followers

Leadership may indeed inhere in leaders, but while it does so, it is effectively dormant, passive. To become effective, leadership has to become active, and in so doing, it leaves the leader and goes out into the organisation, interacting with subordinates – and other leaders – to produce an effect. If leadership has been successfully executed, the effect is the one that is desired: an army defeats its enemies, a political party wins an election, a business achieves its profit targets and so on. However, it does so only if the subordinates 'do their bit' to make the strategy work; as Goffee and Jones (2006) point out, all leadership is relational, that is, it depends on relations between leaders and others. They further argue that this is true regardless of the position of the leader within the hierarchy.

Thus we can posit a model in which leadership requires two elements: the 'going forth', in which the leader transmits his or her views and wishes to the organisation, and the 'coming home', where the organisation interprets those views and wishes and responds accordingly. Leadership becomes *effective* through these two stages, through the interaction of the leaders and the led, and the quality of the leadership and its successful interaction are entirely dependent on the quality of that interaction. The leader exists in a dyadic relationship with his or her subordinates; each is mutually dependent on the other.

It should be stressed that this is something different from the generally accepted argument that leaders must build relationships with their subordinates, and that leadership outcomes depend on the quality of those relationships. This is quite true, but this argument goes further. Instead of seeing relationships with subordinates as an environmental factor which affects successful leadership, it sees them as the vital conduit through which leadership is exercised. The nature of these relationships does not just affect the nature of leadership in any situation, it absolutely determines it. The relevance of all this to action-centred leadership is just this: if leaders do exist in a series of dyadic relationships with their subordinates, then it follows that it is not just the actions of the leader(s) that matter, but also the actions of the subordinates. Action theory shows us how these dyads function.

Action theory

For any strategy to be executed, a set of actions is required. These include actions by the leader, and actions by the subordinates. This is the implementation stage, or what Adair (2002) calls 'making it happen'.

Philosophers of action theory tend to divide actions into two parts: volition, the impelling force behind the action, and the action itself. John Stuart Mill, for example, describes an action as being 'a series of two things:

the state of mind called a volition followed by an effect' (Mill 1843: I.3.5). For instance, if I desire to raise my right arm, I first form the intention to do so – the volition – and then my muscles obey my will and I do so – the action (Hornsby 1980). There has been some argument over this concept, and Mill's theory has been modified to take account of involuntary actions, which are the products of unconscious or subconscious volition. More importantly, the theory has moved beyond the level of the individual, so that inanimate forces or objects can also serve as volition; hence, a strong sonic vibration in mountain air can become the 'volition' that impels an avalanche.

Chains of action and volition interconnect, so that the action of one person creates volition in another, and this brings us back to strategy. If we follow basic action theory according to Mill and his followers, we can hypothesise that the following steps take place:

1 The leader forms a volition, in which he or she intends an action (to carry out the strategy).
2 The leader then takes this action (communicating his or her wishes to subordinates).
3 Subordinates hear the message from the leader and respond to it by forming a volition of their own, the nature of which determines on how well they have understood the message and how they interpret its intent for themselves.
4 Subordinates then take actions as determined by their volitions.

So far so good, and if this were all it took to carry out a strategy, then we would be safe with the basic assumption that leadership is something that inheres in leaders and all it takes to be a successful leader is good judgement, good communications skills and good relations with subordinates. There is a tendency among some of the more formal writers on strategy to assume that this is the case. But if we follow the views of other writers such as Mintzberg (1973, 1989, 2005) or Argyris (1976, 1982), we see that strategy actually unfolds a step at a time, with many rounds of volition and action required to carry it through.

What is more, the process does not just go in one direction. As the strategy unfolds, the actions of the subordinates in turn initiate volition in the mind(s) of the leader(s). Feedback loops are created in which the subsequent volition and actions of leaders are influenced by the prior actions of subordinates, in ways that can have unintended consequences. Let us take one example, a fairly minor one but illustrative nonetheless, from a recent sporting event.

At Old Trafford, Manchester in 2005, on the afternoon of the final day of the third cricket test match between England and Australia, England captain Michael Vaughan proposed to rest one of his bowlers, Andrew Flintoff, who had just bowled five overs and was beginning to tire. Flintoff disagreed with the decision to rest him; in a classic Argyris-type 'defensive routine', he felt that he knew better than his captain whether he was fit to continue, and was in any case hoping to take a wicket he badly wanted, that of the Australian batsman Adam Gilchrist. Vaughan then changed his mind, and let Flintoff continue to bowl (*Guardian* 16 August 2005).

The argument here is not whether Vaughan was right to do so, or whether Flintoff, had he rested then and there, been able to take the final Australian wicket later in the afternoon and so win the match (which ended in a draw). The point is that Flintoff invoked the law of unintended consequences. By interpreting Vaughan's action in his own way, and then taking action according to his own volition, he in turn planted an unexpected volition in Vaughan's mind. The captain's subsequent action was determined by his subordinate – not, as classical leadership theory suggests, the other way around.

We do not actually have to look very far to find many other examples of this happening all around us, in business, politics, sports, the arts, virtually every field of human activity. Actions by subordinates create volition in the minds of leaders, sometimes with positive outcomes, sometimes with negative ones. Either way, the process is a constant one. So it is not just the action of leaders, but the interaction of leaders and subordinates, that creates effective leadership – and, indeed, creates failures of leadership as well. The constant exchange of views through feedback loops, the interplay of action and volition, all affect how any given strategy is executed. Thus it is that 'effective leaders are not simply amalgams of desirable traits, they are actively and reciprocally engaged in a complex series of relationships that require cultivation and nurture' (Goffee and Jones 2006: 15).

Approaches to interactive leadership

That subordinates and their attitudes and behaviour affect the outcome of strategic processes has long been known, and is foundational to several strands of writing and thinking on strategy. In the late 4th century, Vegetius devoted more than a quarter of his *Epitoma rei militaris* to the need for Roman legionaries to be properly trained and inspired to carry out their duties as soldiers (Milner 1993). Fourteen hundred years later, the Prussian general Karl Emmanuel von Warnery wrote in much the same vein in the preface to his *Remarks on Cavalry*: 'if a soldier, whether on foot or horseback, is not animated with ambition, if he has not that patriotic spirit... he cannot be depended upon on any occasion where it is not sufficient to act mechanically' (Warnery 1798).

Writers on business make the same point. Even Frederick Winslow Taylor, whose theory of scientific management is widely (and in this author's view, erroneously) held to treat workers merely as cogs in a machine, argued that no matter how scientifically engineered a production process might be, unless workers understood their tasks and were willing to carry them out, the process would become inefficient (Taylor 1911). In an essay of 1908 entitled *Sweating*, Edward Cadbury argued that workers who were driven or 'sweated' to produce more were always less effective and less efficient than those who worked willingly (Cadbury and Shann 1908). This is a common theme in much of the literature on management and leadership ever since, right up to Sirota *et al.*, who argue that 'employee enthusiasm – a state of high employee morale that results from satisfying the three key needs of workers – results in enormous competitive advantage for those companies with the strength of leadership to manage for real long-term results' (Sirota *et al.* 2005: xxiii).

The receptiveness, enthusiasm, abilities and other features of subordinates affects how well they do their job, and how the strategy is then implemented. What is lacking, however, is an understanding of why this is so: the ways that subordinates interpret or engage with the actions of leaders, the volition that this creates, and how their own actions in turn influence the subsequent actions of leaders. Mainstream management theory tends to treat this as a straightforward action-reaction: the leader leads, the workers follow; the leader gives orders, the subordinates obey them. However, there are several schools of thought, some within management, some outside it, to which we can turn for greater understanding.

Organic approaches

The idea that organisations have parallels with living organisms is a fairly common one, and is often employed by those who are uncomfortable with machine-metaphors (see for example Morgan 1986). It has a considerable historical pedigree, going back at least to the English scholastic and cleric John of Salisbury in the mid-12th century.[1] In the *Policraticus* (1159), a handbook for statesmen and administrators of a type fairly common in its day, John explicitly describes an administrative body (in this case, the state) as being similar to a living organism. He uses the metaphor of the human body to describe how the state is governed; the prince is the head of the state, the senate is its heart, the agricultural workers and soldiers are equivalent to its limbs and so on. The result is an organism whose parts are in a state of mutual dependence; none can function without the others.

In the 19th century the metaphor makes a significant appearance in the work of the British chemist and writer Andrew Ure, who divides his 'philosophy of management' into three sections or three 'principles of action': the scientific, the moral and the commercial. He then goes on to compare the interworkings of these to the inner functioning of biological organisms. The scientific, moral and commercial, says Ure (1835: 55):

> may not unaptly be compared to the muscular, the nervous, and the sanguiferous system of an animal. They also have three interests to sub-

serve, that of the operative, the master, and the state, and must seek their perfection in the due development and administration of each. The mechanical being should always be subordinated to the moral constitution, and both should co-operate to the commercial efficiency. Three distinct powers concur to their vitality – labour, science, capital; the first destined to move, the second to direct, and the third to sustain. When the whole are in harmony, they form a body qualified to discharge its manifold functions by an intrinsic self-governing agency, like those of organic life.

Ure's *Philosophy of Manufactures* was widely read into the 20th century, and it was from Ure that probably the two most important theorists of organic or 'biological' organisation, Harrington Emerson and Herbert Casson, drew their ideas. Emerson, a former mining engineer, was a contemporary of F.W. Taylor and, for a time, equal to Taylor in influence within the fledgling American management movement. Emerson enlarged on Ure's original concept in a whole variety of ways, comparing the different parts of a business to organic cells and noting how cell structures change as the organisation expands and grows. Organisations were composed of living organisms – people – said Emerson, and therefore could be considered as such themselves. The brain, the heart, the senses, the hands and feet are all interdependent (Emerson 1913, 1919).

Notably, Emerson used his organic metaphor to argue against industrial democracy. The hands and feet do not have a vote; they obey the orders of the brain, the controlling agent. But this lack of representation does not mean that the brain, the controlling agent, is not utterly dependent on the 'doers', the limbs of the body or the workers within the organisation. And – most importantly for the discussion here – the brain relies on the senses, such as touch and sight and smell, to provide information. If we are walking and we stumble against something, the brain reacts to the sensory input from the leg and adjusts its actions accordingly. Subordinates provide volition. This tends to reinforce the point that the interactive relationship between leaders and followers exists and is of equal importance regardless of the 'style' of leadership being employed.

Casson, a Canadian-American who worked with Emerson for a time before emigrating to Britain in 1914, took the Emerson theory still further. As well as the organic elements, Casson argued, organisations also had an animating force, something which pulled all the elements together and gave them a common purpose. He likened this animating force to the soul, and this may indeed be one of the first attempts to theorise a 'spirit' of organisation, a set of common shared beliefs, assumptions and goals. In Casson's organisation, the brain, the vital organs and the limbs are all subordinate to this 'soul', and interact in order to carry out its higher purposes (Casson 1917). Another colleague of Emerson, Charles Knoeppel (1918), synthesised the ideas of Emerson and Casson into a full-fledged organic theory of organisation, which he made the centre of his own theories of management (and of a highly successful consulting business).

These are by no means the only theorists to use organic or biological metaphors for business – Thorstein Veblen, Douglas McGregor and Henry Mintzberg have done so, to name but three – but for the purposes of this chapter, they are some of the most significant. Emerson, Casson and Knoeppel all describe something that looks very much like the action theory of the philosophers. It contains volition and action, not once but repeatedly, and through an organisation that is both internally dynamic and affected by its environment. It shows the use of feedback loops in action. And while there are obvious limits to the biological metaphor – in particular, as Emerson points out, it relegates the parts and organs to unthinking status, and allows no room for participation – it nonetheless offers a fully-fledged theoretical perspective on the interactive nature of leadership.

Cosmological approaches

Another theory, which does not come from management but has been enormously influential on management east and west, compares organisations – in a rather roundabout way – with the workings of the universe itself. This theory has its origins in the Chinese school of philosophy known as Daoism. Unlike Confucianism, which stresses control and authority, Daoism argues for a dyadic *yin-yang* relationship of paired opposites, believing that this is the fundamental underpinning of the entire cosmos. Accordingly, the best state of human affairs is one that most closely aligns itself with this natural order. And this is particularly true of leadership and administration, subjects on which the early Daoist thinkers like Laozi (Lao Tzu) had a great deal to say.

The foundational text of the school, the *Daodejing* (*Tao Teh Ching*; the title means roughly 'The Book of the Way and Virtue') develops on a number of themes: the need to avoid conflict and to achieve ends instead through peace and harmony; the need for effacement of the self and the pursuit of inner cultivation rather than striving for things of this world; the essential one-ness of the universe and all things in it; and the belief that true achievement comes not through action but rather through its opposite, *wu-wei*, or 'non-action'. As a philosophy, Daoism likes to play with paradox, and seeks meanings for things in their opposites.

It should come as no surprise, then, to learn that the Daoists believed the art of leadership lay in leading as little as possible. They believed that order and efficiency were natural constants in the universe, and could not be created by human beings. To lead effectively, it is necessary to create the conditions in which order and efficiency can flourish, and that in turn is done by doing as little as possible. Intervention by leaders disrupts the natural order of things. The leader should therefore cultivate *wu-wei*, non-action, and do as little as possible while letting subordinates get on with their lives and work:

> Therefore the Sage says:
>
> I do not make any fuss, and the people transform themselves.
> I love quietude, and the people settle down in their regular grooves.
> I do not engage myself in anything, and the people grow rich.
> I have no desires, and the people return to simplicity (Wu 1990: 84).

The above passage is probably that which caught the eye of the French economist François de Quesnay in the 18th century, and led him to translate *wu-wei*, or non-action, as *laissez-faire*. The rest, as they say, is history. But in whatever language we choose to discuss it, the concept implies a dyad. Daoists saw the leader not as an animating force, but as an empty vessel, a receptacle into which the natural order of the universe could be established. The Daoist leader does not give orders, but exists to respond to the needs of his or her subordinates: 'The Sage has no interests of his own/But takes the interests of the people as his own' (Wu 1990: 72). The best leaders are those of whom the organisation is barely aware (*ibid.*: 25; see also Mak, Chapter 11 this volume), who are there in the background shaping the environment so that the organisation can flourish without need of active guidance. True wisdom, said the Daoists, rests in showing that people do not need to be ruled; they can achieve virtue on their own.

Two very contrasting – and non-Asian – examples of leaders show how this can be put into practice. The first is Ricardo Semler, owner and managing director of the Brazilian light machinery manufacturer Semco S/A. Originally motivated by a desire to reduce his own workload after a serious illness, Semler set up factory committees in order to increase worker involvement. These took time to catch on, especially in the paternalistic business culture of Brazil, but over time the committees began to assume more responsibility. Many factories and business units became self-governing, and profit-sharing was introduced. Dress codes, fixed hours of work and other rules were done away with. Employees turned up for work when they liked and set their own performance targets. Pressure from managers to perform was replaced by peer pressure from team colleagues to add value to the workplace. With some pride, Semler commented that he himself was now completely disposable; the company was managing itself (Semler 1993).

What is particularly important to note about this case is that Semler did not set out with the intention of reaching this near-total devolution of authority. Instead, the transformation happened gradually, with Semler responding to the views of his workers and managers and reacting accordingly (Morgan and

Zohar 1996). The feedback loops were in continuous operation throughout the process, and volition increasingly came from the subordinates, not the leader.

The second example is Gouvion St. Cyr, sometimes described as the most successful of Napoleon's marshals. St. Cyr's leadership style was, quite simply, to let his men get on with it. One of his officers during the French invasion of Russia in 1812, Colonel Jean-Baptiste Marbot, recalled later how at the beginning of a battle, St. Cyr would emerge from his tent only at the last minute. He would spend most of the battle in a prominent position, where his men could see him and where he could see the field, but would only intervene and give orders if it was absolutely essential that he do so (Summerville 2000). Upon the end of the battle, he would return to his tent and disappear once more. Marbot recalls that some officers were scandalised by this, and believed St. Cyr was unfeeling or uncaring towards his men. He was not; as his record over the years showed, he was a very fine soldier indeed. Instead, he knew his men and trusted them implicitly – and equally important, they knew him and trusted him as well. Further, before each battle, St. Cyr met with his commanders, briefed them and ensured that each knew their goals and the plan they were to follow. Like many great generals, St. Cyr knew that success came from letting trusted subordinates get on with things rather than trying to micromanage every aspect of the campaign, and he responded to his subordinates' needs rather then directing them.

What I have called the cosmological approach, above, is not only very complex to do but also rather foreign to the thinking of most of us. It can be difficult, for example, to distinguish between calculated non-action and sheer laziness – particularly in a culture where much work assessment is based on activity as well as achievement. Busy leaders tend to get more credit than quiet ones.

Contractarian approaches

Closer to our comfort zone is the contractarian approach, in which it is recognised that leaders and subordinates are bound together by, for want of a better phrase, a social contract. Invented in classical Greece and 'improved' upon by Hobbes, Locke, Kant, Rousseau and John Rawls, the concept of the social contract is many-layered and complex (Gough 1957; Rawls 1971). For our purposes, the social contract can be summarised as a recognition of mutual interdependence between leaders and subordinates. The social contract recognises the mutual interest of each, legitimises the role of the leader and sets boundaries to that role, and – in theory – establishes the means by which subordinates influence the decisions and actions of the leader.

That most vocal and powerful discussant of organisational contractarianism, Mary Parker Follett, believed that this form of contract was the most important binding force in business as well as society (Follett 1924). As noted, she argued that the contractual relationship between leaders and followers meant that the idea of 'control' is actually an illusion: all control, argued Follett, is in fact coordination. And the idea of coordination itself implies interaction, not the unthinking obedience to orders.

Sometimes social contracts are actual contracts as well. The Greek mercenaries who joined the army of the Persian pretender Cyrus in 401 BC had contracts with their leaders, contracts that required that major decisions be put to a vote and approved by the army as a whole. At councils of war, men made their own views known, and Xenophon, the Athenian officer who took command after the senior Greek generals had been murdered by the Persians, records in his memoirs that such meetings happened frequently, and he often asked his soldiers for their views before formulating orders (Xenophon 1949). Similar practices were employed by some of the *condottieri*, the mercenary armies of late medieval and Renaissance Italy, and it may have been these practices that influenced one of the most important theorists of contractarian leadership, Niccolò Machiavelli.

Often associated – quite erroneously – with the promulgation of despotic leadership, Machiavelli in fact argued that republicanism was a form of government far superior to despotism. Tyranny might be necessary as an emergency measure, at certain places and times, but in general, Machiavelli argues, it is very rare to find a good man who uses bad methods of government. He goes on to give his view that no city or state that did not govern itself, rather than being governed by a despot, has ever prospered. 'The reason is easy to understand; for it is not the well-being of individuals that makes cities great, but the well-being of the community, and it is beyond question that it is only in republics that the common good is looked to properly in that all that promotes it is carried out' (Machiavelli 1531: 1975). Though he does not explicitly use the term 'social contract', that is what he is describing. The tyrant breaks the social contract with the people and acts to serve his own interests; but in a functioning republic, the ruler serves the interests of the people and the city. Volition comes in the first instance from the will of the subordinate, not the will of the leader. Prince and people are locked in dyads of mutual dependency, but also mutual strength; for, says Machiavelli, this is a far stronger system than one where the bonds between prince and people are broken and the former rules only by force and fear.

Contractarian leadership in business has been around for some time, albeit not very widespread. The late 19th-and early 20th-century industrial democracy movement had strong contractarian overtones. The Boston department store owner and armchair management philosopher Edward Filene wrote that he introduced a programme of frequent employee consultation, including votes on major strategic decisions, not because he thought it would improve business performance, but because he felt that in a democracy, his workers had a right to make their voices heard and their views known (Filene 1932). Two other examples, however, show how it is possible to use the social contract as a management and/or leadership tool.

The Birmingham chocolate makers Cadbury Brothers were, in the early 20th century, one of the world's outstanding exponents of industrial democracy. They were also, by a distance, the world's largest confectioner, and one of Britain's most profitable companies. The employee involvement system developed there by George Cadbury and his son Edward took several forms. Directly, employees could make contributions through a suggestion scheme. Suggestions could be put forward for new products, new production methods, new administrative or management procedures, or 'any suggestion on any other subject, so long as it relates to the works at Bournville in some way' (Cadbury 1912: 212). Prizes were given for the best suggestions. Edward Cadbury tracked the number of suggestions carried forward, and found that over time around 20 percent on average were accepted, and 5–10 percent were carried forward and put into practice. Indirectly, employees had a voice through two powerful committees, the Men's Works Committee and the Women's Works Committee. Made up of a mixture of board nominees, foremen and workers and chaired by a director (Edward Cadbury himself chaired the women's committee, the only man to serve on it), the committees had power of scrutiny over plans for new machinery, buildings and other facilities, health and safety, employee complaints, cases of employee distress and many other issues. It is notable that the women's committee had virtually the same powers as that of the men.

The result was not just that the workers made their views known, but also that the employers acted on those views. Herbert Casson, commenting on the Cadbury system, regarded the company as the best managed he had ever seen, largely because of the contribution the workers made to driving the company forward not just through their labour, but through their ideas: 'At Cadbury's, everybody thinks' (Casson 1928: 165). Locked in a series of powerful dyads with their subordinates, the Cadburys used this system of formal and informal feedback loops to generate innovation throughout the company, innovation which they were able to turn into lasting competitive advantage.

The second example comes from what was then Czechoslovakia in the 1920s, where Tomás Bat'a turned a small shoe-making factory into the largest shoe-maker in the world. In order to achieve organisational efficiency, Bat'a adopted a programme of decentralisation. Individual business units were given near-complete autonomy and asked to set their own targets and made responsible for meeting them. Every shop and every department became an independent accounting unit. Relationships between them were handled by a series of contracts, functioning in effect as an internal market, with shops 'selling' 'products' to each other during the various phases of production. Prices for these transfers were set centrally on a six-monthly basis in order to regulate the production flow, but it was up to the business units themselves to negotiate times of delivery, quantity and quality.

In the Bat'a case, contractarianism was extended beyond the relationship between leader and subordinates, and used to establish and define intersubordinate relationships as well. The result was an organisational 'levelling', in which rank and authority counted for less than the strength of a particular relationship. Bat'a himself became an archetypal responsive leader; having designed the architecture of the system, he then let it run; his role as leader became one of monitoring and modulating the system where required. In a famous symbolic gesture, he installed his own office in the lift of the Bat'a factory at Zlín. When someone needed to see the chief executive, they did not come to his office; he brought his office to them.

One of the essences of contractarianism is participation. In any social contract, it is incumbent upon the subordinates to use the authority they are given, responsibly and well. Notions of 'followership' stress that in such systems, where subordinates have power, they must also be educated to use that power for proper ends (who defines what those ends are, of course, is another matter). If subordinates are unable or unwilling to participate, then problems arise. There are also, as Sirota *et al.* (2005) point out, limits to participation. There are certain times and places when people want, even demand, clear orders and objectives from their leaders. But this in itself can be seen as a form of participation. Participative management and/or participative leadership do not derogate or diminish the role of the leader. Rather, they change its emphasis, by focusing on the dyadic interaction between the leader and the led, rather than solely on the good (or bad) qualities of the leader. And as Machiavelli pointed out and Cadbury and Bat'a demonstrated, the dyadic interaction can be a source of real strength. In business as in nature, dyads are usually stronger and more enduring than monads.

The leadership rainbow

The idea that leadership becomes an active concept through a series of interactions between leaders and others has implications for Action-Centred Leadership (ACL). It could be argued that the concept is inherent to the famous three-circles model – task, team and individual – through the notions of the leader meeting the needs of individual and team. Here, however, we will look at the impact on the leadership 'rainbow', the seven generic functions of leadership.

It should be added, in my view, that this idea of leadership as a series of interactions and exchanges supports and strengthens the concept of ACL.

According to ACL, leadership consists in action, and we can include the Daoist concept of non-action here; one of the Daoist paradoxes, of course, is that non-action is a species of action. However, much of the theory of leadership, including leadership in action, has hitherto been focused on the actions of leaders only. If we broaden the concept to embrace the whole of the dyad, to look at the actions of subordinates as well as leaders and – especially – to look at the interplay of action and volition between both parties, we can actually see the rainbow metaphor becoming even more powerful. Rainbows are both tangible and intangible; we can see them and observe them, but we cannot touch or handle them. And rainbows shift as the prism that creates them shifts; they grow and fade and move and change, just as relationships within organisations, between the leader and the led, between the led and themselves, grow and fade and move and change as the endless cycle of volition and action continues.

Each of the seven elements identified by Adair is influenced not only by the action of leaders, but also those of followers, as the limited literature on followership makes clear. For example:

1 Providing direction. As some of the examples above have shown, subordinates help shape direction, either directly when consulted, or indirectly as their present actions influence the future volition and actions of leaders.
2 Setting strategy and policy. Strategy evolves through slow steps, each consisting of rounds of volition and action. How subordinates act in earlier rounds shapes the unfolding of the strategy (particularly if we view strategy as 'emergent' in Mintzbergian fashion).
3 Execution or 'making it happen'. In just the same way, the actions of subordinates contribute to the execution of the strategy. They are just as important – arguably more important – than the actions of the leaders.
4 Organising. Again, leaders may express their wishes as to how a business is organised, but the tasks of organising are carried out by subordinates. In a rigid command-and-control organisation, the wishes of the leader may be regarded as paramount, but in more flexible organisations, subordinates will help to shape the organisation.
5 Releasing the corporate spirit. Once more, the processes of release may be initiated by the leader, but the spirit is created between leaders and led; and ultimately, if Casson's model is followed, becomes greater than both.
6 Bridge-building between the organisation and society. This cannot and must not be the sole prerogative of the leader; subordinates play a major role in projecting the corporate image, and how they do so is reflective of how they interpret such things as the corporate spirit. If subordinates and leader project different images to society, then it is likely that both will have to adapt.

7 Developing the next generation of leaders. Leaders are not just identified, they also identify themselves. Dyadic interactions between present and future leaders are part of the process of leadership development.

What makes for an effective exchange between leaders and subordinates? What is the best way to prepare the ground for this interaction? How, indeed, do we make a rainbow? The prism through which the light is refracted, the mechanism through which the interchange takes place, requires three elements:

1 Consent. Both leaders and led must consent to be part of the same dyad. This can be through a variety of methods: formal or informal contracts, or participative systems, or they may choose to engage with a metaphor such as biological organisms or the cosmos. The method itself is less important, so long as it works, and different methods will be suitable for different organisations. But the need for consent is essential; without it, the dyad fails, and leaders and led are then pitched into strife with one another, rather than working in harmony. As noted above, consent may be obtained in different ways – some of them unsavoury – but it is always necessary to a degree. 'The expert cannot dictate and the people consent. This is the voice of the wax-doll; it has no reality' (Follett 1924: 197).
2 Convergence. As well as consenting to the dyad, all parties have to agree more or less on the nature of the dyad and its purpose, aims and functions: the 'how' and 'why' issues that Adair (2002) refers to. This is true of *any* organisation, regardless of its nature and purpose: symphony orchestras, political parties, Royal Marine commando battalions, animal welfare charities and retail superstore chains are all guided by a common logic and an agreed set of goals. When they cease to be so, then things fall apart. Taken together, consent and convergence mean that both parties agree to join the dyad in pursuit of a shared goal. 'The sage has no interests of his own, but takes the interests of the people as his own' (Laozi, in Wu 1990: 72).
3 Communication. Again, what communications channels and methods and what styles of communication are adopted is less important than the fact there *be* communication. Communication is the means by which knowledge travels in organisations, and that includes knowledge of the wishes, volitions and actions of others. Without communication, neither leaders nor subordinates can fashion an effective response to the other. 'Skillful leaders ensure that they use the *right* mode of communication. This requires a fine appreciation of the message, the context, the people you wish to communicate with, as well as your own personal strengths and weaknesses' (Goffee and Jones 2006: 161).

Leaders on their own can do nothing; no leader can do everything. The most able leader in world history will flounder unless he or she can interact and work with subordinates. Similarly, the best group of subordinates in the world cannot sustain an organisation indefinitely without effective leadership. The French army in the 1940s and Marks & Spencer in the late 1990s are two examples of splendid organisations manned by effective people that declined due to lack of leadership. In both cases, there was no one at the top to provide volition, to set the cycle of volition and action in motion.

Barriers

> With regard to modifying institutions all at once when everybody realises that they are no good, I would point out that, though it is easy to recognise their futility, it is not easy to correct it; for to do this, normal methods will not suffice now that normal methods are bad.
> – Niccolò Machiavelli

Despite the arguments posed above, many leaders will find it hard to accept and embrace the concept of the dyad. This will be due to several reasons. First, many will see it as limiting their own power and authority. In fact, the dyad does not diminish the influence of the leader. In particular, it puts even more emphasis on the power and importance of action. The leader is interactive, not inactive! But human nature is such that many will see this idea as a threat and not an opportunity.

To overcome this, there needs to be something of a cultural change among leaders themselves. Collins and Porras (1994) have pointed out the fallacy of the cult of the 'great' or 'charismatic' leader who functions through the exercise of personal power. But the cult remains strong. Opinion polls among business leaders show that the most-admired leaders are those who are perceived as most powerful, like Henry Ford or Jack Welch. Quieter leaders who function effectively by developing strong inter-active relationships with subordinates, like William McKnight or Carlos Ghosn, do not find favour. Only when we start admiring leaders for the results they get rather than their personal prestige and 'star' qualities will we get away from this problem.

Second, there is tradition. Many business leaders are by nature conservative. They embrace new things slowly, if at all. This seems particularly true of business leadership, where the command-and-control tradition is proving to be very slow to die. Some progress is being made, not every business would agree with Harold Geneen, former chairman of ITT, that participative management is 'baloney' (Geneen and Bowers 1997: xii), but neither would they rush out to embrace it fully. Leaders lead, others follow; it has been thus since Noah led the animals into the ark. For leaders to change their mindset away from this view will doubtless be a serious challenge.

Third, there is a need for a cultural shift on both sides. As noted above, effective interactive leadership requires a capable 'followership' who use their power responsibly. Even enthusiasts for change like Sirota *et al.* (2005) recognise that this can be a serious problem, especially in economies or sectors where skill and education levels are comparatively low.

These problems exist and will be hard to shift, but the effort must be made. Today, more than ever, we are aware of the interdependent nature of our culture and world. To continue to lead as though the leader was a paramount authority is not just a triumph of ego over common sense; it can be downright dangerous. By shifting the emphasis away from the leader and onto the relationship between the leader and the led, we stand a chance of developing a style of leadership that is more flexible, more responsive and better informed: all three essential qualities in the age to come.

Notes

1 In personal correspondence John Adair has pointed out to me that this idea probably has its roots in Plato, and as John of Salisbury was a scholar of Plato, this seems a reasonable assumption; so far, however, I have not been able to find a Platonic source.

References

Adair, J. (2002) *Effective Strategic Leadership*, London: Macmillan.
Argyris, C. (1964) *Integrating the Individual and the Organization*, New York: John Wiley.
Argyris, C. (1976) *Increasing Leadership Effectiveness*, New York: John Wiley.
Argyris, C. (1982) *Reasoning, Learning and Action*, San Francisco: Jossey-Bass.
Bennis, W.G. (1989) *On Becoming a Leader*, Reading, MA: Addison-Wesley.
Cadbury, E. (1912) *Experiments in Industrial Organisation*, London: Longmans, Green & Co.
Cadbury, E. and Shann, G. (1908), *Sweating*, London: Headley Brothers.
Casson, H.N. (1917) *Lectures on Efficiency*, Manchester: Mather & Platt.
Casson, H.N. (1928) *Creative Thinkers: The Efficient Few Who Cause Progress and Prosperity*, London: Efficiency Magazine.
Clausewitz, K. von (1819) *Vom Kriege*, ed. and trans. M. Howard and P. Paret, *On War*, Princeton: Princeton University Press, 1984.
Collins, J.C. and Porras, J.I. (1994) *Built to Last: Successful Habits of Visionary Companies*, New York: HarperCollins.
Emerson, H. (1913) *The Twelve Principles of Efficiency*, New York: Engineering Magazine Co.
Emerson, H. (1919) 'Nature's Type of Organization', *Industrial Management*, 57: 406–10.
Fiedler, F. and Garcia, J.E. (1987) *New Approaches to Effective Leadership: Cognitive Resources and Human Performance*, New York: John Wiley.
Filene, E.A. (1932) *Successful Living in This Machine Age*, London: Jonathan Cape.
Follett, M.P. (1924) *Creative Experience*, London: Longmans.
Geneen, H. and Bowers, B. (1997) *The Synergy Myth, and Other Ailments of Business Today*, New York: St. Martin's Press.

Goffee, R. and Jones, G. (2006) *Why Should Anyone Be Led By You? What It Takes to Be an Authentic Leader*, Boston: Harvard Business School Press.

Gough, J. (1957) *The Social Contract*, Oxford: Clarendon.

Guardian (2005) 'Fearsome Flintoff Raises the Standard', 16 August, p.26.

Hornsby, J. (1980) *Actions*, London: Routledge & Kegan Paul.

John of Salisbury (1159) *Policraticus*, trans. J. Dickinson, *Policraticus: The Statesman's Book*, New York: Knopf, 1927.

Kelley, R.E. (1992) *The Art of Followership*, New York: Knopf.

Kets de Vries, M. (2004) 'Inside the Mind of a Tyrant', INSEAD working paper.

Knoeppel, C. (1918) *Organization and Administration*, New York: McGraw-Hill.

Kotter, J.P. (1990) *A Force for Change: How Leadership Differs from Management*, New York: The Free Press.

Lewin, K. (1948) *Resolving Social Conflicts: Selected Papers in Group Dynamics*, New York: Harper Brothers.

Machiavelli, N. (1531) *Discorsi sopra la prima deca di Tito Livio* (Discourses on the First Decade of Livy), ed. B. Crick, trans. L.J. Walker as *The Discourses*, Harmondsworth: Penguin, 1970.

Machiavelli, N. (1532) *Il Principe* (The Prince), trans. G. Bull, Harmondsworth: Penguin, 1961.

Mill, J.S. (1843) *A System of Logic*, London: Parker.

Milner, N.P. (ed. and trans.) (1993) *Epitome rei militaris* (Epitome on the Arts of War), Liverpool: Liverpool University Press.

Mintzberg, H. (1973) *The Nature of Managerial Work*, New York: Harper & Row.

Mintzberg, H. (1989) *Mintzberg on Management*, New York: The Free Press.

Mintzberg, H., Ahlstrand, B. and Lampel, J. (2005) *Strategy Bites Back*, Englewood Cliffs: Prentice-Hall.

Morgan, G. (1986) *Images of Organization*, Newbury Park: Sage.

Morgan, G. and Zohar, A. (1996) *Ricardo Semler's Transformation at Semco*, http://www.yorku.ca/faculty/academic/gmorgan/semler.html, 12 February 2001.

Rawls, J. (1971) *A Theory of Justice*, Cambridge, MA: Harvard University Press.

Sirota, D., Mischkind, L.A. and Meltzer, M.I. (2005) *The Enthusiastic Employee: How Companies Profit by Giving Workers What They Want*, Englewood Cliffs: Prentice-Hall.

Semler, R. (1993) *Maverick! The Success Story Behind the World's Most Unusual Workplace*, London: Arrow.

Summerville, C. (2000) *The Exploits of Baron Marbot*, London: Constable.

Taylor, F.W. (1911) *The Principles of Scientific Management*, New York: Harper & Row.

Ure, A. (1835) *Philosophy of Manufactures*, London; 2nd edn London: H.G. Bohn, 1861.

Warnery, K.E. von (1798) *Remarks on Cavalry*, London; repr. London: Constable, 1997.

Wu, J.C.H. (1990) *Tao Teh Ching*, London: Shambhala.

Xenophon (1949) *Anabasis*, trans. R. Warner as *The Persian Expedition*, London: Penguin.

5
Gimme Five! Multi-disciplinary Perspectives on Leadership

Tim Harle

Introduction

'I am called to be a priest, not a manager. Discuss'. How would John Adair, whose work synthesises diverse disciplines, react to the implied dichotomy in this essay for aspiring clerics?

Adair has a long experience of such questions. He first explored the relationship between management and the priesthood in published form some three decades ago (Adair 1977). This work built on his experience as first Director of Studies at St George's House, Windsor. He has since worked with a number of bishops and been adviser on strategic leadership to the Church of England's Archbishops' Council. Further afield, he has worked with the World Council of Churches. Among Adair's more recent publications is one considering the legacy of the central figure in Christianity (Adair 2001). He has also co-edited the third collection of essays for the organisation MODEM,[1] which seeks to promote dialogue between the worlds of management and ministry (Adair and Nelson 2004).

Adair's influence in ecclesiastical circles is considerable (see also Chapter 9 by S. Martin Gaskell in this volume). His legacy can be seen in approaches to developing leadership in the church: for example, in what might be referred to as the 'staff college' approach. Another echo of Adair's military background can be seen in the process used by the Church of England for discerning priestly vocations. Although the approach predates Adair, the Church of England's residential Selection Conferences (Sentamu 2001: 110) can clearly be traced back to the War Office Selection Boards, which have spawned a myriad of different assessment centres in the private, public and non-profit sectors.

Some business leaders might question whether anything can be learned from a tradition whose contribution today might be described as somewhere between marginal and irrelevant. Those who believe faith traditions have a contribution to offer might need no further encouragement. Those who believe we have witnessed the death of Christian Britain (Brown 2001) might still allow that an historical approach can be appropriate. Those who, like the author, find sympathies with both groups can bring multiple perspectives to bear.

Approach

This chapter examines the mutual contribution of business and ecclesial leadership by asking three questions prompted by a consideration of John Adair's writings. To help answer these three questions, it examines the interplay between priest and manager through a fivefold framework from two contrasting sources: *Harvard Business Review* (HBR) – more specifically, a *Harvard Business Review* article entitled 'The Five Minds of a Manager' (Gosling and Mintzberg 2003) and the *Ordinal*. Its starting point is a numerical coincidence: each of the sources uses five models, or paradigms, to help paint a holistic picture. I should emphasise at the outset that I am not arguing for a one-to-one mapping between these pairs of five: they simply provide a suggestive starting point for our exploration.

The approach – to call it a 'methodology' would suggest a spurious degree of formality – adopted is that of reflective praxis. 'These days, what managers desperately need is to stop and think – to step back and reflect thoughtfully on their experiences' (Gosling and Mintzberg 2003: 57). Since giving up full-time paid employment in 2003, I have been grateful for an extended opportunity to stop, think, step back and reflect on my experiences as a senior executive, project manager and consultant in the private, public and non-profit sectors. I welcome the brief time I spent at INSEAD, but my main learning has come from years of working with people. To borrow an expression from elsewhere, I am a manager, not a MBA (Mintzberg 2004).

The exploration can be described as both trans-disciplinary, in the sense of transcending individual disciplines, and interdisciplinary, in allowing disciplines to interact and inform one another. It cannot claim complete originality. Alongside John Adair's work, Charles Handy in Europe (e.g., Handy 1997) and Robert K. Greenleaf in North America (e.g., Greenleaf 1977; Greenleaf *et al.* 2002) have long been advocates of widening horizons. Green and Cooper (1998) described one of their four leadership styles as 'priest', the others being 'sage', 'visionary' and 'prophet'. There has been a growth in recent years of interest in the interplay between spirituality – not to be limited to, or confused with, organised religion – and the workplace (e.g., Mitroff and Denton 1999; Lamont 2002; Howard and Welbourn 2004).

What of the intended audience? Higginson (2002: 1) has protested 'against the marginalisation of Christianity by business, and the marginalisation of business by Christianity'. While I am not expecting those familiar with *HBR* and the *Ordinal* to rush out and read one another's writings, my modest hope is that both groups will pause to see if they can learn anything from the other community. Taking this approach runs the risk that those steeped in one tradition or the other may argue about a lack of depth or understanding of their particular viewpoint. Bridge building can be a risky business for a non-engineer.

Lastly, a word about the starting point for the religious exploration. On the basis that our harshest critics with the greatest insights often come from our closest family, my observations come mainly from within the Judaeo-Christian tradition.

Three questions

Although we will find many areas of congruence between priestly and managerial viewpoints in Adair's writings, the aim here is to promote understanding about contemporary leadership by examining three questions prompted by his work.

- Although 'serving to lead' is a favourite Adair theme which features regularly in his writings, does the concept encourage the notion of the 'heroic individual'?
- Team and individual have featured from Adair's earliest writings on action-centred leadership. But does his approach reflect a Western – or Cartesian – worldview, centred on the individual?
- Lastly, does what might be described as Adair's neat hierarchy of team, operational and strategic leadership apply in a contemporary world characterised by chaos and complexity?

To help answer these questions, we first turn to two texts that can provide a framework for our exploration.

The manager's five

At the beginning of 'The Five Minds of a Manager' (Gosling and Mintzberg 2003), the authors recognise the danger of separating management from leadership: 'Most of us have become so enamored of "leadership" that "management" has been pushed into the background' (2003: 54). Adair would agree, tracing the separation to a classic *HBR* article (Zaleznik 1977). At the risk of gross oversimplification, the question posed in the title of the latter article – 'Managers and Leaders: Are They Different?' – has tended to be answered in the affirmative. Adair has elevated this to the formality of 'the Zaleznik Error', by which he means 'the making of a false dichotomy between "leaders" and "managers"' (Adair 2005: 64).

Adair, Gosling, Mintzberg and other thinkers are less inclined to an either/or mindset. Gosling and Mintzberg took their call to the very heart of 'received wisdom'.[2] Elsewhere I have described their article as doing for much of recent leadership thinking what Hans Christian Andersen did for imperial tailoring (Harle 2005: 356). Adair's own work, steeped in the Greek tradition, suggests an alternative to the Scandinavian tale: the Trojan horse. Gosling and Mintzberg offer five mindsets to help managers interpret their world. They do not claim that they are scientific or exhaustive, but encourage us to use them as attitudes which can open up new vistas on our world. The five mindsets are:

- **Reflective.** Organisations do not need 'mirror' people, who see only reflections of themselves, or 'window' people, who cannot see beyond the images in front of them. The both/and approach calls for seeing through our own reflection to see the surrounding world in new ways. Possible new perspectives include seeing products as a service[3] and customers as partners. Using the Latin etymology of 'reflect' (to refold) suggests turning attention inwards so that it can be returned outward. Rather than encouraging introspection, this encourages managers to manage the self by reflecting on experience. Reflective managers can see behind to look ahead: we must appreciate the past if we wish to use the present to produce a better future.
- **Analytic.** Starting with a refreshing reminder that analysis is derived from the Greek to 'let loose', we are reminded that we can't get organised without analysis. Building a pleasure boat is a simple task when compared with the complicated task of building an aircraft carrier. But both involve components and networks which should be predictable. In contrast, the decision whether to deploy an aircraft carrier is truly complex. Managers are encouraged to manage their organisations by moving beyond superficial analysis to deeper meaning. Traditional business schools – and many commercial companies and government organisations – suffer from too much analysis. Unlike the tennis player who watches the scorecard while missing the ball, the analytic manager will appreciate both the score and the crowds, while watching the ball.
- **Worldly.** The authors draw a helpful distinction between a global view (generalisations, disconnect between global and local, blurred differences, cultural convergence) and what they describe as a worldly view (particularity, linking actions to local consequences, plurality of worldview, a patchwork of edges and boundaries). Once again, we see a both/and approach: managers need to be more worldly, in sophisticated and practical ways. Organisations exist in several contexts and managers should be found at the interfaces, or edges: 'to manage context is to manage on the edges, between the organization and the various worlds that surround it – culture, industries, companies' (Gosling and Mintzberg 2003: 59).

- **Collaborative.** The collaborative mindset is contrasted with economic theory that has viewed people as independent actors, 'resources' or 'assets'. The authors note how their Japanese colleagues encouraged them to see the importance not so much of managing *people*, but the *relationships* between them. They contrast heroic management, based on the self, with engaging management, based on collaboration. Reflecting that we talk a lot about networks, but still consider managers on 'top', they encourage managers to be 'throughout'. Who, they muse, manages the World Wide Web?
- **Action.** The metaphor of a chariot pulled by wild horses can be applied to managers. Rather than stirring the horses into a frenzy, they need to be sensitive to the surrounding terrain. Today's overwhelming emphasis on action at the expense of reflection should encourage us to reflect on change and continuity. It is this continuity which brings meaning. The authors note a dominant Cartesian view of managing change: planned strategies lead to action. As an alternative, Gosling and Mintzberg point to Satish Kumar's book, *You Are Therefore I Am*, subtitled *A Declaration of Dependence* (Kumar 2002).

The authors conclude by encouraging us to weave the mindsets together, using a suggestive metaphor of threads, cloths and weavers.

The priest's five

Ordination, in a recent definition, is 'the act of appointing a person to a specific ministry in leadership' (Bradshaw 2002: 342).

Although practice varies across different traditions, it is appropriate here that Anglican (strictly Church of England) praxis should form the basis of our exploration. The Church of England's first service for ordaining priests was produced in 1550, derived from work by the German reformer, Martin Bucer. Revisions followed in 1552 and 1662, when the 'Form and Manner of Making, Ordaining, and Consecrating of Bishops, Priests, and Deacons, according to the Order of the Church of England'[4] was bound in with the *Book of Common Prayer*. The next significant change occurred in 1980, when the *Ordinal* was included in a book of alternative services. This order has recently been revised (Church of England in press); it is this contemporary form[5] which is considered here.

Priests do not have a job description, but The Declaration read by the Bishop in the ordination service provides a reminder to those present which is at once daunting and heartening. In a wide-ranging text, the priests' calling is described using, *inter alia*, five models. Lest anyone worry that this approach reflects either the latest trends or is narrowly English, it is worth noting that each is firmly rooted in Hebrew tradition stretching back more than two and a half millennia (Croft 2005: 13). These five models are as follows.

- **Servants**. The word occurs some 800 times in the Hebrew Bible. Variously meaning worker, slave or political subject, 'servant' may best be summed up as a humble person's self-designation. Particular attention has been given to four poetic passages in the second part of the book of Isaiah. Generally referred to as the Servant Songs, these describe an enigmatic being which has variously been seen as an individual (e.g. Isaiah 52.13ff) or a community (e.g. Isaiah 41.8).

  The primitive church soon came to draw a link between Jesus and the enigmatic servant of Isaiah. In the Matthean tradition, we find 'Behold, my servant whom I have chosen, my beloved' (Matthew 12.18, quoting Isaiah 42.1). In the Lucan tradition, Mary's self-designation is as 'the Lord's servant' (Luke 1.38). And the gospel canticles *Magnificat* and *Benedictus* refer respectively to Israel and David as servants. Jesus' self-designation was as 'one who serves' (Luke 22.27). One of the earliest attempts to understand him after his death – a discipline we would now recognise as christology – can be found in a fragment included by St Paul in one of his letters (Philippians 2.7): Jesus 'took the form of a slave'. Paul frequently refers to himself as *doulos* (translated 'slave'). His *magnum opus* begins 'Paul, a servant of Jesus Christ' (Romans 1.1).

- **Shepherds**. Even those with no religious affiliation may recall 'The Lord's my shepherd' (Psalm 23) from its regular use at funerals, as well as on happier occasions. In a few verses, this poem ranges from pastoral tranquillity ('still waters') to darkest despair ('the valley of the shadow of death'). God is seen as the shepherd of his people, but a shepherd's role is described as at once taking care of both sheep and people. Mediterranean shepherds lead their flock to pasture, caring for group and individual. In a powerful passage, the prophet Ezekiel is told to 'prophesy against the shepherds' (Ezekiel 34.2); the passage goes on to talk of the shepherd seeking out and rescuing their flock.

  The tradition recorded in the fourth gospel applies seven 'I am' sayings to Jesus. Among these is 'I am the good shepherd' (John 10.11). At the end of this gospel, the apostle Peter is given a three-fold charge to feed/tend the sheep/lambs (John 21.15–17). St Paul's farewell to the elders at Ephesus recorded in Acts 20 calls on his hearers to be shepherds of the church.

- **Messengers**. Once again, the book of Isaiah is at the heart of the tradition. 'How beautiful upon the mountains are the feet of the messenger who announces peace, who brings good news' (Isaiah 52.7). In Greek culture, *euangelion* originally applied to a messenger, especially one who brought good news of victory in battle (another military link for our honouree!). The word increasingly came to be seen as the content of the message, and the Christian church harnessed evangel to mean the content of the good news, or gospel. 'Evangelist' is included in New Testament lists of ministries or gifts (*charismata*), e.g., Ephesians 4.11ff.

- **Watchmen.** Looking out from a watchtower for wild animals and thieves to protect the community required an alert, observing role. But the word was used in other contexts. Ezekiel's mortal is described as 'a sentinel for the house of Israel', who, on hearing a word from God's mouth 'shall give them warning from me' (Ezekiel 33.7). Long before the days of multi-sensory experiences, it is fascinating to note that one of the Twelve Prophets is recorded as saying in an oracle that 'I will keep watch to see what he will say to me' (Habakkuk 2.1). Not limited to a passive role, there is more than a hint of prophetic responsibility.
- **Stewards.** The creation stories of Genesis seek to describe the relationship between humanity and the natural environment. They have been used both to inspire and criticise a history of caring for the rich variety of the earth's resources. A steward is also seen as a person having responsibility for a house (Genesis 43.19). This idea is picked up in a parable which describes a shrewd steward, or manager (*oikonomos*, Luke 16.1). St Paul refers to himself and his companions as 'stewards of God's mysteries' and goes on to say that 'it is required of stewards that they should be found trustworthy' (1 Corinthians 4.1f).

Points of congruence

Several links with Adair's approach are apparent. He has a long-standing interest in ecclesiastical concerns. As far back as May 1962, he published an article in the journal *Theology* calling for a staff college for the Church of England. The response was negligible, but in 1966, the doors opened inside the walls of Windsor Castle of what *The Times* called 'a most exclusive, discreet and unusual kind of hotel' (quoted in Adair 1977: 168). St George's House was seen by the then Dean (and future Bishop of Worcester) as 'a genuine attempt by the Christian Church to enter into dialogue with the secular world' (*ibid.*).

Apart from the staff college idea, there are other traces of a military background in Adair's earliest published full-length writing in this area: he refers to a 'corps'[6] of ordained clergy (Adair 1977: 68) and Lao Tzu receives an honourable mention (Adair 1977: 145). After a familiar description of the nature of leadership (qualities, situational, functional) and the interaction of task, group and individual needs, a powerful passage introduces two key New Testament images: the *shepherd* and *servant* (Adair 1977: 142). Adair's interest in etymology is apparent as we are reminded that these terms have come down to us in the words *pastor* and *minister* respectively. He notes the risk of the shepherd promoting sheep-like passivity among followers and suggests this is 'perhaps corrected' by the juxtaposition of the image of the servant.

The idea of servant-leadership is a thread running through much of Adair's work. In a later publication, Jesus is the embodiment of the servant-leader, exemplified in the foot-washing episode (Adair 2001: 142).[7] One of his most recent works (Adair 2005) shares the language of 'growing' leaders with a respected work on developing Christian leaders (Lawrence 2004). Adair's influence extends to monastic communities: a book from Ampleforth, reflecting on the Rule of St Benedict comment that 'Adair and Benedict have a lot in common' (Dollard *et al.* 2002: 66).

The servant is a favourite Adair theme. 'Serve to Lead', the Royal Military Academy's motto, provides not only the title of an anthology (RMA Sandhurst nd), but also chapter titles for more than one book (Adair 2000, 2001). The concept of servant-leadership is especially associated with Robert K. Greenleaf (Greenleaf 1977). The 25th anniversary of the original publication was marked by a new edition (Greenleaf and Spears 2002) with a foreword by Stephen R. Covey and an afterword by Peter M. Senge. Ken Leech (2001: 199–201) addresses servant-leadership; having noted its positive contribution, he warns of 'the danger that exclusive emphasis on the church as servant can obscure other important dimensions' (Leech 2001: 200). Complaining that 'Some use the word "servant" so vaguely that it loses any meaning' (Leech 2001: 256), he highlights the prophetic role and priestly offering of sacrificial love.

Effective communication highlights the messenger's role (Adair 2002a). 'Engaging managers listen more than they talk' (Gosling and Mintzberg 2003: 60) and 'the better the communicator, the more the trust' (Adair 2002b: 52).

'Successful "visions" are not immaculately conceived; they are painted, stroke by stroke, out of the experiences of the past' (Gosling and Mintzberg 2003: 57). Adair has looked in some detail at the vision of Jesus (Adair 2001: 123–37, 149–60). He notes the differences between the Greek and Semitic minds, and how the vision of the Kingdom of God on earth is developed through a number of parables. Everyday images such as house, feast, door and gate are used (2001: 125). And this vision was not immaculately conceived: 'Responding to the opportunity created by John the Baptizer, Jesus took ownership of this vision and made it his own. By his greatness as a teacher and by the example of his own life and death – living the vision – Jesus made it real to those contemporaries who "had eyes to see and ears to hear"' (2001: 149).

Explicit references to stewardship are harder to find in Adair's work, although he implicitly alludes to it in his exposition of the Parable of the Talents (Adair 2000: 22–7).[8] Adair has commented that one important aspect of stewardship he would wish to note is the managing, or 'husbanding', of scarce resources.[9] Others have been more explicit about stewardship. 'Leadership has often claimed to be in service of those they lead, but the leader's "service" took the form of giving direction and protection. Stewardship serves through the form of giving a basic structure and supporting self-direction' (Block 1996: 66). In a Japanese view, 'business unit managers are stewards, rather than owners, of the firm's core competence resources in the same way they are stewards, rather than owners, of the firm's financial resources' (Hamel and Prahalad 1996: 256f). Having admired Greenleaf's servant-leader approach, Raelin nevertheless comments: 'Stewards appear far less divine than servant-leaders, less conspicuous and, consequently, less interested in permanent leadership positions' (2003: 119).

Adair's action-centred leadership trilogy of task, individual and team have links to Gosling and Mintzberg's action, reflective and collaborative mindsets. The collaborative mindset is woven into the *Ordinal*, where the priest's calling is not to an individual role. The latest service (includes a subtle change from previous practice: the plural (servants, shepherds, etc.) is used. Their calling is: 'With their bishop and fellow-ministers'. One could add from observation that this collaborative approach is not always evident among clergy.

Although explicit religious references may be lacking, Adair's deep grounding in a number of cultures has led him to highlight noble notions of leadership. Among these is practical wisdom, *phronesis* (2002b: 73, 2003: 53) and three great values: goodness, truth and beauty (2003: 123ff). I have elsewhere attempted to synthesise the approaches of theology and leadership studies to suggest three new ideas to challenge traditional leadership competencies: serenity, courage and wisdom (Harle 2005).

More generally, the business leadership community has seen a growing trend of those who are no longer prepared to keep their business and spiritual lives apart (Mitroff and Denton 1999; Zohar and Marshall 2000; Lamont 2002; Howard and Welbourn 2004). Such authors emphasise that 'spirituality' should not be confused with organised religion. A second group of authors may not be so explicit about spirituality, but promote an approach that is generally compatible with such an approach (Wheatley 1999; Bennis and Thomas 2002; Robertson 2005). Lastly, it is interesting to note how religious language is used in a business context. Two examples can be offered from many possibilities. First, Rakesh Khurana's writings on the selection of CEOs in North America: *Searching for a Corporate Savior: The Irrational Quest for Charismatic CEOs* (Khurana 2002a) and *The Curse of the Superstar CEO* (Khurana 2002b). Second, in investigating why bad projects are so hard to kill, Royer talks of the 'faith that wouldn't be shattered' and the 'seductive appeal of collective belief' (Royer 2003: 50, 53).

Critical reflections: exploring contemporary trends in leadership

Building on this background of shared perspective, we can begin to look for contrasts – areas to explore and enrich our understanding. This may involve challenging and stretching our zones of comfort. We will do this by asking three critical questions which arise from Adair's work.

The heroic individual?

As we saw above, serving to lead is a favourite Adair theme, not least because of links with the Royal Military Academy's 'Serve to Lead' motto. It is a constant theme in his books (Adair 2000: 128–41; 2001: 138–46). But does the concept encourage the heroic individual?

We can ask whether being a hero and servant are mutually exclusive: can one be a heroic servant or servant-hero?[10] Here we encounter changing attitude in society, with implications for language. We can note how servanthood (serfdom, slavery) has been subject both to grave distortion in practice and trenchant criticism philosophically. Researching similarities and differences between leaders two generations apart, Bennis and Thomas refer to the 'end of heroic leadership' (2002: 79). One question they asked was about heroes. While the older leaders (the 'geezers') had influential heroes in their formative years, their younger counterparts (the 'geeks') tended to refer to family members.

It is good for British readers to be reminded that Mediterranean shepherds are to be found ahead of, rather than behind, their flocks. I vividly remember seeing shepherds in the arid mountains around the Eastern Mediterranean leading their sheep to find food and water, and defending them (with stones!) from attack. This is a long way from the image of 'One Man [sic] and his Dog' herding their flock into a pen. The biblical image of a shepherd includes dealing with the range of emotions from still waters to death's dark vale – a tough life rather than pastoral idyll.

The collaborative mindset 'means getting away from the currently popular heroic style of managing and moving to a more engaging style' (Gosling and Mintzberg 2003: 60). They quote John Kotter's response about the Harvard Business School class of 1974: 'these people want to create the team and lead it to some glory as opposed to being a member of a team that's being driven by somebody else'. 'That', they note, 'is not the collaborative mind-set' (*ibid.*). One report of recent research, which is severely critical of the transformational hero as leader, includes a chapter entitled 'The End of Superman – Don't be a Hero' (Binney *et al.* 2005).

One of the unexpected findings of research on enduring companies (Collins and Porras 1994) was that they did not all have what, in today's language, would be called 'charismatic CEOs'. (Another interesting finding, which we do not have time to pursue here, is that the 'visions' of these companies were not necessarily in place from the start but evolved over time, for example 3M and Hewlett-Packard. Note the parallel with Gosling and Mintzberg's comments above on visions). Collins went on to look at leaders of enduring companies and coined the term 'Level 5 Leadership'. A Level 5 Executive 'builds enduring greatness through a paradoxical blend of personal humility and professional will' (Collins 2001: 20). One key to profound change in an organisation with whom I worked came when a CEO described as an 'autocratic bully' was replaced by one who demonstrated vulnerability. Research on executive selection with its preference for outsiders – often linked with quasi-religious terms such as faith and salvation – confirms the doubt about the enduring impact of the heroic charismatic figure (Khurana 2002a, 2002b).

In reaction to the heroic leader, the idea of the quiet leader has been gaining ground. Badaracco (2002: 169ff) identifies three quiet virtues: restraint, modesty and tenacity. Another increasingly used phrase is the 'defining moment' (Badaracco 1997). Bennis and Thomas noted the importance of transformational events across the generations: they coined the term 'crucible' for these and linked them to 'defining moments' (2002: 161). They refer to the 'ability to extract wisdom from experience is a skill honed in the crucible' (2002: 109). Note the similar language to Adair's *phronesis*, or practical wisdom. My own work with leaders at various levels confirms that getting people to talk about their lives often reveals similar experiences.

Adair refers to a concept with some similarities to the defining moment: the 'inspired moment' (Adair 2003: 179). 'A leader with such a deep understanding – however intuitive – will be able to sense the inspired moment, that window of opportunity that opens up briefly where, if he or she does or says the right thing, the switch is thrown on the electrical circuit and that spiritual energy kicks in that enables people to transcend their previous limits'. However, the focus is on the leader, rather than the external environment. This leads on to our second question.

A Cartesian worldview?

Does Adair reflect an overly Cartesian worldview? Individual and team have featured from his earliest writings on action-centred leadership and it would be churlish to focus on one at the expense of the other. But does the approach reflect a Western egocentricism: *cogito ergo sum*? In searching for certainty, Descartes fell back on the fact of his own conscious existence. We might add that he went on to argue for the existence of God, which militates against a totally egocentric philosophy.

Charles Handy addresses this question. 'The idea that true individuality is necessarily social is one of the oldest propositions in philosophy... To be ourselves we need other people. What I term a "proper selfishness" builds on this fact that we are inevitably intertwined with others' (Handy 1997: 86f). However, the (properly selfish) I is still at the centre. African and other thinkers have for some time been pressing for an alternative perspective: 'I am known, therefore I am'. Satish Kumar uses the Sanskrit dictum *So Hum* to advocate a perspective of 'You are, therefore I am' (Kumar 2002). 'In stewardship and in collective leadership, people think of themselves in the context of the community' (Raelin 2003: 116f).

Gosling and Mintzberg's collaborative mindset emphasises relationships, which is also fundamental to Goleman's work on Emotional Intelligence. 'The art of relationships is, in large part, skill in managing emotions in others' (Goleman 1996: 43). The last of his four groups of Leadership Competencies is Relationship Management (Goleman *et al*. 2002: 255).

A useful perspective on individual and communal roles is provided in an important work on strategic futures: 'A company full of highly socialised, like-minded clones is unlikely to create the future; on the other hand, neither is a company full of self-interested renegades. What is needed are *community activists*, individuals who are not afraid to challenge the status quo, not afraid to speak out, but who also have a deep sense of community and a desire to improve not only their personal lot but that of others as well. The notion of a community of activists brings together the seemingly contradictory ideas of common cause and individual freedom.' (Hamel and Prahalad 1996: 320, italics in original).

Is it significant that Adair's reference to an 'inspired moment' uses a parallel with electricity? The Newtonian worldview is being challenged by a quantum approach, characterised by uncertainty, complexity and chaos. Followers of what is sometimes referred to as 'new science' prefer organic analogies (swarms of bees and ant-hills are two favourites). In particular, such concepts as complex adaptive systems, strange attractors, self-organisation and emergent properties emphasise afresh how relationships and interactions between agents can produce highly creative results (Wheatley 1999; Pascale *et al*. 2000; Olson and Eoyang 2001; Robertson 2005).

In considering the relationship between individuals, the theologians have a contribution to make. '[This essay] proposes Christian thought *in principle* as a profound, flexible and still-credible tradition which can secure the value of each individual person within the control of an equally secure relational and social vision. This vision has its origin in the nature of God and his [sic] relatedness' (White 1997: 159, italics in original). For Christians, the doctrine of the Trinity provides a model to explore relationships, though any application must bear in mind both Nicholls' (1989) historical perspective and Hunt's (2005) contemporary theological one.[11]

The Trinity has formed the basis of sociopolitical paradigms. A foremost exponent of the relational model has been Leonardo Boff, a Latin American theologian and former priest (e.g., Boff 1988). We will have particular reason to consider Boff below in his relations with the Roman Catholic hierarchy: 'Well did John Paul II say... "Our God, in his most intimate mystery, is not a solitude, but a family".... We must see human societies, the social relationships among their members... as impulses poured forth into history by the most holy Trinity' (Boff 1992: 69). Fiddes (2000) talks both of a personal God, who makes a community, and a triune God, who deals with questions of power and authority.[12]

Another perspective comes from the Orthodox tradition of iconography. One widely known icon is Andrei Rublev's (c1360–1430) of the Old Testament Trinity.[13] Three figures – ostensibly angels visiting Abraham[14] – point subtly to one another in their equality. They are gathered in a circle around the table: the space at the table is on the viewer's side. Through the device of inverse perspective (Baggley 1987: 80), we are invited to join the group, to complete the circle. A good metaphor to integrate individual, team and relationships.

A neat hierarchy?

Lastly, does Adair's neat hierarchy (2002b: 82, 2005: 44) – from *hieros*, sacred, and *archos*, one in authority – of team, operational and strategic leadership speak to a world characterised by complexity and chaos? We should not overplay the dichotomy between traditional hierarchies and complex adaptive systems. The latter 'always has some similarity at all levels of the system – individual, group, organization... Thus learning about a system on one level provides information about all of the other levels. For example, different departments in the same organization will share values, procedures, or communication habits' (Olson and Eoyang 2001: 105). But we can ask how far the 'neat hierarchy' helps or hinders leadership 'at the edge', or from marginal positions. 'Leaders are not just at the top but in the middle of a complex network of relationships. Living leaders recognise this interdependence' (Binney *et al.* 2005: 242).

Discussing the worldly mindset, Gosling and Mintzberg talk of learning through 'immersion in a strange context' (2003: 59). Referring to the module of the International Masters Program for Practicing Management undertaken in India, they comment that 'being there, especially among fellow managers from Indian companies, takes the non-Indian participants past the nice abstractions of economic, political, and social differences down onto the streets, where these differences come alive' (*ibid.*). Mention of 'down onto the streets' might evoke images of Mother Theresa in Calcutta, and a myriad unsung Mothers Theresa on the streets of the world. Adair refers to Mother Theresa, and Albert Schweitzer, in a section headed 'From periphery to centre' (2001: 153f). To a theologian, 'down on the streets' might prompt contemplation of the Christian doctrine of the incarnation, which sees its leader born and die on the margins of society. 'Showing some vulnerability is a key element in leading' (Binney *et al.* 2005: 48). In recent and contemporary politics, we can think of how, for many years, certain authority in South Africa emanated from a prison cell on Robben Island. Or how a significant source of authority in present day Myanmar comes from a suburban house in Rangoon.

And as for business, 'I can think of several organizations, particularly customer-oriented ones, that brag about how a single customer enquiry or the suggestion of one employee directed them into entirely new product lines that became very successful. There was no preplanning, no long-range strategic objectives, that led into these markets. Just the creativity of one or two individuals who succeeded in getting the attention of the organization and then watched the suggestion *amplify* to the level where the company reorganized or responded to it' (Wheatley 1999: 88, italics added). One could add the oft-quoted story of the invention of Post-Its by 3M employees, though it is important to note the underlying corporate culture that encouraged such off-beam developments.

A book on Christian ministry captures something of the approach in its title. *Eccentric Ministry* (Moody 1992) refers to the technical meaning away from the centre (though it could perhaps double for a collection of clerical biographies). Moody makes use of the model of the shepherd. A contemporary research project, Encounters on the Edge,[15] looks at lessons to be learned from the margins. Leech (2001: 166–201) addresses the issue of marginality from his experience in the East End of London and elsewhere. His critical theological reflections do not make comfortable reading. Although he makes few explicit references to leadership, Leech raises questions which are highly relevant to our purpose. Having described ministry on the margins, he reflects on the significance of theology at the edge of chaos. 'It seems to me that "the edge of chaos" is where we are in theology and pastoral care. Yet much of our pastoral work has been shaped within a framework of a culture of order, and of a Church obsessed with tidiness' (Leech 2001: 190). Leech then raises the pertinent question of whether the church is of the centre or of the margins. We can recall that, in the worldly mindset, managers are at the edge: 'To manage context is to manage on the edges, between the organization and the various worlds that surround it – cultures, industries, companies' (Gosling and Mintzberg 2003: 59).

Leech reserves some of his harshest criticism for the institutional church and of 'the increasing dominance of the centralised executive church model' (2001: 195). He quotes a major critic of this model, Richard Roberts: 'My fear is that all marginal ministry will be disallowed in favour of ministry that is in conformity with central "vision" statements and subject to deskilling managerial enforcement... There will be no place for nonconforming figures in a rationally managed church driven from the centre by executive power' (*ibid.*). Roberts' criticism of a centralised executive church model was directed at the Church of England. But the Roman Catholic church provides a telling illustration of his fear that nonconforming figures will be driven from the centre. Consider the experience of Leonardo Boff, whose relational model of the Trinity we considered above. Boff left – or was driven from, depending on your perspective – the Roman Catholic priesthood in 1992, but continues his trenchant observations. It is arguable that what finally led to the parting of the ways was not a disagreement about theology, but a disagreement over authority, and hence leadership. Boff railed against the centralising tendency of the Roman church.

'To be in a collaborative mind-set means to be inside, involved, to manage *throughout*. But it has a more profound meaning, too – to get management beyond managers, to distribute[16] it so that responsibility flows naturally to whoever can take the initiative and pull things together' (Gosling and Mintzberg 2003: 60, italics in original). A proponent of leaderful (sic) organisations writes: 'In the twenty-first-century organization, we need to establish communities where everyone shares the experience of serving as a leader, not sequentially, but concurrently and collectively' (Raelin 2003: xi).

In closing this section, we can reflect that Adair's three levels of leadership – strategic, operational and team – are seen in hierarchical terms (see, for example, the diagram in Adair 2005: 44). Given the widespread use of overlapping circles – for task, team and individual in the context of Action-Centre Leadership – our exploration raises the suggestive possibility of plotting these three 'levels' of leadership as overlapping circles, rather than in a hierarchy.

Closing reflections

In closing, we can note the significance of *change* in linking religious and managerial perspectives. In a recent book he co-edited, Adair highlights the importance of change in moving from management to leadership (Adair and Nelson 2004: 5). Over a quarter-of-a-century earlier, he noted, in a section headed A Theology of Change, that 'Change introduces an element of uncertainty... Confidence in God should encourage the churches to take risks and to explore, which means to accept the unknown and uncertain' (Adair 1977: 231). Excellent theology and in tune with contemporary approaches to uncertainty. What of the reality?

An Anglican Bishop asked about my professional work. When I said it involved helping people and organisations through change, the bishop responded, 'Ah, change and decay!' He was reflecting a common word association, derived from the Victorian hymn, *Abide with me*, by H.F. Lyte (1793–1847). The bishop was in good company in his negative attitude. One of the biggest selling *HBR* reprints during the 1990s was 'Leading Change: Why Transformation Efforts Fail' (Kotter 1995).

Such an attitude to change is, at the least, paradoxical; because many religions have change at their heart. Myths of (re)creation talk of bringing about new realities, whether order out of chaos (as in the first Genesis account, where the earth was a formless void until the breath of God moved over the turbulent waters) or the Noble Path leading to final enlightenment, or *nirvana*.

The Christian tradition conceives of the breath, or Spirit, of God as animating, sustaining and renewing the whole of creation. There is talk of conversion. A multi-valent word, its richness of meaning is diminished if it is applied in too narrow a context. Exploring one of the Greek words it translates, *metanoia*, reveals an interplay between process, event and attitudinal change. The concept covers both change of mind and behaviour. Conversion of life forms a fundamental thread running through the Rule of St Benedict, and *conversatio morum* is one of the three vows taken by a novice on entering the community (Parry and De Waal 1990: xxii). 'The call to conversion of life is in effect a vow to change, to never remain still either in self-satisfied fulfilment or self-denying despair' (Dollard *et al.* 2002: 201).

We find the same idea in a business context in the subtitle of a recent book: *Why Reinvention and Change are Prerequisites for Business Success* (Robertson 2005). Or more starkly, 'Equilibrium is death' (Pascale *et al.* 2000: 19). Two respected authors on strategy comment that 'Enormous managerial energy, and acres of newsprint, have been devoted to turn-arounds, rescues, and massive "change" programs, yet isn't the real goal to avoid a crisis-sized transformation problem by creating a capacity for continuous renewal deep within the company?' (Hamel and Prahalad 1996: x).

In closing, we might take heart from two sources which have helped guide our exploration. Benedict used three images to describe an Abbot: shepherd, healer/doctor, and steward (Dollard *et al.* 2002: 52ff). More than 14 centuries later, Wheatley (1999: 165) offers a '*very* partial list of new metaphors to describe leaders: gardeners, midwives, stewards, servants, missionaries, facilitators, convenors' (italics orig.). Two of the priest's five models appear and 'missionary' is suggestive,[17] even if it is a term rarely used in discerning ecclesiastical circles today. It looks as if managers and priests might indeed learn from one another.

Notes

1 MODEM. See www.modem.uk.com
2 Searching the Harvard Business School publications' website (www.hbsp. harvard.edu) reveals a rather different picture. Entering 'leadership' yielded 7,171 entries; 'management' produced 13,269 (searched 12 February 2006).
3 A change I noted while working for a major UK utility in the 1990s. Traditionally perceived by an engineering approach as delivering a product, a new perspective prompted some, but not all, to revision themselves as delivering a service to customers.
4 The origins, development and contemporary application of the so-called three-fold order of ministry are topics of considerable debate, which take us well beyond the bounds of our current consideration.
5 I am grateful to Canon Jeremy Fletcher of the Church of England Liturgical Commission and Sue Moore at Church House for arranging for me to receive prepublication copies of the new text.

6 I am grateful to John Adair for reminding me (in a private communication, September 2005) that 'corps' is derived from *corpus*, body – a word closely associated with the writings of St Paul.
7 Recorded in John Chapter 13. This passage contains the origins of Maundy Thursday traditions. In Great Britain, the command (*mandatum*) to love one another symbolised through foot-washing is now expressed in the symbolic giving of Maundy money.
8 Recorded in Matthew Chapter 25 and Luke Chapter 19.
9 In a private communication, September 2005.
10 If the role is allowed, Jesus would be an obvious candidate.
11 We can note how appropriate such a model is for someone whose writings have been characterised by trios: team/task/individual, strategic/operational/team, qualities/functional/situational leadership... to name but three.
12 Such an overly-compressed summary runs the risk of dualism. For other perspectives from differing religious traditions, see Zizioulas (1985) and Volf (1998).
13 The original is in the Tretyakov Gallery, Moscow (www.tretyakovgallery.ru/english/about).
14 Recorded in Genesis Chapter 18.
15 Headed by George Lings (www.encountersontheedge.org.uk).
16 My colleague David Lewis (www.edeninsight.co.uk) has recently developed a Distributed Leadership Assessment, based on a short questionnaire. Pilot results suggest that this provides a powerful tool to help organisations wrestling with this concept.
17 As is 'gardener'. See John 15.1.

References

Adair, John (1977) *The Becoming Church*, London: SPCK.
Adair, John (2000) *How to Find Your Vocation*, Norwich: Canterbury Press.
Adair, John (2001) *The Leadership of Jesus and Its Legacy Today*, Norwich: Canterbury Press.
Adair, John (2002a) *Effective Communication*, London: Macmillan.
Adair, John (2002b) *Effective Strategic Leadership*, London: Macmillan.
Adair, John (2003) *The Inspirational Leader: How to Motivate, Encourage and Achieve Success*, London and Sterling, VA: Kogan Page.
Adair, John (2005) *How to Grow Leaders: The Seven Key Principles of Effective Leadership Development*, London and Sterling, VA: Kogan Page.
Adair, John and Nelson, John (eds) (2004) *Creative Church Leadership*, Norwich: Canterbury Press.
Badaracco, Joseph L. (1997) *Defining Moments: When Managers Must Choose Between Right and Right*, Boston, MA: Harvard Business School Press.
Badaracco, Joseph L. (2002) *Leading Quietly: An Unorthodox Guide to Doing the Right Thing*, Boston, MA: Harvard Business School Press.
Baggley, John (1987) *Doors of Perception: Icons and their Spiritual Significance*, Oxford: Mowbray.
Bennis, Warren G. and Thomas, Robert J. (2002) *Geeks & Geezers: How Era, Values, and Defining Moments Shape Leaders*, Boston, MA: Harvard Business School Press.
Binney, George, Wilke, Gerhard and Williams, Colin (2005) *Living Leadership: A Practical Guide for Ordinary Heroes*, Harlow: FT Prentice Hall.

Block, Peter (1996) *Stewardship: Choosing Service Over Self-Interest*, San Francisco, CA: Berrett-Koehler.

Boff, Leonardo (1988) *Trinity and Society*, Tunbridge Wells: Burns & Oates.

Boff, Leonardo (1992) *Good News to the Poor*, Tunbridge Wells: Burns & Oates.

Bradshaw, Paul F. (ed.) (2002) *The New SCM Dictionary of Liturgy and Worship*, London: SCM Press.

Brown, Callum G. (2001) *The Death of Christian Britain*, London & New York, NY: Routledge.

Church of England (in press) *Common Worship: Ordination Services*, London: Church House Publishing.

Collins, Jim (2001) *Good to Great: Why Some Companies Make the Leap... and Others Don't*, London: Random House.

Collins, Jim and Porras, Jerry I. (1994) *Built to Last: Successful Habits of Visionary Companies*, London: Century Business.

Croft, Steven (2005) 'Leadership and the Emerging Church', *Focus on Leadership*, York: Foundation for Church Leadership, pp.7–41.

Dollard, Kit, Marett-Crosby, Anthony OSB and Wright, Abbott Timothy OSB (2002) *Doing Business with Benedict*, London & New York, NY: Continuum.

Fiddes, Paul S. (2000) *Participating in God: A Pastoral Doctrine of the Trinity*, London: Darton Longman & Todd.

Goleman, Daniel (1996) *Emotional Intelligence*, London: Bloomsbury Publishing.

Goleman, Daniel, Boyatzis, Richard and McKee, Annie (2002) *The New Leaders: Transforming the Art of Leadership into the Science of Results*, London: Little, Brown [Published in the USA as *Primal Leadership*].

Gosling, Jonathan and Mintzberg, Henry (2003) 'The Five Minds of a Manager', *Harvard Business Review*, November 2003, pp.54–63.

Green, Sebastian and Cooper, Patrice (1998) 'Sage, Visionary, Prophet and Priest: Leadership Styles of Knowledge Management and Wisdom', in Gary Hamel *et al.* (eds) *Strategic Flexibility: Managing in a Turbulent Environment*, Chichester: John Wiley & Sons.

Greenleaf, Robert K. (1977) *Servant Leadership: A Journey into the Nature of Legitimate Power and Greatness*, New York, NY: Paulist Press.

Greenleaf, Robert K., Beazley, Hamilton, Beggs, Julie and Spears, Larry C. (eds) (2002) *The Servant-Leader Within: A Transformative Path*, New York, NY: Paulist Press.

Greenleaf, Robert K. and Spears, Larry C. (ed.) (2002) *Servant Leadership*, 25th *Anniversary Edition*, New York, NY: Paulist Press.

Grint, Keith (2005) *Leadership: Limits and Possibilities*, Basingstoke: Palgrave Macmillan.

Hamel, Gary and Prahalad, C.K. (1996) *Competing for the Future*, Boston, MA: Harvard Business School Press.

Handy, Charles (1997) *The Hungry Spirit*, London: Hutchinson.

Harle, Tim (2004) 'Lessons from the Margins', *The Reader*, 101(1), 14–15.

Harle, Tim (2005) 'Serenity, Courage and Wisdom: Changing Competencies for Leadership', *Business Ethics: European Review*, 14(4), 348–58.

Higginson, Richard (2002) *Questions of Business Life: Exploring Workplace Issues from a Christian Perspective*, Carlisle: Authentic.

Howard, Sue and Welbourn, David (2004) *The Spirit at Work Phenomenon*, London: Azure.

Hunt, Anne (2005) *Trinity*, Maryknoll, NY: Orbis.

Khurana, Rakesh (2002a) *Searching for a Corporate Savior: The Irrational Quest for Charismatic CEOs*, Princeton, NJ: Princeton University Press.

Khurana, Rakesh (2002b) The Curse of the Superstar CEO. *Harvard Business Review*, September 2002, 60–6.

Kotter, John P. (1995) 'Leading Change: Why Transformation Efforts Fail', *Harvard Business Review*, March–April 1995.

Kumar, Satish (2002) *You Are Therefore I Am: A Declaration of Dependence*, Dartington: Green Books.

Lamont, Georgeanne (2002) *The Spirited Business: Success Stories of Soul-Friendly Companies*, London: Hodder & Stoughton.

Lawrence, James (2004) *Growing Leaders: Reflections on Leadership, Life and Jesus*, Oxford: Bible Reading Fellowship.

Leech, Kenneth (2001) *Through Our Long Exile: Contextual Theology and the Urban Experience*, London: Darton Longman & Todd.

Lipman-Blumen, Jean (2005) *The Allure of Toxic Leaders: Why We Follow Destructive Bosses and Corrupt Politicians – And How We Can Survive Them*, New York, NY: Oxford University Press.

Mintzberg, Henry (2004) *Managers not MBAs*, Harlow: FT Prentice Hall.

Mitroff, Ian I. and Denton, Elizabeth (1999) *A Spiritual Audit of Corporate America*, San Francisco, CA: Jossey-Bass Wiley.

Moody, Christopher (1992) *Eccentric Ministry: Pastoral Care and Leadership in the Parish*, London: Darton Longman & Todd.

Nicholls, David (1989) *Deity and Domination: Images of God and the State of the 19th and 20th Centuries*, London: Routledge.

Offermann, Lynn R. (2004) 'When Followers Become Toxic', *Harvard Business Review*, January 2004.

Olson, Edwin E. and Eoyang, Glenda H. (2001) *Facilitating Organization Change: Lessons from Complexity Science*, San Francisco, CA: Jossey-Bass/Pfeiffer.

Parry, Abbot OSB and De Waal, Esther (1990) *The Rule of St Benedict*, Leominster: Gracewing.

Pascale, Richard T., Millemann, Mark and Gioja, Linda (2000) *Surfing the Edge of Chaos*, London and New York: Texere.

Raelin, Joseph A. (2003) *Creating Leaderful Organizations: How to Bring Out Leadership in Everyone*, San Francisco, CA: Berrett-Koehler.

Robertson, Peter (2005) *Always Change a Winning Team: Why Reinvention and Change are Prerequisites for Business Success*, London: Marshall Cavendish Business.

Royal Military Academy Sandhurst (n.d.) *Serve to Lead*, Sandhurst: RMA.

Royer, Isabelle (2003) 'Why Bad Projects Are So Hard To Kill', *Harvard Business Review*, February 2003, 48–56.

Senge, Peter, Scharmer, C. Otto, Jaworski, Joseph and Flowers, Betty Sue (2005) *Presence: Exploring Profound Change in People, Organizations and Society*, London: Nicholas Brealey Publishing.

Sentamu, Margaret (2001) 'Selection', in Gordon W Kuhrt (ed.), *Ministry Issues for the Church of England*, London: Church House Publishing, pp.107–16.

Tourish, Dennis (2005) *Transformational Leadership and the Perils of Coercive Persuasion*. Paper presented at the 4th International Conference on Studying Leadership, Lancaster University Management School.

Tourish, Dennis and Vatcha, Naheed (2005) 'Charismatic Leadership and Corporate Cultism at Enron: The Elimination of Dissent, the Promotion of Conformity and Organizational Collapse', *Leadership*, 1(1), 455–80.

Volf, Miroslav (1998) *After Our Likeness: The Church as the Image of the Trinity*, Grand Rapids, MI: Eerdmans.

Wheatley, Margaret J. (1999) *Leadership and the New Science*, San Francisco, CA: Berrett-Koehler.

White, Vernon (1997) *Paying Attention to People*, London: SPCK.

Zaleznik, Abraham (1977) 'Managers and Leaders: Are They Different?', *Harvard Business Review*, May–June 1977.

Zizioulas, John D. (1985) *Being as Communion: Studies in Personhood and the Church*, Crestwood, NY: St Vladimir's Seminary.

Zohar, Danah and Marshall, Ian (2000) *SQ – Spiritual Intelligence The Ultimate Intelligence*, London: Bloomsbury Publishing.

Part II
Adair's Influence on Institutions

6

Action-Centred Leadership in the Royal Air Force: Final Landing or New Horizon?[1]

Sir Brian Burridge

Introduction

For today's cohort of senior military officers, John Adair's ground-breaking work on Functional Leadership (as Action-Centred Leadership was then known) represented the starting point of many personal leadership journeys stretching over more than 30 years. The recognition that tyro officers needed to understand what a leader actually *does* as well as recognising the qualities that a leader should possess seems axiomatic in today's world. Yet in the 1960s, this requirement was far from clear. The military world, then in the grips of the Cold War, seemed a much more ordered place but there was a growing recognition that more needed to be done to equip young officers for the leadership challenges that lay ahead. As a result, first Sandhurst then Cranwell[2] and soon Dartmouth adopted the Adair approach. It profoundly altered our training and gave us a much-needed toolbox with which to face the future.

This chapter takes as a baseline, the nature of leadership training at the Royal Air Force College Cranwell in the early 1960s then briefly looks at the impact of the introduction of Functional Leadership. It then defines today's leadership context for the Royal Air Force and assesses the extent to which the Functional approach has stood the test of time. It also examines whether the approach has developed a broader relevance in today's military world. It therefore seeks to add to the debate on whether the context in which military leadership now takes place has altered so fundamentally that the Action-Centred Approach has lost its relevance (final landing), or whether the approach is so fundamental that it is capable of application regardless of context (new horizon).

Minor public school – good at games!

The ethos of officer training in the Royal Air Force was defined by Lord Trenchard, the architect of what was the world's first independent air force.

In creating the Royal Air Force College at Cranwell, he saw the output as being officers who had 'been trained for the Air Force rather by general culture than by instruction in special technicalities' (Haslam 1982: 21).[3]

Perhaps unsurprisingly, therefore, the 1964 edition of Notes for the Guidance of Flight Cadets – the bible for new entrants to Cranwell – paid scant attention to leadership. Rather, the document made the implicit assumption that, if an individual understood the responsibilities of being an *officer*, then all would be well. This rather superficial approach was very much trait orientated. But it met head-on the enigma of whether leaders are born or made, an aspect deeply embedded in the Service's folklore. Writing about leadership in the Battle of Britain, fighter ace Johnny Johnson wrote of fellow ace, Douglas Bader, that:

> The elusive, intangible qualities of leadership can never be taught, for a man either has them or he hasn't.

Yet the Royal Air Force then (as now) prided itself on being a meritocracy and thus the explanation in Notes for the Guidance needed to finesse the issue: the result was predictable:

> One often hears the expression 'an officer and a gentleman'. There have been many invidious and inaccurate definitions of a gentleman. A simple definition is ... one who puts other people at their ease. The great asset of this definition is that it is not necessarily confined to any particular class of society.

This statement has its roots in the distinct nature of the Royal Air Force when it was formed as an independent Service in 1918.

> The development of warfare itself ... called for a system of command which, ... increasingly demanded a degree of technical, administrative and professional expertise that was not necessarily to be found among the traditional officer-producing classes. Further, it demanded among all ranks a degree of intelligent co-operation and devolution of authority, very different from the instant and unquestioning obedience, which the old hierarchy had expected and very largely got. The new Royal Air Force, in particular, with its increasing dependence on technology, very quickly found that a structure of command based on rigid distinctions between officers and other ranks simply did not work (Howard 1996).

From the outset, officer selection processes recognised this difference from the other two Services. While the pre-World War II mantra for the selection of pilots of 'minor public school – good at games' had a tinge of class recognition about it, the Cranwell of the 1960s did understand that there was a need to develop leadership, albeit bound-up in the notion of 'officership'. However, the consequent approach was rather vague. It dwelt on the rules and conventions governing the conduct of an officer. In other words, *attributes* were given prominence at the expense of the *role* that either leaders or officers undertake. John Adair recognises this dichotomy in his latest book when discussing 'the manager as leader' (Adair 2005: 31). He points out that the issue is not whether managers have leadership attributes. Rather, it is a question of whether they understand the role or of a leader across all facets or are they simply fixated solely on the task. So, *Notes for the Guidance of Flight Cadets* gave stern advice under headings such as professional competence, personal appearance (particularly the need for good taste in clothes) and speech, which the document acknowledged was a delicate subject! The paragraph describing the necessary 'Code of Behaviour' states boldly and then with a sting in the tail that:

> As an officer, you will be recognised as a leader ... It must be emphasised that nobody wants to destroy individuality and to produce stereotyped officers. There are many brilliant individualists playing rugby, but they all follow the same rules.

The associated pedagogy therefore centred largely on the requirement for instructor officers to represent role models. Success depended on an individual cadet's ability to conform and willingness to do so. The result was a leadership style that was directive and hierarchical; this was entirely in line with the deferential nature of society at the time. Given the subsequent career success of the Cranwell output, it worked tolerably well but, by the mid-1960s, cracks were beginning to show. Moreover, the rapid expansion of university education throughout the 1960s meant that there were progressively fewer young men (and they were all men at that stage) who were willing to spend three years in an institution such as Cranwell without gaining a university degree. Hence, by 1970, the traditional Cranwell cadet intake had been replaced by a graduate entry scheme.

The age of Aquarius[4]

The introduction of John Adair's Action-Centred Leadership model (as Functional Leadership was then termed) represented a paradigm shift in both the delivery of training and in the resulting leadership acumen of young officers beginning their careers. The model was introduced just ahead of the onset of the graduate entry scheme. This was fortuitous as it was highly unlikely that young people imbued with the culture of the 1960s who had been to university during a period of particular radicalism would have willingly conformed to the old approach. Action-Centred Leadership made it possible to teach what leaders actually do. As a result, young officers were equipped with a toolbox that allowed them to lead the planning, execution and monitoring of leadership tasks within a structured framework. Such was the power of the Adair approach and the skill of the instructors that even the most reticent of students could generate the confidence to grasp the nettle of leadership.

More broadly, within ten years or so, the lexicon of Action-Centred Leadership was universal in the Royal Air Force. There was a remarkable alignment of expectations on how officers should perform as leaders. This, in turn, added robustness to the annual appraisal process making assessment easier and development more prominent. The current *Officers Joint Appraisal Report* which serves all three Services has clear roots in the functional approach. Management is assessed separately from leadership with the latter being almost exclusively about addressing task and team needs. Individual needs are catered for under a separate heading of subordinate development. But the appraisal process is deemed to take a holistic approach in assessing an officer across the entire spectrum of competencies within which leadership is prominent. It is, of course, axiomatic that military officers are faced with real leadership challenges on a daily basis, providing a highly relevant context for both development and assessment. So, as the new millennium approached, the Action-Centred model, coupled with a robust appraisal system, had served the RAF well for more than 30 years. But there was much discussion on whether the same approach would serve us so well for the next 30 years.

Contextual flux

By the late 1990s, new factors had significantly altered the context of military leadership. First, the nature of military action had changed profoundly. The rigid and predictable objectives of the Cold War where bipolarism set the agenda had been replaced by the ambiguity of operational theatres like the Balkans, Sierra Leone and Iraq. In these cases, end states were less easy to define in tangible terms. Unpredictable and asymmetric enemies rendered conventional, precooked planning useless. The latter are usually non-state actors who do not conform to the norms or legal conventions of war. The need to generate overwhelming tempo to get inside the very rapid decision-action cycles of such adversaries required commanders to capitalise on fleeting opportunities. Overall, a ponderous, hierarchical and directive style of command and leadership which might have worked in the Cold War was no longer relevant. Nevertheless, Britain's military success throughout this period is testament to the leadership acumen of both officers and NCOs. Clearly very task orientated, they retained a clear focus on the objective while other nations, who were new to these novel missions in ambiguous circumstances, became fixated on aspects such as their own protection to the detriment of the task.

The return of Prussian doctrine

To cope with this unpredictable military environment, the notion of Mission Command grew in prominence. This has it roots in the Prussian General Von Molke's doctrine of 'Auftragstaktik' which sought to empower even the most junior commanders to grasp the moment and capitalise fleeting opportunities without the need for specific permission. In its modern form, it promotes a decentralised style of command, freedom and speed of action, and initiative but with a strong emphasis on teamwork. It operates on the basis of a 'loose-tight' fit with superior direction. It has clear parallels with the doctrine of empowerment that was sweeping through the flatter structures and matrix-managed organisations of the 1990s. But the elements of Mission Command are clearly defined in British Military Doctrine:

- First, a commander ensures that his subordinates understand his intentions, their own missions, and the strategic, operational and tactical context.
- Second, subordinates are told what *effect* they are to achieve and the reason why it is necessary.
- Third, subordinates are allocated sufficient resources to carry out their missions.
- Fourth, a commander uses a minimum of control so as not to limit unnecessarily his subordinates' freedom of action.
- Finally, subordinates decide for themselves how best to achieve their missions.

In broad terms, in any organisation (military or civilian), this approach requires leaders to engage in robust analysis so as to define their intent and test it for relevance at every level within the organisation. It calls for the ability to communicate that intent in a form that is digestible at every level. It requires resources to be provided to match the task, a facet of empowerment that is often ignored. It also relies on the ability of leaders at all levels to stand back and not to meddle. These aspects clearly have implications for the Action-Centred Approach which are examined after considering other contextual changes.

Making every pound count

The quest for efficiency in the public sector has made huge advances in the last 20 years. Looking back to the 1960s, it seems bizarre that resource control for Defence and the Armed Forces was completely centralised. There was no understanding of costs by those on the frontline who actually consumed the resources. By the late 1980s, the New Management Strategy emerged which sought to align financial authority with accountability for output. This approach achieved some success but it was introduced against the backdrop of the Cold War when, by comparison with today, resources were less problematic. The Cold War represented a real threat to vital national interests and western governments expected to pay the necessary premium. Since then, Defence has had to compete more starkly with other aspects of public expenditure. More importantly, the number of 'bucks' in the 'bang for the buck' equation has to be regarded as a measure of the relevance of armed forces in the modern world. By necessity, the Royal Air Force had adapted well in this situation; combat aircraft are expensive to buy and to maintain in service.

The majority of the non-commissioned element of the Royal Air Force is primarily involved in logistic support at the producer level. Equally, a significant proportion of the commissioned population either manages logistic support or relies on it as a means to achieve a task. Logistic support costs over a 25-year period are often 3–4 times the initial procurement cost of the fleet of aircraft concerned. Much focus in the past has been directed towards reducing the cost of logistics support by changing both process and structures. Few have been as successful as the recent Logistics Transformation Programme. The key here has been the involvement of even the most junior personnel in the Royal Air Force. Unsurprisingly, it is they who have the understanding of the imperfections of the current processes. They also bear the frustrations of inefficiency. This knowledge was unlocked by the consultants (Simpler)[5] who used Value-Stream Analysis and Rapid Improvement Events amongst those who actually do the logistics work. This degree of involvement not only generated enormous buy-in but also unlocked the innate but dormant creativity that existed at lower levels of the Royal Air Force. This process has had very beneficial effects on the sense of empowerment (which aligns with mission command) and hence the self-esteem in the junior ranks. So, the contextual challenge is how do we continue to unlock this creativity without endangering the distinct military ethos that is inherent in a hierarchical command structure? In other words, how should we adapt our approach to the Action-Centred Leadership model to generate this culture without allowing anarchy to rule? Keith Grint's work on 'constructive dissent' (Grint 2005: 111–13) is relevant and leads to the notion of creating a heterarchy[6] rather than a hierarchy where 'responsible followers' possess high commitment aligned with high independence. This, in turn, calls on individuals to exercise significant self-discipline. These aspects are now covered in the leadership training of our most junior personnel under the heading of 'followership'. But to understand the impact on the Action-Centred approach, we need to delve deeper into the nature of the individual who is either leading or following.

Generation X lives on[7]

Generation X is deemed to be those born between 1965 and 1979. The earliest representatives are now in mid-seniority leadership positions in the Royal Air Force. Generation X characteristics include: a greater acceptance of the shortcomings of others; reluctance to accept the concept of all-knowing leadership; and a deep scepticism towards the degree of trust that can be placed in institutions. They represent the irreversible shift in the UK from a 'deferential' to a 'referential' society. Unsurprisingly, they have views on leadership and followership that vary markedly from the cohort of officers who were first introduced to Action-Centred Leadership in the 1960s.

These aspects were explored during a major study[8] in 2003 aimed at revising the RAF's approach to leadership training and development. The study found that the Action-Centred approach was effective in producing officers who were task-orientated and entirely comfortable taking charge of like-minded individuals. In other words, development favoured leadership

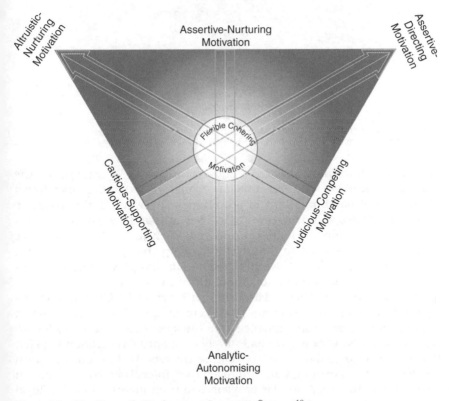

Figure 6.1 The Strength Deployment Inventory® arrow[10]

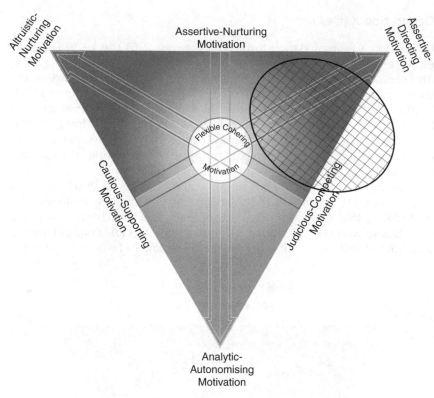

Figure 6.2   The SDI® arrow with results cluster

of peer-group teams to achieve short-term goals. By extension, the prevalent leadership style was autocratic which worked well in operational situations but had limitations in peacetime activity and during training. However, the deeper integration of Civil Servants and civilian contractors into Royal Air Force structures means that even junior Royal Air Force leaders will be exposed to different leadership styles. Equally, they are required to adopt approaches other than 'I'm in charge' when dealing with these groups. Of particular note, junior officers were found to have inadequacies in managing their relationship with Senior NCOs. The former's style was very much peer-group related, making it difficult for them to either stimulate or absorb guidance from the more experienced but hierarchically lower NCO cadre. We had simply developed a generation who felt that they had to be right and have all the answers. This sat uneasily with the psyche of Generation X and led to a rather 'forced' approach lacking in depth of confidence. A similar problem had been identified in the Royal Australian Air Force (Thomas 2000) where there was an identified need to move away from the command/management leader-centred style to a relationship and entrepreneurial style.

Given the importance of this relationship issue, useful (if immature) data are emerging from assessment using the Strength Deployment Inventory® (SDI®).[9] The SDI® is a paper-based questionnaire founded on Relationship Awareness Theory® derived by Dr Elias Porter in the 1960s. Although a self-report test, it is deemed by users to be accurate in terms defining motivation rather than just categorising behaviour. The test cohort was some 100 officers of squadron leader rank, the majority of who were in their thirties (the leading edge of Generation X). SDI® seeks to identify personal strengths in relating to others in two sets of circumstances; first, when everything is going well; and secondly when faced with conflict. Individual inventory scores are plotted on the Interactive Triangle at Figure 6.1 with the relevant descriptors at Table 6.1. The main scatter of results is shown at Figure 6.2. The main cluster was around the Assertive-Nurturing axis with significant concentration (including 80 percent of the pilots) in the central Flexible-Cohering area.

Table 6.1 Summary of relevant value systems®

	Value System	Value-Relating Style	Rewarding Environment
Assertive-Nurturing	• Concern for protection, growth and welfare of others through task accomplishment and leadership	• Actively seeking opportunities to help others • Persuading others to ensure maximum growth and development of others • Being open to proposals for creating welfare and security for others • Creating enthusiasm and support in tackling obstacles to success	• Openness, mentoring, enthusiastic, friendliness, sincerity, trust, compassion • Respect for others, supporting the underdog • Positive, progressive initiatives for the growth and development of others
Flexible-Cohering	• Concern for flexibility • Concern for group welfare • Concern for members of the group and belonging in the group	• Being curious about what others think and feel • Open-minded and willing to adapt • Experiments with different ways of acting	• Friendly, involving, sociable, democratic, playful, changing, flexible • Encouraging interaction • Being heard and listening

Table 6.1   Summary of relevant value systems® – *continued*

Value System		Value-Relating Style	Rewarding Environment
		• Proud to be a member • Likes to know lots of people • Likes to be known by a lot of people • Likes to be known as flexible	• Sensitivity to feelings • Consensus building
Altruistic-Nurturing	• Concern for the protection, growth and welfare of others	• Being open and responsive to the needs of others • Seeking ways to bring help to others • Trying to make life easier for others • Trying to avoid being a burden to others • Ensuring others reach their potential • Ensuring others are valued • Defending the rights of others	• Open, friendly, helpful, considerate, supportive, enhancing, trusting, socially sensitive, sincere, loyal, compassionate, respectful, humanitarian • Being needed • Being appreciated

The theatre of 'I'm in charge'

These results need to be judged against the hypothesis that the Action-Centred Approach has led to a cohort of task-orientated RAF officers whose comfort zone lies in taking charge of the like-minded individuals. Based on their initial training, they believe that they are expected to display (as in a theatrical production) the style of leadership depicted in their early experiences at Cranwell (the script) to the same type of people with whom they trained (the cast). For this to be true, more individuals would have been on the right-hand side of the triangle towards the Assertive-Directing, Judicious-Competing and Analytic-Atomising axes. These axes have a greater task focus than do the other axes which are more aligned with the Team Needs and Individual Needs represented in the Action-Centred model. Even given the small sample size and the prospect of some collective wish to adhere to group norms, these results would seem to undermine the 'task-orientated' hypothesis. It is thus possible that this generation of leaders engage in 'theatre' by seeking to adhere to what they believe to be the expectations of a 'can-do' (hence task-orientated) organisation such as the Royal Air Force. But it is clear that the preferred approach to leading others is to focus particularly on team aspects and on the value of the individual. As a Commander-in-Chief, I am reassured by this. As an aside, the close clustering of pilots in the Flexible Cohering domain indicates the value they attach to the sense of squadron identity and 'belonging' that this inspires.

Conclusion – final landing or new horizon?

In assessing the relevance of the Action-Centred model for the future, we need to make judgements over its ability to embrace the following:

- Mission Command
- Constructive Dissent
- An organisational culture that balances task-orientation with team and individual needs

The last bullet was precisely the underpinning logic of John Adair's model when it was introduced in the 1960s. Two factors have caused difficulties in applying the model over the years both in the Armed Forces and more broadly. First, initial teaching must stress that the model is dynamic. There are occasions where the importance of the task outweighs all but minimum focus on team or individual needs (a frequent military requirement in combat). But such a situation cannot continue indefinitely if the organisation's performance is to be sustainable (again a frequent military requirement). In other words, the three circles often need to be of different and changing sizes. Secondly, there is a general shift towards an output focus in the public sector and beyond. Granular performance indicators with league tables that name and shame (driven by a cynical media) is now a common feature of the leadership environment. This acts as a catalyst towards a culture of task-orientation whilst failing to recognise team and individual needs as ingredients of sustainable success. For Armed Forces, continual exposure to operations (across the spectrum of conflict) also drives task-orientation. So, as the first element of a new horizon, the model remains a powerful tool by which to maintain a balanced approach.

To judge the model's applicability in a new leadership paradigm (or new horizon) that embraces Mission Command and Constructive Dissent, it is appropriate to examine this aspect against John Adair's original 'Sandhurst List' of the functions of a leader (Adair 2005: 18–19). The latter represents the initial teaching of the model in its earliest form to officer entrants to the

Table 6.2 The Sandhurst List versus the new horizon

Function	Sandhurst List	New Horizon
Planning	• Seeking all available information • Defining group task, purpose or goal • Making a workable plan (in right decision-making framework)	• Define intent – what is the end-state? • Decide on degree of freedom of action to be given to subordinates • Make a plan appropriate to your level of leadership • Check resource constraints
Initiating	• Briefing group on the aims and the plan • Explaining why aim or plan is necessary • Allocating tasks to group members • Setting group standards	• Communicate intent in a way that is digestible at every level • Brief on the 'effect' that subordinates are to achieve • Encourage brainstorming • Agree feedback requirements
Controlling	• Maintaining group standards • Influencing tempo • Ensuring all actions are taken towards objectives • Prodding group to action/decision	• React to requests for further direction • Check whether the context and constraints have changed • Monitor synchronisation between the different parts of the organisation • Encourage novel and creative solutions
Supporting	• Expressing acceptance of persons and their contribution • Encouraging group/individuals • Disciplining group/individuals • Creating team spirit • Reconciling disagreements or getting others to explore them	• Stand-back and do not meddle • Encourage freedom of action • Create a sense of common purpose • Resolve conflicting priorities over resources • Let people make their own mistakes and give them confidence to do so
Informing	• Clarifying task and plan • Giving new information to the group, i.e., keeping them 'in the picture' • Receiving information from the group • Summarising suggestions and ideas coherently	• Clarify direction as time moves forward and new facts unfold • Listen to feedback and check for coherence with intent • Spread best-practice • Act as a style exemplar
Evaluating	• Checking feasibility of an idea • Testing the consequences of a proposed solution • Evaluating group performance • Helping the group to evaluate its own performance	• Checking feasibility of an idea • Testing the consequences of a proposed action at every level • Listen to the self-evaluation of performance

Army in 1968. In so doing, this is not to suggest that the list is set in stone; as Adair states, 'a fixed list would ossify what should be living material'. But the comparison at Table 6.2 shows that the model itself needs no adaptation to meet the requirements. Rather, it is a matter of thinking through the individual activities that make up the three circles to meet the requirements of the current context. Thereafter, there needs to be a periodic sanity check to ensure balance between the three circles over time.

A common and powerful thread running through all aspects of Action-Centred Leadership is that, in learning and understanding the model itself and in applying it successfully in early leadership situations of high ambiguity, young officers gain the confidence to grasp the nettle of leadership in a way that was absent before the introduction of the model. The conclusion is therefore that the Adair Action-Centred Leadership approach represents a timeless model which should continue to be the bedrock of RAF leadership teaching and development. It is more than capable of adapting to the requirements of the new horizon and is by no means on the approach to its final landing.

Notes

1   The views expressed in this chapter are those of the author alone. They do not necessarily reflect the views or policy of either the Royal Air Force or the Ministry of Defence.
2   RAF Henlow, then training Direct Entry officers adopted the Adair approach in 1968 just ahead of Cranwell. Similarly, the RN introduced it to officer candidates drawn from the ranks ahead of its formal introduction at Dartmouth.
3   Extract from a report on Preliminary Education of Candidates for Royal Air Force Commissions quoted in Haslam (1982).
4   The end of an era and the dawning of a new exciting age as enshrined in the 1968 West End musical *Hair* introducing nudity to the conventional London stage for the first time. Undergraduate culture of the late 1960s readily grasped both notions.
5   Simpler® Consulting Limited. www.simpler.com +44(0)1427 874456 with detail on SDI on www.personalstrengths.co.uk
6   A structure consisting of highly committed followers with significant independence under the guidance of a Socratic leader.
7   Generation X is regarded as the modern cohort from mid-twenties and mid-thirties who have grown-up in a technological and materialistic society. The hypothesis deems them to be emotionally scarred, alienated from the values of their elders, rejecters of conformity and obsessed with the search for a deeper meaning to life.
8   The RAF Leadership Development Team conducted 135 focus groups involving 990 personnel (2 percent of the trained strength).
9   The Strength Deployment Inventory® (SDI®) is protected by worldwide copyright and is registered to Personal Strengths Publishing Inc. www.personal-strengths.co.uk +44(0)1780 764776.
10 Adapted from the Interactive Triangle © Copyright 1973, 1996 by Personal Strengths Publishing. All rights reserved in the US and worldwide.

References

Adair, J. (2005) *How to Grow Leaders*, London: Kogan Page.

Grint, K. (2005) *Leadership: Limits and Possibilities*, Basingstoke: Palgrave Macmillan.

Haslam, E.B. (1982) *The History of Royal Air Force Cranwell*, London: HMSO (Her Majesty's Stationary Office).

Howard, Sir Michael (1996) 'The Armed Forces and the Community', *RUSI Journal*, August, pp.9–12.

Johnson, J. (1956) *Wing Leader*, London: Chatto and Windus.

Thomas, K. (2000) *Leadership Development: A Case Study of the Relative Effectiveness of Educational Mechanisms*, (EISAM Paper).

7
Public Sector Leadership Centres – a Variant of Groundhog Day?

Ewart Wooldridge

Introduction

Since 1999 when I took up my role as Chief Executive of the Civil Service College (then to become a directorate of the Centre for Management and Policy Studies, now the National School of Government), we have witnessed the birth – and rebirth – of leadership centres for the public sector at the rate of more than one per year. We now have in existence (and this may not be an exhaustive list) centres dedicated to the leadership development needs of the civil service, local government, schools, health, police, defence, further education and higher education (to which I moved as founding Chief Executive 18 months ago). Is this a wasteful proliferation of overlapping bodies or an assertion of the crucial importance of diversity and context to leadership development? Devolution has also prompted the creation of public service leadership centres in Scotland and in Wales, and their cross-sector experience (especially in Scotland) may be of particular interest to the debate prompted by this chapter.

The references to the film *Groundhog Day* may sound slightly flippant, but there is a sense of déjà vu as some of these centres set out their models of – or approaches to – leadership development. We may find strong similarities in the techniques used (such as the ubiquitous 360° feedback and regular recourse to action learning, coaching, and mentoring), the priority subject areas such as project management and user/customer focus, and the models of leadership. Leadership Centres usually deny that a single model is used and then proceed to set out a construct, or framework of competencies, closely akin to a model! But is there a single model of public sector leadership which has the same elegance and simplicity as John Adair's three interlocking circles?

In parallel with these developments, we have an ongoing rhetoric from government (which entered the language largely at the same time I joined the Civil Service College) about 'joined up government' and the quest to transform the leadership and delivery of public services generally. This can be tracked back to the launch of the Modernisation programme and values in 1998, which was followed up by Civil Service Reform, the work of the Prime Minister's Delivery Unit under Professor Sir Michael Barber, and the Office of Public Service Reform under Wendy Thomson. This rhetoric, and those institutions, have prompted a growing level of activity within the Cabinet Office, to make a genuine and practical attempt at finding ways of increasing collaboration and cooperation between the various public service leadership centres, coordinated by the Public Services Leadership Consortium (PSLC). This activity also led originally to the creation of the Public Service Leaders Scheme and now to its successor that embraces private and public sectors, called 'Leaders UK'. Later on in this chapter, I will be examining the nature of those developments and the opportunities that the PSLC is seeking to achieve a greater sense of cross-sector joined up working.

Aims and issues

My aim in this chapter is to give a more public airing to the debates about public service leadership development, which are largely going on behind closed doors. We need to promote a much more active and open dialogue about issues which are of real concern to those who are funding and running leadership development organisations in various parts of the public sector. These issues include: (1) Unnecessary reinvention and duplication (i.e. the 'Groundhog Day' phenomenon). Are we seeing an inefficient proliferation of leadership centres, all developing similar generic skills? Or, on the other hand, are they doing nothing more than manifesting one of the essential issues about leadership, that it is highly specific and contextualised? (2) In the very worthy activities being pursued at the centre of government to try and promote cross-sector collaboration and understanding, are we simply encouraging a lot of technical (ultimately low impact) activity about leadership **development** processes and procurement, and missing the wider point about promoting joined-up **leadership**? (3) Do we need to commission research on the activity of public service leadership itself, reflecting on the impact of eight years of sustained focus on modernisation, reform and joined-up delivery in the public services? Amongst other things, this study might stimulate a wider public debate about the desirability of encouraging some forms of joined-up public sector **career** under which a small but significant cadre of people (particularly in 'fast stream' type positions) move from one part of the public sector to another as they climb up the leadership ladder. Or is this 'public sector career' an eternally elusive concept that will be forever thwarted by a combination of professional silo thinking and problems over incompatible salary, bonus and pension arrangements?

A personal interest

Clearly I, need to declare my own personal interest in this. I spent five years leading the Civil Service College/CMPS during the formative period of much of this activity, and for the last two years have been establishing the newly created Leadership Foundation for Higher Education. However, the cross-sector dimension of all this is fundamental in my experience. Indeed my own organisation has as one of its underlying values the maximisation of **cross-sector themes** and activities and **collaboration** both in the UK and internationally. Indeed, I hope to bring a unique experience to this debate, having been involved over my career in executive and HR leadership roles in both the private sector and various parts of the public sector – local government, central government and now higher education, with also a spell in the not-for-profit 'voluntary' sector as Director of Operations at the South Bank Arts Centre. Not only will I be drawing upon various source documents and conversations I have had with leaders of these leadership institutions, but will be incorporating my own personal experience of leadership in a number of different sectors.

What does 'leadership' mean?

It may be important at this stage to undertake some definition of terms. By leadership, I mean a process that can happen at a variety of levels in an organisation, from chief executive to the frontline of delivery. Since it is almost by nature distributed and shared, it has to embrace quite large aspects of what we call 'management' as well as 'governance'. In certain sectors – particularly local government and central government – there is the added dimension of elected members (either councillors or MPs) who undertake leadership roles in their local authority cabinets or government departments. We should also be quite firmly aspirational. We are not looking simply at ways and means of propping up routine leadership processes. The debate in the public service is about **transformational leadership** that can cope with the most complex processes of change and the most demanding of stakeholder environments. We are looking beyond just the ability to deliver the standard competencies associated with effective leadership. Since a lot of my own formative leadership experiences were in the creative industries, let me illustrate that with a quote from Richard Attenborough on leadership, who wrote as follows: 'Acting – as in leadership – has two massive ingredients, one is a passionate commitment, not in terms of tramping over people, but a determination to succeed. The other is courage. You have got to be prepared to dare. You have to be prepared to venture' (Forrest and Tolfree 1992: 20).

So I am setting the bar high, because this whole debate about leadership centres is not about tidying up the business between allegedly overlapping organisations, but about exploring whether different arrangements can genuinely produce a new breed of highly effective, committed and passionate leaders for the public sector.

The Civil Service journey

I would like to start with the Civil Service because clearly I have an intensive experience of this process over the last few years. My series of quotes at 'milestone' points in the history of the process of equipping civil servants to deliver to the needs of government starts with the following:

> That the Permanent Civil Service, with all its defects, eventually contributes to the proper discharge of the function of Government, has been repeatedly admitted by those who have successively been responsible for the conduct of our affairs. All, however, who have had occasion to examine its constitution with care have felt that its organisation is far from perfect, and that its amendment is deserving of the most careful attention.[1]

This is from the Northcote-Trevelyan Report of 1853. We then move on over 100 years to the second quote, drawn from the hugely influential report of the Committee on the Civil Service under Lord Fulton in 1968 which led directly to the creation of the Civil Service College:

> This combination of major teaching and research functions should enable the College to fulfil a role which we believe is greatly needed. It should become a focus for the discussion of many of the important problems facing the Civil Service as a whole – discussion in which we hope that many outside the Civil Service will share.[2]

We then move on six years later to when the Civil Service College has been established, for a comment which reveals the challenges facing such institutions in the public sector:

> The College is not an elitist Institution. If it had been it might have found it easier both to establish its repute with some of its more demanding critics and to fulfil the research and promotional roles proposed for it. On the contrary, it was proposed by the Fulton Committee, and accepted by two successive governments, that it should be a large scale, broad based institution... It is as though the same institution was expected to combine the roles of All Souls and Adult Education Centre,

with some elements of technical education and teacher training thrown in for good measure.[3]

What do these quotes tell us about earlier approaches to leadership development in the civil service? First of all, they show a strong commitment to the process of management development, acknowledging a close link between the direct performance of civil servants and the effectiveness of government. Secondly, Fulton in particular reveals that the existence of such an institution is not there just to deal with skills and capabilities, but to be a focus for discussion of important problems. This implies the need for an organisation – call it a corporate university or whatever – that is dealing with learning in a much wider sense – a forum for debate, a place where values are defined, a safe environment in which those at the very top can go offline. However, in the third quote, the reference to the tension between the roles of 'All Souls' and 'an Adult Education Centre' reveal a long-standing debate about the civil service's leadership development institutions. Are they essentially for those with top leadership roles, or do they have a much wider, almost 'democratising' inclusive remit, spreading both competence and values to a very large constituency of civil servants?

These issues have certainly been at the heart of the debate about the Civil Service College and subsequently CMPS, and now the National School of Government. The transformation of the senior development programmes in recent years has created much more of a sense of a career and development journey fuelled by a High Potential scheme and the Fast Stream, and culminating in the Top Management Programme for those destined for the most senior positions in the senior civil service. Beyond that, for those at the Permanent Secretary level, there is the prospect of such programmes as the Chevening Programme which brought them together, under Chatham House Rules, with the most senior representatives of other walks of life. When CMPS was launched in 1998, the then Director General, Professor Ron Amann, was absolutely clear what the advantage was – he was particularly enthusiastic about the integration of policy-making, as opposed to management skills alone, into the remit of the new organisation, and he used these words at the launch of the organisation: 'The formation of CMPS gives us the opportunity to apply a joined-up approach to a range of issues that will make government more responsive, effective and, most importantly, customer focused.'[4]

He then went on to explain that the college, as a directorate of CMPS, had been refocused much more precisely around the new civil service reform programme. The development programmes of the civil service college would, 'better reflect the competencies required to achieve the civil service that the Prime Minister and Sir Richard Wilson had described through the modernising Government White Paper and the Sunningdale agenda, which committed the civil service to strong leadership, better business planning, sharper performance management, improved diversity, greater openness to people and ideas, and a better deal for staff'. Taking these reforms as its themes, the college directorate's recent package of programmes, 'Making it Work', was a practical and comprehensive approach to achieving organisation change through people development – crucial to the civil service reinventing itself now and in the future.

The most significant aspect of so much of that rhetoric, was the reference to the very precise linkage between the programmes of CMPS, either through the Civil Service College or its other departments, and the needs of the government's modernisation, civil service reform, and delivery agenda.

Seven years on in 2005, I attended the launch of the new National School of Government, which takes over the responsibilities previously covered by the Centre for Management and Policy Studies. In this new iteration, there is a clearly signposted intention to make a step change, particularly away from the high volume courses and programmes associated with the Civil Service College dimension of CMPS. But still there is a strong emphasis on the particular needs of the civil service. As Sir Andrew Turnbull said at the opening, 'we will not allow our key training and development provider to become divorced from the corporate development aim of the civil service. The School will therefore have a specific role in ensuring that we invest in high quality development of current and future leaders of the civil service'.[5]

At the same time, the rhetoric includes reference to obligations across the wider public sector. In referring to a document from Sue Street, Permanent Secretary of DCMS, about the kind of leaders they needed in the civil service of tomorrow, there is reference to 'building a greater sense of common leadership community and eventually across the wider public sector'.

At the same launch ceremony, there was also reference to work that was going on within the Cabinet Office, with the support of Ministers, in looking at opportunities for greater collaboration in the area of public sector leadership – but the commitment to that broader view perhaps fell short of a larger aspiration for public sector leadership and leadership development that he could have announced. The words were as follows:

> In order to deliver on the Government's objectives for more customer-focused public services, all the players in the chain of delivery, which stretches from Ministers, through civil servants to the wider public sector, need to work more closely together. So I want to see much better exchange of knowledge and skills between sectors and across the public service. To address this, some people call for the creation of a single public sector academy. I do not favour this but I do believe that the National School [of Government] should take on the role of promoting closer working with its counterparts in other sectors such as the Defence

Academy, the new Leadership Centre for Local Government and NHS University (from July this year part of the NHS Institute for Innovation and Improvement) and the National Centre for School Leadership.[6]

So during this period, we have seen in the Civil Service **two tracks of activity**. On the one hand, a focus on developing the skills of civil servants to **meet the specific needs of government** and to create that sense of common purpose and common values across the service. In parallel with that, we have seen a growing activity around looking at **relations with the wider public sector**. Most particularly, we saw about three years ago the development of the Public Service Leaders Scheme which involved collaboration between the civil service, the NHS, the police and local government. Now we have the launching of 'Leaders UK', which brings a broader consortium of public service organisations together along with a private sector dimension. At the same time – and we will refer to this in more detail later – there was a continuing level of activity going on within the Cabinet Office about trying to find practical areas of collaboration and cooperation between the various leadership agencies.

These two tracks are not incompatible. The concern is that this worthwhile area of activity to broaden the area of collaboration will not really make a fundamental difference to all that is going on independently in the various agencies across different parts of the public sector. This is primarily due to the fact that the main focus of these discussions is on leadership **development** rather than stepping back and looking at **leadership** itself. The activity at the centre is tending to be an administrative and process-driven one about building better training courses and getting improved collaboration on procurement and value for money rather than allowing it to be driven by a vision for leadership in the public sector. It is at this point in the chapter that we need to step back and look at some of the issues in public service leadership. Is there a construct that will command a sensible and practical consensus that is more than a bland list of competencies? Does it provide a better set of building blocks around which we could then establish a fresh and more collaborative approach to public service leadership development? Let's seek out some issues about which an agenda can be developed.

Leadership in the public services – defining a fresh agenda

Public service leadership has not prompted a large amount of research. One of the more systematic studies in recent years was undertaken by the Performance and Innovation Unit (2000) of the Cabinet Office. Whilst the report in many ways fell short of making the major impact it was expected to, its analysis (and particularly its report of the outcomes of its workshops) provided a lot of useful material about the issues of contemporary

Table 7.1   PIU Workshop findings – cross-sector leadership qualities

Leaders:
- are reflective – they are self-aware of their own behaviours and actions, and the impacts they have on others
- know that they cannot lead alone
- draw on multiple perspectives
- believe in us more than we do ourselves
- have courageous patience
- take time
- ignore ridicule
- know how to create trusting relationships
- treat the short term as if it were the long term
- are consistent
- demonstrate integrity/independence
- can dissent for the sake of the task
- use feedback
- rely on and know how to foster our commitment and creativity
- know we are only motivated by meaningful work
- desire to be included and fear being left out
- know how to support and appreciate
- are gladly accountable
- state what really counts
- give an account of what they've done (retrospectively)
- hold themselves accountable for the whole
- fail – and learn from failure

In organisations, leaders:
- know that it is the identity of an organisation which determines its outcome, and hence focus on defining and reinforcing that
- use participative processes to solve intractable problems
- value multiple perspectives
- focus on creating possibility rather than identifying and fixing problems
- make organisations safe for people who don't 'fit' and, by so doing, add richness and perspective
- communicate by coordinating behaviour
- have minimum standards and act decisively when breached
- are connected to the daily reality of their staff and users
- know that the public they serve are the meaning, not the problem
- use political demands as catalysts for doing what really matters, not as an end in themselves
- push control down
- know outcomes are too important to be left to measures alone

Working with other organisations, leaders:
- use different models of partnership (cooperative, collaboration, co-evolution) depending on the circumstances
- seek strong partners, and build 'fair trades' between them
- recognise that intermediaries can distort, and buffers protect
- know they can't do it on their own
- understand that making connections is core business
- build community

Source: PIU (2000).

public sector leadership and the contributions which high quality leadership development might make. If nothing else, this report could provide a useful starting point for the agenda of a new research programme into (or national debate on) the dilemmas and issues of 21st century public service leadership and the contribution of leadership development. It is worthwhile reminding ourselves of some of these issues and observations.

Many are well known territory. What I want to encourage is a process which takes them beyond the statement of the obvious (e.g., risk aversion, multiple stakeholder relationships and blame cultures) and challenges us to identify not a sterile list of competencies but the **attributes and behaviours** of those who **successfully work through these barriers to effective leadership**.

A good starting point is to be found in section 3 of the PIU Report, which sets out a very interesting schematic diagram of the findings of the workshops on 'cross-sector leadership qualities'. There is so much to unpack in Table 7.1 (much of it still relevant) and the report never really did it justice.

There are some very useful concepts which merit further study, such as:

'**Courageous patience**' – how many senior leaders in the public sector know just how long such courageous patience has to be sustained on some occasions? It has the same tension in the term as such phrases as 'tough empathy'. How do we develop it?

'**Are gladly accountable**' and '**hold themselves accountable for the whole**' – the crucial issue here is how this attribute in public sector leadership can be sustained without being allowed to atrophy into risk aversion.

'**The value of multiple perspectives**' – we all know that public sector leaders need to be able to handle multiple stakeholder relationships, but the emphasis here is on the word 'value'. We need to see how it enhances outcomes, and is not just an excuse for procrastination through endless stakeholder consultation.

'**Use different models of partnerships (cooperative, collaborative, co-evolution)**' – how much work has really been done on looking at the specific qualities of leaders to handle external and collaborative and partnership relationships? (In the Leadership Foundation for Higher Education, we have developed specifically a programme focusing on those skills, whether they be for research collaborations, knowledge transfer with industry, or partnership at a regional, local, government or community level).

Elsewhere the report focuses on the more customary areas of public service leadership experience and invites, but never takes far enough, the more detailed analysis that should now be undertaken. In this context, I would include such issues as:

Aversion to risk – a long-standing factor associated with the culture of public sector management and leadership, but what we will be seeking will be the role models of those leaders who manage to work through this issue and still maintain and develop entrepreneurial behaviours.

Blame culture – so often a characteristic of working within the public sector but what are the tactics that effective leaders in the public sector use successfully to transform a blame culture into a learning organisation? **Lack of organisational space** – so often leaders in the public sector feel hemmed in simply by the process of politics and other constraints that surround them – what are the techniques that successful leaders use to create more effective working space around them in order to achieve and make impact?

Attributes and behaviours of successful public sector leaders

This process of identifying the attributes and behaviours of successful leaders reminds me of research which I commissioned from the School of Public Policy at Birmingham University when I was at the Civil Service College. The research was undertaken by Professor Sue Richards who now is Director of Strategic Leadership at the National School of Government. The outcomes have very much stood the test of time and I hope she will forgive me if I blend into the findings certain other conclusions drawn from my own experience and further development work.

The essence of this research was to take about 15 frontline leaders in the public services drawn from the police, teaching, local government, regeneration projects and the NHS. In every case, these public service leaders were recognised as successful. The qualitative research took that perception as a given and then, through in-depth interviews, tried to identify what were the attributes of success – and behaviours associated with – successful leadership at the frontline in public services. Five critical features emerged and, as I said earlier, they have been reinforced by further development work I have undertaken in the public sector.

Firstly, these individuals who were working very close to the operational frontline had the capacity to **change gear between the strategic and the operational** with great ease. In other words, rather like a helicopter that can hover at different levels, they could engage at a strategic level with key policies and strategies of their organisation and internalise them, and then when engaging with their own direct frontline staff, share that vision and that strategy in a way that those staff understood. It is a characteristic that is uniquely important to success in the public services where too often there is a perceived mismatch between the policy and strategic direction at one level (often the domain of politicians and the top executive team) and the reality of implementing and delivering at the frontline. It is what I would call 'connected' or 'engaged' leadership.

The second really important characteristic was the capacity to understand and **use the power of information to unblock resistance to change.** This is an interesting use of a very traditional public sector value (the deployment of evidence and information) and applying it to the vital process of unblocking resistance to change.

The third area, also related to the management of change, was the ability of these successful public sector leaders to **understand the WIIFM – or 'what's in it for me?'**. In other words, they demonstrated a capacity to see things very clearly from the point of view of those who are on the receiving end of change and from that to have a shrewd idea as to where opportunity and advantage could be identified in an otherwise negative situation. There are strong links here with emotional intelligence.

The fourth characteristic was that these frontline leaders were well-disposed to **invest in the personal and professional development of their staff**. This again showed a shrewd understanding of the nature of the public sector, where conventional reward may not be that generous. However, they could see the value of investing in other ways in the employability of their staff, again therefore predisposing them to be more positive towards change because they were better equipped to cope with it.

The fifth quality was associated with **storytelling**. These leaders seemed very effective not only at narrating the storyline of the need for change (which related back to their ability to understand and embrace the broader strategy) but also to tell the stories of success as change became implemented.

Although it could be argued that some of these are generic qualities to be found in successful leaders in any sector, what is important about them is that they seem to be particularly effective in the context of the constraints found in the public sector.

Career focus – the public sector psychological contract

The other frame of reference which I would like to bring to this reassessment of public sector leadership, is a concept that I worked on for many years with Professor David Guest, now of King's College London, when looking at the quality of the employment relationship. It was what we called the **'psychological contract'**. It is a concept which was originated by Professor Chris Argyris (Argyris 1960) and was developed further by Professor Denise Rousseau in the US in the 1980s (Rousseau 1990). We applied it in the early 1990s to assess the health of the employment relationship, particularly in the private sector, in the wake of the major recession and redundancies in the late 1980s and early 1990s. The psychological contract goes to the heart of the employment relationship by focusing on the mutual expectations of employee and employer in the employment relationship. It is about reciprocity and the exchange and delivery of promises, which is often referred to more briefly as 'the deal'.

David Guest's research provides a unique picture of the development of the quality of the psychological contract across all sectors (Guest and Conway 2001). The research was developed around a telephone survey of a statistically valid sample of private and public sector employees. It focused on issues such as perception of leadership, the quality of employment relationship and dignity and fairness at work. The research spanned nearly ten years and the most interesting outcomes were in relation to the public sector. In the early stages of the research, the psychological contract was understandably most unhealthy in the private sector as the major disruption of the recession and the redundancies continued. However, by the end of the 1990s, the position had reversed. Despite the greater stability of employment prospects and pension arrangements in the public sector, the psychological contract was undeniably less positive in the public sector. There appeared to be a strong link between the perception of leadership, particularly at senior levels, and the healthiness of the psychological contract in the public sector.

Hopefully, these examples of successful attributes and behaviours in public service leadership set out above can provide at least a starting point for a fresh debate and/or research programme.

What does all this mean for those running public sector leadership centres?

It is important for all of us who are involved in running specific leadership centres across the public sector to pool our experience of how we strike that balance between the contextual and the generic. There is no doubt from the purely practical experience I have had both in higher education and the Civil Service, that contextualisation is a very strong factor. Let me reflect on my experiences of the last 18 months in setting up the Leadership Foundation for Higher Education.

In most cases, these centres have been established after an intensive process of enquiry, and debate, – maybe research – and quite a lot of politics. The net result is a real sense that investment has to be shown to pay off specifically for the sub-sector concerned. Higher Education was no exception. In HE the pressure at the outset was to engage very actively with clients and stakeholders to generate a specific agenda for change. There was a lot of emphasis, quite naturally, on practical, operational and behavioural outcomes. A return on the specific investment is naturally sought. All this militates against a process which attempts to say to the particular sector 'your problems are generic and therefore the processes of developing leaders in this sector should be generic'. Key clients and stakeholders will want solutions that they can own and feel and that are within the culture of their part of the public sector specifically. This is reinforced by the fact that one of the most effective forms of leadership development is through the process of organisational development and happens inside particular institutions or agencies, working with their leadership teams. This naturally leads to highly contextualised processes.

The Leadership Foundation for Higher Education was very conscious of these issues when established. One of the general principles established right at the outset was that anything we did had to take account of cross-sector and cross-cutting opportunities both nationally and internationally. Interestingly, even that has proved difficult due to a tendency for the sector to want to see its own issues and problems (and therefore solutions) as unique to itself. Nonetheless, we are persisting with these cross-cutting policies and hope they will substantially bear fruit.

In putting together this chapter, we have been in touch with most of the other specific leadership centres in the public sector such as defence, police, NHS, and local government. All have demonstrated the same tensions. On the one hand, they have developed models and worked methodologies in very close consultation with their own clients and stakeholders. This has inevitably contextualised both their approach to leadership attributes and the activities they undertake of a leadership development nature. Some sectors have particularly good reasons for seeing themselves as having very precise agendas, such as the police and defence leadership centres. The most recently created local government leadership centre on its own website places huge importance on its connection directly with the sector. However, to be fair to all those other leadership centres, they are actively part of the process within the Cabinet Office that is attempting to improve coordination and the sharing of perceptions of and resources across the public sector.

Will a 'joined-up' approach make a difference?

This brings me really to my final point, which is the extent to which current initiatives on joined-up public sector leadership development are likely to make a real difference against a background of pressures for contextualisation that I have mentioned.

The Cabinet Office has taken the main responsibility over the last few years for coordinating this activity and has undoubtedly made some significant progress, both in bringing parties together and developing more specific initiatives for collaboration. The most overt of these is the new cross-sector programme called 'Leaders UK'. This has as its origins the public service leaders scheme which was developed by CMPS a few years ago. It has now been widened to include the CBI and representatives of the private sector, and for the first time will produce a genuinely all sector (public, private and voluntary) leadership scheme involving intensive workshops, coaching, mentoring and attachments over a two-year period. All public sector leadership partners are signed up to participating in this programme.

There are other activities, mainly of an investigatory nature, looking at issues such as diversity and leadership across the different parts of the public sector, the concept of 'customer' or user focus in public sector delivery, and the issue of more efficient procurement of leadership development programmes and support (through gaining a better understanding of the market for leadership development).

There is no doubt that there are useful outcomes from this work programme, and I particularly hope Leaders UK will be a successful cross-sector programme. There is nonetheless a feeling that this activity is still marginal to the whole picture. It has tended to look at small and specific issues – one relatively small scale programme of development, one aspect (e.g., diversity) and administrative issues such as procurement. What is lacking here is a contemporary analysis through research of the broader issues of public service leadership in the first decade of the 21st century. It is also an activity that is largely being carried on 'behind closed doors' in the Cabinet Office and should definitely come out of that closet, engaging more directly with leaders in the public arena.

A way forward?

So how do I draw together the strands of this chapter as a basis for a way forward?

1. There is no doubt that Groundhog Day is in the ascendant. However generic and common many of the learned leadership development processes may be, the expectations of stakeholders and the absence of any solid evidence to the contrary is forcing most of these leadership development centres down a route which is contextual and specific. Those clients and stakeholders will not be shaken from that view unless there is substantial evidence from research to the contrary.
2. The Cabinet Office have initiated over the last few years a set of processes that are bringing about a new level of cooperation and collaboration across the leadership centres and across different parts of the public (and indeed private) sectors. This work will undoubtedly lead to continued collaboration on a programme such as Leaders UK and on processes to improve the efficiency of procurement and training needs analysis. But it will not change the essential nature of the game.
3. The process needs to come much more out into the open, and
   (a) **engage with current leaders** across the public sector in a more open forum (something that is happening quite effectively in Scotland where there is a cross-sector Scottish Leadership Foundation);
   (b) address **the issue of the public service career**, and look afresh at the scope for new forms of **multi-sector careers journeys** for high potential individuals moving between such areas as civil service, local government, health, and higher education leadership;
   (c) **commission fresh research about the attributes and behaviours of successful public service leaders**, using as its starting point a challenge to some of the current assumptions I identified earlier;

(d) **promote much more activity in the area of cross-sector organisational raids, cross-boundary mentoring, and project-led learning**
of the kind developed in the HE 'Change Academy', jointly run by
ourselves and the HE Academy;

(e) **create an open forum/conference for cross-sector exchange,**
bringing together leaders and leadership developers in an annual
round-table debate and ideas exchange.

None of us should feel guilty that we may seem to be victims of a
Groundhog Day syndrome. But we should be enthusiastic about investing
much more effort and energy into refreshed cross-sector collaborative
processes because at the end of the day, the result may be not only a better
joined-up public sector, but an opportunity to create a development
process led by public sector leaders rather than leadership developers. As
John Adair said in his critique of this chapter, there is a lack of fundamental thinking about the nature of leadership itself in the public sector. Bring
the leaders (not the leadership developers) together and let the debate
begin!

Notes

1 Report on the organisation of the Permanent Civil Service – 23 November 1853
(Northcote Trevelyan Report).
2 Report of the Committee on the Civil Service – 19 June 1968 (Fulton Report).
3 Civil Service Training – 17 September 1974 (Heaton Williams Report).
4 Amann, Professor R., Director General, Centre for Management and Policy
Studies. *Overview August/September 2000*, pp.6–7.
5 Turnbull, A., Launch of National School of Government – 20 June 2005.
6 Turnbull, A., as above.

References

Argyris, C. (1960) *Understanding Organisational Behaviour*, Homewood, Ill: Dorsey.
Forrest, A. and Tolfree, P. (1992) *Leaders – the Learning Curve of Achievement –
Sir Richard Attenborough*, London: Industrial Society Press.
Guest, David and Conway, Neil (2001) *Organisational Change and the Psychological
Contract: An Analysis of the 1999 CIPD Survey*, CIPD Publications.
Performance and Innovation Unit (2000) *Strengthening leadership in the public sector. A
research study by the PIU*, Cabinet Office.
Rousseau, D.M. (1990) 'New Hire Perceptions of their Own and their Employers'
Obligations: A Study of Psychological Contracts', *Journal of Organisational Behaviour*
II, pp.389–400.

8
Leading the Way in Higher Education: A 20-year Journey from the University of Surrey to the Leadership Foundation

Robin Middlehurst, Tom Kennie and David Faraday

Introduction

John Adair held the first professorial appointment in Leadership Studies in the world at the University of Surrey from 1978–83 and subsequently became a Visiting Professor in the Civil Engineering Department for a further five years. During his time at the University, Professor Adair initiated a national programme of leadership courses for heads of academic departments in universities and subsequently for Vice Chancellors and Registrars and contributed to leadership programmes and seminars at other universities. In parallel, he inspired a group of young lecturers to design Action-Centred Leadership (ACL) courses for students, initially in the Engineering disciplines. Two of the former Surrey staff members involved in these courses (Tom Kennie and Dave Faraday) write about their experiences as case studies within this chapter.

From 1986, Professor Adair led a research programme with funding from the Department of Education and Science (now DfES) to evaluate and develop his programmes for University leaders; the principal investigator at the time (Robin Middlehurst) is the main author of this chapter. Each of these early research and developmental initiatives have blossomed and borne fruit as Adair's former colleagues have taken his ideas deeper into higher education and other sectors. In higher education, Adair's pioneering work in leadership development spread through the sector and contributed to the argument and business case for establishing a Leadership Foundation for Higher Education which opened in 2004. The Foundation is owned by the sector's representative bodies, UniversitiesUK and the Standing Conference of Principals (SCOP) and received start-up funding from all the UK's higher education funding bodies.

This chapter charts the early history of John Adair's work at the University of Surrey and traces the expansion of leadership development in higher education through the medium of research as well as training and development. It also highlights the parallel strands of leadership development work with students, young graduates, alumni, academic and professional staff in higher education and beyond. While the story reveals the importance of Action-Centred Leadership, it also illustrates the influence of wider leadership theory on developments that flowed from Adair's work and the integration of leadership development with wider academic and professional training. The story is also a personal testament to Professor Adair's influence and continuing support in that the three authors began their own leadership work at the University of Surrey and have since expanded it into the territories of professional services, business and industry, and higher education, nationally and internationally.

The chapter is organised into five sections. The first throws a spotlight on the arrival of leadership studies at the University of Surrey, drawing parallels with current issues and debates. The second section focuses on Adair's early work – with academic staff and students – and includes a case study of developments in the disciplines of Engineering at the University and subsequently in engineering industries, written by Dave Faraday. In the third section, Tom Kennie illustrates how the early developments in Engineering were taken forward into the surveying profession and wider professional services sectors. Robin Middlehurst, in section four, discusses Adair's legacy in higher education and subsequently, in section five, explores Adair's particular contribution in the light of wider leadership theory and approaches to leadership development.

1 Bringing Leadership Studies into the University

The initial response of members of the academic community at the University of Surrey to the idea of a professorial appointment in Leadership Studies has some parallels to the varied reactions of university leaders more recently to the establishment of the Leadership Foundation in Higher Education in 2004. In 1978, members of the University's Senate and Council voiced a spectrum of opinion, from hostility to enthusiasm. The sceptical voices questioned whether leadership, as a characteristic of individuals, could be taught and asked what the value of leadership studies might be in a technologically-focused university. The proposed chair in leadership studies also had no precedent: the next professorial appointment in Leadership (the Konosuke Matsushita Chair at Harvard Business School) was not established until 1981.

The more positive among the physical and social scientists and engineers saw the proposal as a potentially interesting venture, but did not at that time see any particular relevance to themselves as academic leaders, to their students or their disciplines. The idea was eventually carried on the basis that external sponsorship would support the position for a five-year period; John Adair had raised the necessary £40,000 from industry and charitable sources including Shell, the Prudential, the Dulverton Trust and the Industrial Society (now Work Foundation).

At Surrey, the new professorial position in Leadership Studies was initially located in the Department of Psychology. John Adair recollects that colleagues were friendly and tolerant, but noted that there was little common ground and no interest in his subsequent work with the engineering departments. Another interpretation of this context is that Adair's approach to leadership studies did not sit comfortably with the epistemological bases and empirical approaches to research in Psychology at the University at this time. Adair's combination of experiential knowledge, thoughtful scholarship and multi-disciplinary perspectives made him 'an outsider' in relation to the research traditions of the department. There are resonances here with today's debates about pure and applied research and scholarship and the relative value placed by universities on different forms of knowledge generation.

2 Developing Leadership Studies at the University of Surrey

Adair had a clear vision of how leadership studies in general and Action-Centred Leadership in particular could add value to students on university courses. This was based on his experience of providing effective leadership training for young people aged 18–20 in the armed services before they took up their first appointment in a command role (Adair 1968). His ideas for universities are set out in a book chapter entitled 'Leaders for Tomorrow: the Universities' Contribution' (Adair 1988). Adair's vision and arguments remain topical since his aim was to equip young graduates with the personal transferable skills that were sought by employers and that graduates would need to make a full contribution to society. Across the range of his work, Adair has sought to map these skills, describing them as a constellation that together make up the 'human side of enterprise' (building on the work of McGregor 1961). For Adair, the constellation of skills includes decision-making, motivation, innovation and creativity, problem-solving, team-building and time-management. In the late 1980s and early 1990s, the Enterprise Initiative of the then Department of Education and Science echoed many of these themes and they remain in 'the Employability' agendas of today (HEFCE 2003).

Adair's thinking went further in three key directions. First, he suggested that universities should develop 'the whole person not just the brain' (Adair 1998: 118) and his use of experiential exercises in leadership training illustrated how traditional university pedagogies might be transformed to move closer towards this goal. Second, he argued that the *quality* of students' learning was enhanced through a partnership between academics and managers with practical experience of leadership and management in professional contexts. Thirdly, Adair identified practical ways in which leadership studies could provide for 'bridge-building between academic and industrial life' (Adair 1998: 122). He saw a role for managers as tutors and mentors within university courses and identified mutual benefits for universities and companies. He noted three sources for potential manager-tutors: companies and organisations in the neighbourhood of the university, companies involved in taking students on placement for their professional training year (a special feature of the University of Surrey) and former graduates already working in industry. Adair's ideas were two decades ahead of the Lambert Report (2003) that focused on the continuing need for such 'bridge-building' between industry and higher education. The case study below illustrates how Adair's thinking was put into practice at Surrey by committed junior academic staff who were inspired by the potential of Adair's ideas and excited by the opportunity to experiment and innovate in their approaches to learning and teaching.

Action-Centred Leadership and Engineering at Surrey: A Case Study by Dave Faraday

In the early 1980s, Adair pioneered the introduction of Action-Centred Leadership training in Civil Engineering[1] with the assistance of Dr Peter Gardiner and Mr Mike Huxley (former colleagues of the authors whose reflections were captured through conversations undertaken as part of the preparation of this chapter). The two-day course introduced second year undergraduate students to the generic role of a leader: the leader's areas of responsibility as represented by the three circles – achieving the task, building and maintaining the team and developing and supporting the individual; and, what the leader has to do, the functions – defining the task, planning, briefing the team, controlling, motivating, evaluating, organising, setting an example and reviewing (Adair 1983, 2002). The course was experientially-based, giving students many opportunities to practice and develop their own leadership skills in preparation for their forthcoming period of professional training. The leadership exercises were both classroom-based, including the now well established Span Contract,[2] and outdoor-based, exercises such as Acid Test and Crossed Poles. In addition, a unique element to the Surrey courses was the half-day multi-tasked exercises which involved the students solving problems and undertaking orienteering-style tasks across Guildford and beyond. These longer exercises tested the physical, mental and emotional abilities of students. The Civil Engineering students responded very positively to the training, as course evaluations consistently indicated. ACL provided a solid foundation for students to understand, experience and practice leadership and teamwork at an introductory level. This success was reflected quickly across the whole of the then Faculty of Engineering, with Chemical Engineering,[1] Mechanical Engineering[1] and Electrical and Electronic Engineering[3] incorporating similar versions of this course into their undergraduate programmes before the end of the 1980s.

Development and expansion

Throughout the 1990s all four engineering disciplines developed their ACL training programmes to suit their own specific needs. Civil Engineering and Electrical and Electronic Engineering adjusted elements of their two-day course to reflect the needs of their students and fulfil the requirements of their professional training employers, bringing in more team working and communication elements. In Mechanical Engineering, the course was moved off-campus, to the New Forest in Hampshire. A two-and-a-half day residential course was developed, supported by industry, and was jointly delivered by departmental staff and external training organisations, again remaining true to the core principles of ACL training.

The greatest development and expansion occurred in Chemical Engineering. The basic two-day ACL programme was expanded into a three-day course, retaining all elements of the ACL programme, but introducing additional material in teams and team working, communication and problem solving; establishing ACL as the core of the personal skills development programme. In 1990, the basic course was supplemented with a six-day residential course located in the Brecon Beacons area of Wales. This expansion was supported extensively by the department's professional training employers. Many outdoor-based activities were included, but the core was centred round a 'chemical engineering' project which tested the application of the principles of functional leadership, as well as the three-circles model, to the limits which could be expected of second year undergraduates.

In 1995, five of the alumni of the Brecon course embarked for Nairobi, Kenya, on the first of four East African projects between 1995 and 2001. These projects concerned a wider skills agenda, including technical and professional skills, but again had ACL at their core. Over the four expeditions, specific projects were identified in higher education institutions, with start-up companies, with charitable organisations and major companies across three countries: Kenya, Tanzania and Malawi. These projects included essential oils distillation, environmental testing and monitoring and, of course, ACL training, delivered by the graduates to staff from the host organisations.

A further expansion of ACL training took place in all the engineering disciplines with the development of courses for postgraduate and final year students to train them as team tutors to help in the delivery of training to the second year undergraduate students. A more detailed account of the programme developed by Ron Schulz and David Faraday can be found as a Case Study in Effective Leadership Development (Adair 2006).

The benefits and the legacy

The impact of ACL training on the engineering disciplines is undeniable. A glance through any University of Surrey prospectus from the late 1980s onwards will reveal many photographs of students undergoing ACL training and information outlining the importance of this training to contemporary engineers. Furthermore, feedback from students (Figures 8.1–8.3, below) attending the Chemical Engineering version of the ACL course between 1991 and 2000 also highlights a change in attitude and culture. Over this period, the percentage of students rating the course delivery as very good or excellent rose from 63 percent in 1991 to 86 percent in 2000, while for the leadership exercise it rose from 48 percent to 91 percent. However, the most significant indicator of the change in attitude and culture is the rating for relevance to future work. The percentage of students rating this a very good or excellent course for this purpose rose from 40 percent in 1991 to 83 percent in 2000.

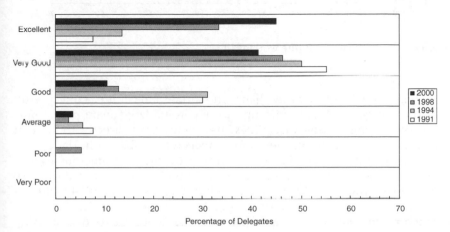

Figure 8.1 Course delivery

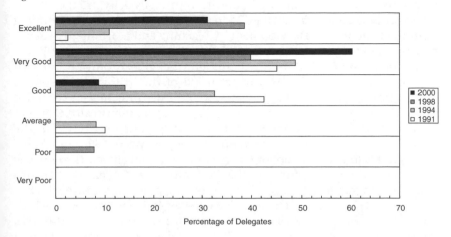

Figure 8.2 Leadership exercises

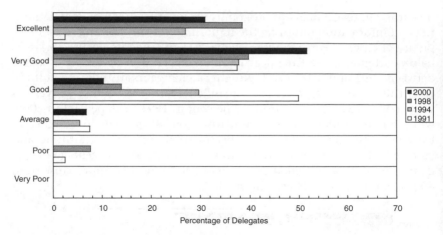

Figure 8.3   Relevance to future working life

There is no doubt that this change in attitude and culture, a direct result of the inclusion of ACL training in the core undergraduate programme across the engineering disciplines, has contributed directly to student recruitment. In addition, the staff members responsible for initiating and developing these courses have been recognised through numerous awards. Most significantly, Ron Schulz and David Faraday were awarded the Esso Partnership Award for Transferable Skills in Engineering in 1994 and I was the inaugural recipient of the Frank Morton Medal for Excellence in Teaching in Chemical Engineering in 2001; Action-Centred Leadership featured strongly in my submission. Our success in leadership training also helped us attract grant funding from within the University, from commercial organisations and from HEFCE.[4] In the latter case, we secured funding from the Fund for the Development of Teaching and Learning to disseminate this best practice to other higher education institutions in the UK.

The final part of this story highlights a further global contribution with contemporary resonance. As a direct result of the ACL training courses in Chemical Engineering, 12 graduates from the department were seconded to the United Nations through the Foreign and Commonwealth Office to work as Biological and Chemical Weapons Inspectors for UNSCOM (the United Nations Special Commission to Iraq) between 1994 and 1998. Through this link, the School of Engineering now annually hosts the Surrey Phase of the Organisation for the Prohibition of Chemical Weapons Associate Programme. This is a three-week long programme, into which is incorporated the current version of the two-day ACL training course which was first introduced by Adair and colleagues in 1983. However, in this case, the course is delivered to 24 academics and industrialists, most of them in senior positions and all from different developing countries. The positive and enthusiastic appreciation of this training and the recognition of its application in their own environments undoubtedly secures the ongoing contribution of ACL training in the new millennium.

The core principles of Action-Centred Leadership and John Adair himself have been a guiding influence on my own development as an academic, a professional engineer, an entrepreneur and leadership trainer. He inspired us to inspire our students to do great things. Our graduates inspired us to inspire others.

3 From the University of Surrey to the professional services' sector

Through his work with the Engineering disciplines in the 1980s, John Adair had demonstrated how leadership development could be included into the early stages of education and training for undergraduates studying professional disciplines. He had also advocated the continuing role of leadership development as part of continuing professional development. Once again, Adair was ahead of his time. The importance of leadership development for the professions was a strong theme in the recent work of the joint DfES and DTI funded Council for Excellence in Management and Leadership (Gold *et al.* 2001). Indeed, Recommendations 12 and 15 of the Council's Final Report (2002) refer directly to undergraduate education and continuing professional education and the responsibilities of professional bodies and universities and colleges. Recommendation 12 points to the need for Professional Associations to introduce elements of management and leadership development into prequalification and CPD programmes. Recommendation 15 states that undergraduates of all disciplines should have the option of acquiring management and leadership skills. The case study below illustrates one way in which these recommendations were addressed several years earlier by developing John Adair's ideas at the University of Surrey.

Action-Centred Leadership and Developments in the Surveying Profession: A Case Study by Tom Kennie

In parallel with the enthusiastic take up of ACL and leadership training for undergraduates and then graduates across the Engineering Faculty at Surrey was the application of these models to other professions, firstly the surveying and latterly the legal profession. I was a lecturer in surveying within the University's Civil Engineering Department in the early to late 1980s and took forward these initiatives with colleagues.

The origins

Where the value of management studies (if not leadership training) was already recognised by the Engineering professions in the middle 1980s, this was not yet the case in other professions. For example, the route to qualifying as a professional surveyor was through academic achievement followed by a structured period of professional experience; a final dissertation was then examined as part of a 'Test of Professional Competence'. Any notion that other attributes might be required to demonstrate 'professional competence' had yet to develop.

As an early enthusiastic adopter of leadership training, the opportunity to pilot the process with young recently qualified surveyors occurred in 1985 through what was at the time called the Junior Organisation (JO) of the Royal Institution of Chartered Surveyors (RICS). Tom Kennie, as a member of the national JO committee, encouraged the JO to support a series of regional one-day events for young graduate surveyors. The existing Surrey programme for young engineers was adapted with the support of Dr Peter Gardiner, Dr Bob Griffiths and Dr Jeff Keir (all Surrey colleagues at the time and subsequently contacted in relation to this chapter). This adaptation proved highly effective. The combination of Adair's practical, yet powerful exercises combined with discussion of the lessons of experience as they applied to the particular contexts of the participants helped to raise the critical importance of leadership, team work, motivation and communication skills in the delivery of professional work. A chapter describing this initiative was also well-received within the profession and won the 1986 RICS 'President's Prize Chapters' competition (Kennie 1986).

The RICS, encouraged by the positive feedback from those who attended the events, then invited the Surrey team to design and facilitate an event for 150 surveyors at their annual weekend conference in Edinburgh in 1988. The Saturday provided an opportunity to consider some of the basic ACL principles before participating in a grand 'black tie' dinner. Sunday was quite a different experience, as Dr Gardiner recalls. 'Twelve teams of twelve professionals rotated clockwise through twelve intellectually and physically demanding activities (particularly following the previous night's dinner...) which were spread over a wide geographical area. The twelve supervisors (8 trained by the Surrey team) rotated anti-clockwise so that each participant and each supervisor undertook each exercise. The logistics for this (before the advent of text messaging or mobile phones), involved a claxon horn sounding various coded messages around the Firth of Forth as the exercise started, stopped, debriefed and transferred'.

These experiences helped to raise awareness of the value of leadership development for those at the beginning of their career (Kennie and Gardiner 1988). But they also had wider impact, leading to the Surrey team being invited to work with the Chief Executive of the RICS at the time and his senior management team to develop their team-working and leadership skills.

By the mid-1990s, the use of ACL had become a feature of both the pre-qualification training and post-qualification continuing professional development (CPD) activities at many of the larger surveying practices. Having left the University of Surrey to move into the private sector and ultimately become HR Director of one of the larger firms of property professionals, Kennie noted the significance of this kind of experiential training for those graduates we recruited who had not had the opportunities offered by Surrey for a year's professional work-experience or the intensive leadership training provided for undergraduates.

Recent developments

By the mid-1990s, the surveying profession had recognised the value of leadership and management development for more senior staff. A research project on the leadership skills adopted by Partners and Directors of successful small and medium sized enterprises (SMEs) led in 1996 to the publication of a series of Practice Management Guidelines for surveying practitioners (Kennie and Price 1997, updated 2003). Leadership lies at the heart of the framework (see Figure 8.4). The guidelines also follow the Adair philosophy of encouraging leaders to reflect and develop self-insight by focusing on a series of self-assessment questions. As co-author of the guidelines, I pay tribute to the impact of my early experience of working with John Adair. John has a great capacity to challenge people to self-reflect and think deeply about 'being' a leader and 'doing' leadership, while also being tremendously supportive. Both capabilities (being and doing) are critical to success in influencing professionals (particularly in SMEs) where the leadership and management role is often perceived to be a part-time role.

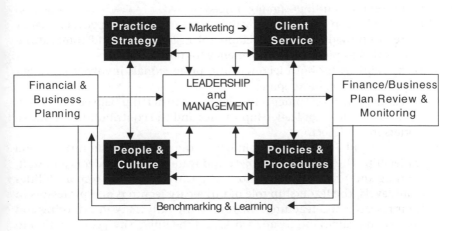

Figure 8.4 Leadership and management framework

The take up of leadership training and development in the surveying profession can also be traced in other areas of the professional services sector (Middlehurst and Kennie 1995, 1997). Leadership training forms part of the expectations placed on those who wish to practice as solicitors and many would argue, has been central to the success of many of the large UK-based international legal practices which dominate the profession globally. Leadership skills are also now expected of barristers and are included in the recently published 'competency framework' for Queens' Counsel as part of 'Working in the Team' (http://www.qcapplications.org.uk). They show striking parallels to the basic concepts contained within Adair's ACL model.

In summary, John Adair has directly and indirectly had a significant influence on the debate about the value and importance of leadership within the professions, through his lectures and writing and through his support for others who have taken his work forward in new directions.

4 Applying leadership development and research in universities and colleges

In Adair's inaugural lecture at the University of Surrey in 1980, he outlined five elements of leadership development that had emerged from his work at Sandhurst (Adair 1968) translating them into the context of universities (reported in Adair 1988: 119–25). He made a strong link between leadership courses for staff, students and graduates. The five elements of a systematic approach, he argued, included:

- The Leadership Course: a short course in leadership studies to raise awareness of key concepts and skills. (Adair's first course for staff was a one-day experimental leadership course that sparked the interest of the two case study authors, among others).
- Field Leadership Training: using the professional training year offered by Surrey to provide further development in leadership and communication as well as professional experience for undergraduates.
- Staff Training: for both lecturers and professionals involved in leadership training and development.
- Research and Development: involving a partnership between the academic contribution of leadership studies and the contributions of practitioners from all sectors.
- Structure and Ethos: the ways in which the university can further good leadership. These included project and teamwork for students and staff, training and preparation for those who carry leadership responsibilities at all levels, the leadership role of university lecturers and professors in their research and teaching, the role of the university in exploring and discovering values for life and work, and the university's contribution to developing the leaders of tomorrow.

Under the heading of 'Staff Training', Adair made reference to the University of Surrey's positive approach to staff development, noting that several future heads of department had attended external leadership courses and that senior technicians participated regularly in the Action-Centred Leadership course for scientists, run jointly by the University and the Industrial Society (now Work Foundation). This early support for leadership development for staff continued as the University Secretary at the time, Leonard Kail, and his assistant, James Strawson, asked Professor Adair to design an in-house course for Heads of academic departments. Adair preferred this to be open to all universities and a national programme was launched at Farnham Castle in 1984. The Farnham courses were developed from Adair's experience of leading study groups on 'leadership in universities' (offered in 1983 to the heads of colleges and schools of the University of London, including the large teaching hospitals). The national courses for Heads of academic departments were residential, lasting two days. The content reflected Adair's 'leadership constellation' described earlier. The learning activities were based on Adair's belief in experiential and participative learning; they included plenary and small group discussions, film, case studies, practical exercises and role-play.

In his work for universities, Adair contributed to and built upon a slowly changing climate both in respect of attitudes to leadership in academic organisations and the university's role in developing the leaders of tomorrow. A speech by Lord Flowers, quoted in Adair (1988: 128) captures the start of this spirit of change. 'We have to look to our leaders of the future...[to create]...a climate in which leadership can flourish, rather than be restrained by precedent and the safety belt of committee decisions'. Lord Flowers' words anticipated the findings of the Jarratt Report which investigated the efficiency of management and decision-making in universities and recommended changes in the structure and governance of institutions (CVCP 1985). There are also resonances with the more recent Lambert Report (2003).

In 1985, Adair and the University of Surrey added a new pilot national Leadership Seminar for Vice Chancellors, Pro Vice Chancellors, Registrars and Secretaries to the portfolio of programmes. It was organised jointly between the Universities of Surrey and Kent, with participation from Brunel and Exeter Universities. This initiative sowed seeds that later grew into Exeter's current Centre for Leadership Studies. By 1986, seven national courses for Heads of academic departments had been run, attended by 175 people, and discussions were in train to expand the suite of programmes to Heads of support departments and to add new content. New resources were needed and a successful grant application to the DES was made to evaluate the courses and develop them further. The Final Report to the DES (see Middlehurst 1989, 1993) includes an in-depth study of participants' responses to the leadership courses and offers a detailed analysis of the types of impact of Adair's leadership model and ideas on academic leaders from a range of disciplines.

The evaluation of Adair's programmes included analysis of course feedback sheets from 12 courses (where immediate responses to the courses were collected), a questionnaire survey of all participants on the 12 courses mounted between 1984 and 1987, and interviews with a sample of participants (to gauge intermediate responses). Response rates were high (81 percent for the postal questionnaire survey to academic heads and 49 percent for the survey to more senior staff). At the individual level, the majority of respondents reported satisfaction with course content and its relevance to their leadership roles. For example, for the nine Head of Department courses surveyed, 79 percent of respondents found the course helpful in clarifying their managerial or leadership role; 77 percent in providing new knowledge about leadership; and 85 percent in providing a forum for discussion with peers about similar issues and problems. The course was also reported as relevant to a range of leadership and management activities from strategic thinking and planning to decision-making, time-management and managing change. The overall positive evaluation of the course was reflected in the fact that 70 percent of respondents had recommended it to colleagues and 84 percent said they considered the course useful to senior university staff (particularly at the onset of leadership and management responsibilities).

The wider impact of the courses on institutional performance was not assessed in this research, although individual comments from the questionnaires and interviews attest to the changes that individuals were making to their practice. In several cases participation on the national programme was a precursor to the development of in-house provision.

The evaluation also threw up specific criticisms of the courses, some personal and some related to the focus of the course.

The developmental side of the project sought to address some of these difficulties. First, course content was adapted to include a new course on finance and marketing for Heads of academic departments, and university staff assisted with the design of the learning activities to tailor them more closely to the university context. Second, the project undertook a wider exploration of perspectives and practice in relation to leadership and management in universities. This fed into the courses themselves and into the wider promotion (through conferences, seminars and networks) of relevant leadership and management development in the sector. Finally, the research included a comparative study of approaches to leadership development in other sectors: Local Government, the Civil Service, schools, further education and the polytechnic sector. Some of these sectors had a wider conception of leadership and management development than existed in the higher education sector at the time. This wider perspective was reflected in the Report's recommendations for action in higher education.

The two-year DES-funded study (1986–88) along with Adair's programme of courses provided a platform for leadership development in the university sector. Several groups around the country, particularly in the north of England and in Scotland, built on Adair's early work and developed both in-house and regional programmes. In addition, some of the funding for the project enabled Professor Adair to stimulate a strategy for leadership development in the sector. A Summit meeting was held between the heads of the University Grants Committee (UGC) and the Committee of Vice Chancellors and Principals (CVCP), the Minister for Higher Education and Adair himself. The outcome of the meeting was agreement to establish a national Training and Staff Development Unit (USDU) to promote staff development at all levels and to continue to develop the leadership courses begun by Adair at Surrey. The Unit opened in 1990, based at the University of Sheffield, where strong institutional support for leadership and management development had emerged through the efforts of Professor Bob Boucher (now Vice Chancellor of Sheffield) and Dr Pat Partington (the first Director of the Unit).

The DES-funded study offered the Unit and its member universities a range of recommendations for action that are still relevant, for example:

- The new Unit should play a leading role in encouraging a training culture in all universities, in monitoring and disseminating good practice from all sectors and countries...
- Management and leadership development should be a formal and explicit part of institutional policy, linked to the implementation of that policy as well as contributing to its formation...the focus of 'development' should move from its current emphasis on individual needs to a closer alignment with institutional agendas and ethos...
- The responsibility for leadership development rests ultimately with leaders – in providing funds, in setting an example (in practice and through continuing professional development), in establishing a learning climate and a strategy for training and development, and acting as mentors and teachers...
- Universities could benefit from mutual collaboration and exchange with other sectors in the field of management and leadership development. This should not however preclude the continued shaping of strategies relevant to the specific nature, traditions and future of the academic enterprise.

These recommendations have been implemented in a number of universities; they are also embedded in the design and practice of the new Leadership Foundation for Higher Education that incorporated (in 2004) the organisation that started life as USDU.

The wide scope of the DES project produced a wealth of data and information relating to leadership and management practice and attitudes in universities. It also provided insight into the personal and institutional experiences of change as universities began to move from more collegial cultures and structures towards more executive and corporate approaches to leadership and management. The initial project prompted a bid for further research, and a second and related study focusing on senior management levels (also supported by the DES) investigated 'The Changing Roles of University Leaders and Managers: Implications for Preparation and Development' (Middlehurst *et al.* 1991, 1992). Subsequently, these studies were consolidated into a book on leadership and leadership development in universities, *Leading Academics* (Middlehurst 1993). Adair's functional leadership model was included in this book and this provided an opportunity to review the contribution of Adair's thinking and that of others to the practice of leadership in universities (these issues are discussed further in section 5, below).

Adair continued to offer national programmes through the new Unit (for example, a programme for Pro Vice Chancellors) and to contribute to leadership seminars mounted by other universities such as the University of London, working in partnership with some of his colleagues from Surrey. From 1992, these colleagues took over the leadership elements of the week-long London programme for Heads of academic departments (continuing with these programmes for a further ten years) and expanding the work at head of department level for other universities and regional consortia as well as other countries including Sweden and South Africa. Typically, in this period of the mid-1990s, universities individually or in groups were mounting their own programmes and were drawing on external presenters and facilitators from inside and outside the higher education sector to deliver the leadership and management content.

At the more senior levels of higher education, the main providers of management and leadership training and development in the UK in the 1990s included national professional associations (such as the Conference of Registrars and Secretaries) and the Committee of Vice Chancellors and Principals (CVCP) and Committee of Directors of Polytechnics (CDP). The second DES-funded study (Middlehurst *et al.* 1991, 1992) reported on the level of provision at senior levels in the early part of the decade, providing comparisons again between levels and forms of provision in higher education and other sectors and countries. The findings illustrated the greater quantity and quality of provision, for example, in the US through the American Council on Education, in continental Europe through the Conference of University Rectors and in the Local Government and Health sectors. Whether stimulated by these findings or not, senior members of the Committee of Vice Chancellors and Principals working with the central Unit (now called the Universities and Colleges Staff Development Agency, UCoSDA), advertised for consultants to design and deliver two senior-level programmes. The first was a development programme for women leaders ('Room at the Top') which ran once in 1998, and a strategic leadership programme. From 1999 these were merged within a new Top Management Programme for Higher Education (TMP@HE). Through this programme, Adair's legacy was continued since the team that designed and has delivered the TMP@HE since 1999 is led by two of Adair's former Surrey colleagues (Robin Middlehurst and Tom Kennie). The background to the programme, with details of its design features, early development and evaluation were reported in a Briefing Chapter (HESDA 2001).

The final links in the chain of research and development that joins Adair's early work to the establishment of the Leadership Foundation took place between 2000 and 2003. The key links were a sector-wide survey of senior management development in the higher education sector (Middlehurst and Garratt 2000) and a subsequent working group report which was led by senior Vice Chancellors and lay governors.

5 Adair's contribution in the light of wider leadership theory, practice and development in higher education

The case studies and early research in higher education described above provide a range of insights into the impact and value of John Adair's work. Table 8.1 provides a brief review of his major contributions.

Table 8.1   Review of John Adair's major contributions

Type of contribution	Nature of impact or value

Innovative conceptual frameworks which have contributed to leadership research and scholarship	• The ACL model developed a three-dimensional framework (concern for task, team and individual) that is arguably more useful in practice than the two-dimensional frameworks developed in the US at the time (see Blake and Mouton 1964, 1991 – concern for task, concern for people).
	• Adair identified and mapped key leadership skills: communication, decision-making, motivation, team-building, time-management, creative thinking. These are included in many current development frameworks for managers and leaders.
	• 'Functional leadership' focused on action rather than personality. The concept opened up the leadership field in four important ways:
	  – by proposing that leadership could be learned and developed
	  – by emphasising that leadership was a function needed by organisations and working groups, the potential for leadership roles to shift or to be shared according to expertise, skill etc.

Table 8.1 Review of John Adair's major contributions – *continued*

Type of contribution	Nature of impact or value
	emerged, foreshadowing work on 'distributed leadership' (Gronn 2002) – the ACL model highlighted the relational aspects of leadership and foreshadowed work on 'leader-follower relations' (Hollander 1978; Graen and Scandura 1987); – focusing on the *exercise* of leadership allowed for this key function to be performed by anyone (with the requisite skills) in any context or situation where the three sets of needs came together (i.e., need to achieve a task, to be kept together as a working group and to achieve individual satisfaction). Adair's concept therefore embraced formal and informal leadership.
Practical value in range of contexts	• There is evidence reported in this chapter as well as in the success of Adair's books and lectures that people in different professional and disciplinary contexts, in different roles, at different levels of the organisation, at different stages of their career and from different countries and cultures found the three circles concept and the nine functional responsibilities of leaders to be of practical value in their work.
Pioneer in studying and making links between the idea of leadership, its application in practice and the ways of developing leadership capacity and capability	• Adair has given equal weight in his work to the study of leadership as a concept, to the ways it can be applied in practice and to the ways in which it can be developed. His notion of development is broad and encompasses the individual and the organisation (Adair 1988, 2005). There is much commonality between his approach to leadership development and that of the Centre for Creative Leadership (2004).
'Action-centred' pedagogy	• The variety of experiential exercises used in Adair's ACL training test a range of skills, but also highlight other qualities and attitudes. This active and discovery-based approach to teaching echoes Dewey (1938) and provides a rich learning experience which gets beyond purely cognitive and intellectual skills.
Mentor and guide	• Adair has acted as mentor and guide to many people, particularly young people, and has supported them in their efforts to be leaders and to 'grow leadership' in different contexts. He has 'practiced what he preaches' through his consistent level of personal support to individuals.

As can be seen from the table, Adair's contribution has been wide-ranging and important for many individuals, organisations and sectors. Yet, there are also gaps and differences between his work and the wider leadership literature that remain to be explored and tested and in some cases, strengths can also be perceived as weaknesses. For example, the practical value of Adair's work in a range of contexts – which is noted in the case studies above and in many of the evaluation responses in the higher education research – would suggest that ACL can be applied successfully in any context, culture or situation. This stands in opposition to 'contingency theories of leadership' which propose that approaches to leadership vary (and may need to vary) according to a range of variables (Northouse 2004). The ACL model and John Adair's writing does not explore directly the impact of specific contexts or conditions on the application of the ACL model.

- Leadership style (the three-circles model is 'style-neutral', yet how leadership is exercised and what styles are appropriate for what conditions is an important issue for practitioners and researchers. Adair does however, address different styles of decision-making).
- Power, authority and influence (the relative balance of power between leaders and followers or the ways in which leadership is practiced and interacts at different levels of an organisation are an important focus of current research).
- 'Transformational' aspects of leadership (the ACL model represents a functional approach to the practice of leadership and does not make a distinction between different forms of leadership such as 'transactional and transformational' and their relative effect on individuals and organisations). Arguably, one of the wider failings of the leadership field is that there are too few attempts to integrate different theories, perspectives and models or to point to contradictions and dilemmas.
- Ethics and leadership (the ACL model is again 'neutral' in ethical terms, although the application of the model is designed to achieve 'effective' leadership. In his wider writing, Adair highlights the importance of integrity as a feature of effective leadership at the individual level).
- Impact of different organisational models (the relationship between leadership and types of organisations or stages of development of organisations is an important domain for current research).
- Gender and leadership (a strength of the ACL model is its 'neutrality' in relation to gender or culture. However, these issues are significant in the research agendas of today).
- Substitutes and neutralisers for leadership (the ACL model assumes the need for leadership in all working situations involving groups of people. Some research has specifically sought to investigate conditions and contexts where leadership might not be needed or where other social influence processes are effective in reaching intended outcomes).

Researchers adopting a different conceptual or analytical frame address some of the themes identified above. Contingency theories have focused on the contexts and situations in which leadership is practiced and have thrown light on a range of leadership styles. The varied literature on, for example, servant leadership (Greenleaf 1977) or charismatic and heroic leadership (Bryman 1992; Grint 1997) can add value to Adair's functional model. A related and equally significant concept is that of 'power' and its place within the exercise and impact of leadership. The dynamics of power, its use and abuse by leaders, its role in organisational, national and party politics, its impact in group-dynamics and its implications for 'diversity' make it a key variable in leadership. The ACL model does not provide ready answers for practitioners or researchers eager to understand these issues so there are rich opportunities for contemporary researchers.

The wave of studies on transactional and transformational leadership touches on issues of both power and ethics (Bass 1990; Northouse 2004). These studies explore questions of leadership style, but also dig more deeply into how individual and group motivation, sense of purpose and identity are influenced by different approaches to leadership. In describing leadership as 'the management of meaning', Bennis and Nanus (1985) capture some of these ideas and other writers such as Kouzes and Posner (1987) and Badaracco and Ellsworth (1989) have also made useful contributions that address the role of values and emotion in leadership. In his stories of leaders (for example, in *Great Leaders*, 1989) Adair does refer to and reflect on these dimensions, but his work needs further development.

An important issue when one seeks to understand the exercise of leadership in different organisational settings is how context influences practice. For example, small and large organisations have different levels of complexity in their structures and systems, service organisations differ from manufacturing organisations in the nature of their operations and the staff they recruit, 'business start-ups' often require different skill-sets from mature organisations and multinational conglomerates or networked consortia also differ in their organisational and staffing needs. If one adds a cultural dimension to any of the above, then variety and complexity potentially increases. These different organisational and cultural dimensions are likely to have an impact on leadership style and behaviour. Hierarchy may give way to a matrix-style where leadership responsibility is split. Leadership roles may be highly distributed at different levels and may vary in form (from managerial to thought leadership). Leadership positions may be temporary, part-time or differentiated (as in many universities and the health sector) and there are likely to be important differences in how leadership is practiced (and the skills involved) when followers are 'close-by' or 'at a distance' (Gardner 1995). While the ACL model is clearly transferable to different contexts, it does not deal with the implications of some of these variations and complexities.

Finally, and perhaps unsurprisingly, Adair does not discuss the notion of 'substitutes for leadership' (Kerr and Jermier 1978). Kerr and Jermier investigated situations in which neither 'task-related' nor 'relationship-oriented' behaviour on the part of leaders had any effect on followers' satisfaction, motivation or performance. In some organisations, there were elements that substituted or neutralised leadership. Substitutes included the nature of the task (which could be intrinsically motivating), the characteristics of followers (perhaps autonomous professionals) or the structures and norms of the organisation or unit. Neutralisers, Kerr and Jermier argued, either prevented leaders from acting in particular ways or counteracted the effects of leadership. Such variables might include lack of control over rewards, the competence of subordinates, inflexible organisational policies and procedures, or political controls over organisational activities. Many of these elements are evident in higher education (Bensimon *et al.* 1989; Birnbaum 1992) and in the wider public sector in the UK (PIU Report 2000). In some cases these features may obviate the need for leadership, in others the leadership role may shift between people according to expertise, and in other cases, the need for leadership may be strong but the task difficult, necessitating a subtlety or range of approaches. The contribution of leadership research in the future remains one of investigating these themes to help us understand the impact, interactions and implications of contexts, situations and people on the practice of leadership.

6 Conclusion

Adair has made a wide-ranging contribution to leadership thinking and leadership development in higher education and beyond. There is still much depth to plumb in Adair's work and there is scope for further interpretation and development of his ideas in the light of the wider literature. Adair's colleagues from the University of Surrey have drawn on and worked with his ideas through research, scholarship, practice and development in different organisations and at different levels. Over the last 20 years, they have interpreted and applied his model and ideas, as well as wider research, in order to spread an understanding of leadership in all its nuanced richness. The Leadership Foundation for Higher Education will continue this exploration, providing new opportunities for individuals, institutions and communities of practice.

Notes

1 Part of the School of Engineering since 2001.
2 Dr Bob Griffiths changed the original Industrial Society 'Tower Exercise' using Lego bricks to a more demanding bridge-building exercise, 'The Span Contract'. Due to requests for the bricks, the Lego company now produces a standard 'bridge-building' kit for leadership trainers.
3 Part of the School of Electronics and Physical Sciences since 2001.
4 Fund for the Development of Teaching and Learning, TRANSEND Project, in partnership with University College London, the University of Birmingham and the University of Newcastle.

References

Adair, J. (1968) *Training for Leadership*, Guildford: Talbot Adair Press.

Adair, J. (1983) *Effective Leadership*, Aldershot: Gower.

Adair, J. (1988) *Developing Leaders*, Guildford: Talbot Adair Press.

Adair, J. (1989) *Great Leaders*, Guildford: Talbot Adair Press.

Adair, J. (1998) *The John Adair Handbook of Management and Leadership*, London: Thorogood.

Adair, J. (2002) *John Adair's 100 Greatest Ideas for Effective Leadership and Management*, Chichester: Capstone.

Adair, J. (2005) *How to Grow Leaders*, London: Kogan Page.

Adair, J. (2006) Effective Leadership Development, London: CIPD, 137–43.

Badaracco, J.L. and Ellsworth, R.R. (1989) *Leadership and the Quest for Integrity*, Boston: Harvard University Press.

Bass, B.M. (1990) 'From transactional to transformational leadership: Learning to share the vision', *Organizational Dynamics*, 18, 19–31.

Becher, T. and Trowler, P. (2001) *Academic Tribes and Territories: Intellectual Inquiry and the Culture of Disciplines* 2nd edn, Buckingham: SRHE/Open University Press.

Bennis, W. and Nanus, B. (1985) *Leaders: The Strategies for Taking Charge*, New York: Harper & Row.

Bensimon, E., Neumann, A. and Birnbaum, R. (1989) *Making Sense of Administrative Leadership: The 'L' Word in Higher Education*, Washington, DC: ASHE-ERIC Higher Education Reports, 1.

Birnbaum, R. (1992) *How Academic Leadership Works*, San Francisco: Jossey-Bass.

Blake, R.R. and Mouton, J.S. (1964) *The Managerial Grid*, Houston: Gulf Publishing Co.

Blake, R.R. and Mouton, J.S. (1991) *Leadership Dilemmas: Grid Solutions*, Houston: Scientific Methods Inc.

Boyer, E. (1990) *Scholarship Reconsidered*, New York: Carnegie Foundation for the Advancement of Learning.

Bryman, A. (1992) *Charisma and Leadership in Organizations*, Newbury Park, CA: Sage.

Centre for Creative Leadership 2nd edn (2004) *Handbook of Leadership Development*, Greensboro: CCL.

Committee of Vice Chancellors and Principals (1985) *Report of the Committee on Efficiency Studies in Universities*, London: CVCP.

Council for Excellence in Management and Leadership (2002) *Managers and Leaders: Raising our Game* Final Report, London: CEML.

Dewey, J. (1938) *Experience and Education*, New York: Collier and Kappa Delta Pi.

Gardner, H. (1995) *Leading Minds: An Anatomy of Leadership*, London: HarperCollins.

Gibbons, M., Limoges, C., Nowotny, H., Schwartzman, S., Scott, P. and Trow, M. (1994) *The New Production of Knowledge: Science and Research in Contemporary Society*, London: Sage.

Gold, J., Rodgers, H. and Smith, V. (2001) *The Future of the Professions*, London: Council for Excellence in Management and Leadership.

Graen, G.B. and Scandura, T.A. (1987) 'Towards a Psychology of Dyadic Organizing' in Cummings, L.L. and Staw, B.M. *Research in Organizational Behaviour*, vol. 9, Greenwich, CT: JAI Press.

Greenleaf, R. (1977) *Servant Leadership*, San Francisco: Jossey-Bass.

Grint, K. (1997) (ed.) *Leadership: Classical, Contemporary and Critical Approaches*, Oxford: Oxford Management Readers.

Gronn, P. (2002) 'Distributed leadership as a unit of analysis', *The Leadership Quarterly*, 13, 423–51.

HEFCE (2003) *Graduate Employability Study*, HEFCE R&D Reports, Bristol: HEFCE (http:www.hefce.ac.uk/pubs/rdreports/2003/rd13_03/)

HESDA (2001) *Insight into HESDA's Top Management Programme for Higher Education (UK)*, Briefing Chapter 95, pp.1–6, Sheffield, HESDA.

Hollander, E.P. (1978) *Leadership Dynamics: A Practical Guide to Effective Relationships*, New York: Free Press.

Jarratt, Sir A. (1985) *Report of the Steering Committee for Efficiency Studies in Universities*, London, CVCP/UGC.

Kennie, T.J.M. (1986) *Some thoughts on leadership and management training for chartered surveyors*. Winner of the Ryde Memorial and President's Prize in the Royal Institution of Chartered Surveyors Prize Chapters Competition. 25pp.

Kennie, T.J.M. and Gardiner, P.F. (1988) *Leadership training for chartered surveyors in the United Kingdom – A review of a programme of continuing education*. International Federation of Surveyors (FIG), Commission 2 Symposium. Madrid.

Kennie, T.J.M. and Middlehurst, R.M. (1995). *Leadership and Professional Organisations*. Tertiary Education and Management, 1(2), 20–32.

Kennie, T.J.M. and Price, I. (1997) *Practice Management Guidelines. Key Questions for the Leaders and Managers of Professional Practices*. RICS Guidance Note. RICS Books, 88pp. (2nd edn, 2003)

Kerr, S. and Jermier, J.M. (1978) 'Substitutes for Leadership: their meaning and measurement', *Organizational Behaviour and Human Performance*, 22, 375–403.

Kouzes, J.M. and Posner, B.Z. (1987) *The Leadership Challenge: How to get extraordinary things done in organizations*, San Francisco: Jossey-Bass.

Lambert, R. (2003) *Lambert Review of Business University Collaboration*, London: Department of Trade and Industry.

McGregor, D. (1961) *The Human Side of Enterprise*, New York: McGraw-Hill.

Middlehurst, R. (1989) Leadership Development in Universities, 1986–1988. *Final Report to the Department of Education and Science, University of Surrey* (also published in CORE, (1992) 16, 1, Fiche 3, B01).

Middlehurst, R. (1993) *Leading Academics*, Maidenhead. SRHE/Open University Press.

Middlehurst, R. and Garratt, R. (2000) *Developing Senior Managers in Higher Education*, Summary Report and Vol. II: Supporting Evidence, available through the Leadership Foundation (www.lfhe.ac.uk).

Middlehurst, R. and Kennie, T.J.M. (1995) *Leadership and Professional Organisations*. Tertiary Education and Management, 1(2), 20–32.

Middlehurst, R. and Kennie, T.J.M. (1997) 'Leading Professionals: Towards new concepts of professionalism', in Broadbent, J., Dietrich, M. and Roberts, J. (eds) (1997) *The End of the Professions? The restructuring of professional work*, London: Routledge, 50–68.

Middlehurst, R., Pope, R. and Wray, M. (1991) The Changing Roles of University Leaders and Managers: implications for preparation and development. *Report to the Department of Education and Science, University of Surrey* (also published in CORE, (1992) 16, 1, Fiche 5, E11).

Middlehurst, R., Pope, M., Wray, M. (1992) 'The changing roles of university leaders and managers: implications for preparation and development', *CORE*, 16(1).

Northouse, P. (2004) *Leadership: Theory and Practice* 3rd edn, London: Sage.

Performance and Innovation Unit (2000) *Strengthening Leadership in the Public Sector: A research study by the PIU*, London: Cabinet Office.

Wheatley, M.J. (1992) Leadership and the New Science: Learning about Organization from an Orderly Universe, San Francisco: Berrett-Koehler Publishers Inc.

9
John Adair and Church Leadership

S. Martin Gaskell

Introduction

John Adair's contribution to church leadership is closely connected, and intertwined, with his involvement in St George's House, Windsor Castle, from where I write this contribution. John recalls, as a schoolboy, often walking over the playing fields from Slough to attend sung Evensong in St George's Chapel; shortly after the opening of St George's House he joined its staff, on secondment from the Royal Military Academy, Sandhurst; and, over the subsequent 40 years of its history, he has contributed to the work of the House, most notably today through his involvement with the Windsor Leadership Trust.

St George's House was founded in 1966 by the then Dean of Windsor, Robin Woods, and His Royal Highness the Duke of Edinburgh as a place for consultation, 'where men and women of responsibility and serious intent could discuss where their world was going and what they could do about it', and as a place for the in-service support of clergy of all denominations. It was, as Dean Woods later reflected, 'a genuine attempt by the Christian Church to enter into dialogues with the secular world' (Adair 1977: 168). To that dialogue, and through his commitment to the Church, John Adair has contributed extensively and significantly. This chapter seeks to review his initial thinking on the subject of church leadership and the importance of those ideas in the formation of St George's House; it will describe how those ideas were implemented at Windsor and how, subsequently, they evolved, reflecting the debate about in-service education and training for leadership in the Church; the chapter will conclude with an assessment of how John Adair's ideas and work on leadership in the Church have developed over the years and how they have influenced the current movement for, and debate about, leadership in the Church of England.

And, at the outset, as the above summary has already demonstrated, there is a confusion and conflation of terminology between 'Church' and 'Church of England'. John Adair speaks of 'church' leadership, and I am sure he sees his thinking of relevance to the whole Christian Church; but in reality, and inevitably given his own personal commitment and involvement with the Church of England, his contribution has focused on the Church of England. Undoubtedly, John Adair's work has influenced thinking in other denominations, but, within the constraints of this chapter, it has not been possible to assess that; rather, it will focus on the Church of England. So there is need for an apology, and explanation, as to when 'Church Leadership' is used as short-hand for 'Leadership in the Church of England'. Even the most committed Anglican would not consider the Established Church in this country to be co-terminous with the Church. However, that is the context to which this chapter is confined.

In 1962 John Adair had published in the journal *Theology* an article entitled 'A Staff College for the Church of England' (Adair 1962). In that article, Adair explained the concept of the 'staff college' as it operated in the Army, and examined its potential application to the Church; for there is a real sense in which the Church is 'like a mighty army'. Adair suggested that students on such a course might start with a study of the Church as 'the body of Christ' and the ways in which it responds to concrete situations and the needs of the world. The structural organisation of the Church of England would be reviewed in terms of the total work of the Church, as a theoretical introduction to the roles of rural deans, archdeacons and bishops. Utilising the instructional model of the Army Staff College, it was proposed that participants would work together in small teams of eight with an instructor and would study, with the help of sociologists and management consultants, the present functions of the staff within the Church of England. Specialist work might involve subjects such as the sociology of large organisations, methods of personnel selection, office management, lateral and scalar communications, and ecclesiastical law. To balance these practical group investigations, some lectures on more general topics, such as church history and world politics, would be added to the course. Through all this, Adair sought to train those who might be called to high office within the Church, so that they could be more effective in their posts and thus contribute to a more effective National Church.

This was radically different from anything offered in the Church of England at that time. Nevertheless, it was an idea and a concept that was to influence Robin Woods when he became Dean of Windsor in that year. On arrival, he felt immensely frustrated that 'so little was happening, and that the whole place seemed to be allowing itself gently to collapse, as it were, with too little money, houses in gross disrepair, and nothing going on'. At the same time, Robin Woods was not part of the 'old establishment', despite his antecedents, and his prior experience was very different to that of his predecessors. As Archdeacon of Sheffield, he was Chairman of Industrial Mission and, on the national scene, Vice-Chairman of the Church Assembly Board of Social Responsibility.

There were two other major factors. The first was the introduction, in the last years of the War, mainly under the inspiration of Field Marshall Earl Alexander (who was later to be so influential in the setting-up of St George's House), of the whole concept of leadership training for lay people, with the setting-up of leadership schools in Rome, Trieste and Hamburg. Robin Woods, as a senior Army Chaplain, had been involved in this and it had very much affected his ministry. Secondly, in the 1950s and '60s there was developing in the Church of England, for the first time, 'Specialist Ministries' – Industrial Mission Chaplains, Hospital Chaplains and Prison Chaplains – and for Army Chaplains there was the setting-up of the Army Chaplains Training Centre. But while all these things were happening, Woods felt that the main body of the Church of England was not really having a rethink.

Looking back, Robin Woods recalled that he got himself into early trouble on appointment and arrival at Windsor by talking about the necessity of a 'staff college' for the Church of England. Having served in the army, he was impressed by the military pattern of service staff training. So he developed, at an early stage, a plan for really teaching and helping people to assume senior appointments. In doing so, he hoped that the Church was 'sufficiently humble to say that if Colonels, Brigadiers needed training on appointment, so did we'.

In taking these ideas forward, Robin Woods was encouraged by his discussions with The Duke of Edinburgh, who impressed on him his own experience of the Naval Staff Course, and who suggested that something along these lines might be helpful for mid-career clergy. Prince Philip was critical of the fact that clergy training took place on 'entry', when the people concerned had absolutely no knowledge or experience of their intended profession. They obviously had to learn, but Prince Philip maintained that you learnt even more against a background of practical experience. There was also, he argued, a big difference between doing a junior job 'under command', as it were, and taking on a senior job with responsibility for others. As Prince Philip put it: 'The staff course is not so much "instruction" as getting people to take their noses off the grindstone for a moment and to have a look around the wider countryside'.[1]

So St George's House was born out of concerns about 'leadership', particularly in the Church of England. The earliest ideas were essentially about teaching and training; but, over the first three years of Robin Wood's time as Dean of Windsor, these nascent ideas broadened into the concept that was to become St George's House. That this was so was largely due to the influence and encouragement of The Duke of Edinburgh, and the detailed discussions that he and the Dean had had over that time. As a result, by the time the House opened in 1966, one of its twin aims was: 'To be a place where clergy of all denominations could come together for courses which could incorporate the understanding gained in the total work of the House'.[2]

The Appeal Brochure to secure funds for the establishment of the House had set out that, in addition to consultations for lay people, there would be conferences for clergy only:

> Those for whom St George's House is particularly intended are those in the 40–55 age group who may understandably have become weary of well-doing and exhausted by unrewarded effort. St George's House will seek to reinstruct, re-equip and reinspire them for their ministry.
>
> There are staff colleges for the armed forces, management courses for executives and a great volume of further training in the professions, but not much is done for the clergy. Once he is ordained he is 'launched on to the open seas and given little help in navigation.'
>
> St George's House will seek to meet this need.[3]

Inevitably, the initial clergy work at the House was rather *ad hoc* and fairly specifically focused. The House needed to move quickly to fill the weeks with clergy-related operations, between the weekend general consultations. In its first year of operation, the House held consultations for people from similar backgrounds and with similar interests – Archdeacons, Country Parsons, Suburban Clergy and Clergy from New Towns. And increasingly, both the ministry and the laity of the Free Churches and the Roman Catholic Church were sharing in this. Quickly a range of activities became established and by the end of the '60s there was a rich and regular pattern of courses for clergy at St George's House.

Valuable though were these weekday courses for different groups of clergy and laity in the Church, and though some of them had begun to address issues of leadership in the Church, they did not meet the challenge of the fundamental concern which Prince Philip had so clearly identified. Tenacious as ever, he continued to encourage Robin Woods in the pursuit of the idea of 'a staff college for clergy', against the resistance of others in both the Chapter and the Council of St George's House. So, after much discussion, it was agreed during 1968 to act on John Adair's suggestion that the House would mount the first four-week Clergy Course in the following year.

For by that time John Adair had joined the small group of people responsible for turning the concept of St George's House into reality, effectively the Warden, along with the Dean and those of the Canons sympathetic to the project. He was there on secondment from the Royal Military Academy, Sandhurst from January 1968 until July 1969. John had already been involved in thinking about how the House could best contribute to the continuing education of the clergy. In 1966, as Vice-Chairman of the Ministry Committee of the Advisory Council for the Church's Ministry, he had been invited to a consultation for 15 Diocesan Bishops at which Prince Philip was present, regarding the need for the Church to change. So when John suggested to Dean Robin Woods that he might spend his sabbatical period at St George's House, the response was receptive. Robin Woods was aware of the work he had been doing in the Church of England on Adult Education and Laity Training. He knew of the two-week 'group dynamics' programme that John Adair had conducted for 120 Anglican Bishops in Toronto in 1963. With his position established as Adviser in Leadership Training at Sandhurst, John Adair came to St George's House to contribute to its intellectual creativity, and to develop his ideas for clergy support along lines with which both the Dean and The Duke of Edinburgh were sympathetic.

So when, in 1969, St George's House launched its first extended Clergy Course, it was not surprising that the course reflected the concept and character for such a course that John Adair had set out in his 1962 article. However, the nomenclature of 'staff college' had been dropped, and the more prosaic, comfortably Anglican terminology of 'Clergy Long Course' was adopted. As a result of this timely conjunction of interests and ideas, John Adair's original proposals on church leadership were being brought to fruition.

Of course, there had been criticism, if not outright hostility, from some in the hierarchy of the Church of England, who felt it was presumptuous on the part of St George's to think they could identify the Church's future leaders, even though participants had been identified by their Bishops. However, the majority of Bishops were positive and encouraging, and fears of élitism, which have always dogged St George's House, were overcome. John Adair had personally promoted the cause in one-to-one meetings with individual Bishops and, sometimes, with their respective Bishops' Councils. In the event, 20 dioceses nominated men for the first course, and the Methodist Church sent two. There was, indeed, a sense of positive enthusiasm from all involved.

A variety of people contributed to the planning of the course syllabus, including some bishops and the heads of staff colleges and business schools. From Dr Norman Leyland, the founder and first Director of the Oxford Centre for Management Studies, came the necessary advice and confidence to require the participants to spend time, in the six months before the course, preparing a written project, which has remained a constant and important element in the clergy courses to this day. The programme for the course itself fell into three phases: what was happening in the world; the role and purpose of the Church; and, how the purpose and aims of the Church could be more effectively achieved in the world.

The course included visits to the Army Staff College at Camberley, the Administrative Staff College at Henley and the Urwick Management Centre in Slough where the philosophy of 'management by objectives' was explored. The Archbishop of York, Dr Coggan, came to comment on the first group of syndicate reports, and the Lady Margaret Professor of

Divinity in the University of Cambridge, C.F.D. Moule, led the Bible studies on such themes as leadership, teamwork and organisation. As a result, the participants were encouraged, by the end of the course, to reflect on the ways in which the purpose and aims of the Church could be more effectively achieved in a world revealed by the lectures and discussions of the first week. The presentation of projects, in both small groups and plenary sessions, occupied much of the later part of the course (a characteristic of the 'staff college' model, and a continuing feature of clergy courses to this day). The course ended, again as they do today, with a comprehensive and challenging survey by the Dean of Windsor.

So was established the model for what was to become known as the Mid-Service Clergy Course, which took forward the initial ideas of John Adair. Though, of course, in both detail and in emphasis, and in terms of concept, it has changed over the years. John Adair left Windsor, at the conclusion of his sabbatical term, immediately at the end of this first Clergy Course. Others took them forward, and, over the next decade, the pattern was established of holding the Mid-Service Clergy Course twice a year, and alongside these the House designed the Senior Clergy Course for those who were in that important age group of 50 to 55 when many were often undertaking their longest and most important period of sustained ministry in one place. In addition, for those who had been called to be Bishops or placed in other positions of high clerical or lay responsibility in the Church, the House annually ran the Senior Church Leaders Course to study the exercise of their responsibility in contemporary church and society.

In 1972, the Reverend H.W. Moore (a member of the first Clergy Long Course) wrote a research thesis evaluating the Courses (Moore 1972). Embracing the expectations of Bishops as well as participants, he identified consequent creative activity stemming from the courses, and, on the other hand, cases where participants felt let down because nothing had happened in response to their efforts. However, overall, he reported 'an overwhelming assertion of confidence and appreciation' for the Mid-Service Clergy Courses. The sceptics and critics in the Church were being confounded, and the initial vision was being realised.

The original template for the Clergy Courses remained remarkably pervasive. Perhaps inevitably, over time, the emphasis of the courses changed, and they moved away from the concept of 'the staff college' preparing men for senior leadership positions. Rather, the Clergy Courses increasingly embraced the ideas running through the other work of the House, and came to be opportunities for the clergy to reflect, first and foremost, and in different ways, on what God was saying to them through the world.

This view of the Clergy Courses was taken forward at St George's House in the 1970s and remains influential to this day. However, the organisational structure of the courses, as established by John Adair, has remained largely intact and certainly influential, though the remit of the courses shifted into a more self-critically reflective mode. The debate about the respective benefits and values of these different approaches to clergy in-service work has continued as a leit-motif through the history of St George's House. It has similarly been reflected, more widely, in the debates in the Church of England over the intervening 40 years about continuing education and clergy leadership training.

John Adair propelled that debate, and in 1977, in his book *The Becoming Church* (Adair 1977), he reviewed achievements and reflected on the way forward. Of course, that book is about much more than just Church Leadership. The conviction underlying the book was that the Church as a whole was not in the grip of a single crisis, but was in a process of developing or 'becoming' through continuous creative interaction with its environment. And the dominant factor in that environment was the subtle but persistent shift of values towards secularisation. Adair argued that the Churches had not, at that time, sufficiently understood their changing situation, and had not fully or properly responded to the need to engage the laity. He examined the statistics of institutional decline and the staffing problems of the Church of England, and he concluded that the essence of the parochial system, in the form of one man, one building, one area, could and should survive, but the whole system needed to be developed. In considering how that could happen, he, not unexpectedly, paid particular attention to training and organisation:

> Leadership is an important principle in the Christian enterprise, as in any other, but it is by no means the whole story. It is only within the context of other positive developments in an organization of community – structure, communications, training, morale – that good leadership becomes really effective. A wise organization, while never leaving everything to its leaders or blaming all misfortunes upon them, learns to value good leadership as an essential resource.(*ibid.*: 157–8)

Applying his now well-known and well-established paradigm for good leadership to the Church, he concluded that the Church of England was in a position where it had to choose between a painful period of readjustment, or enter into a long period of peaceful decline. He then suggested a third alternative, in which really good relations between people enabled them to work together towards common aims and objectives, which he believed could be achieved through the application of honest and sympathetic appraisal:

> It is not easy to give such leadership, especially as the Christian leader may have become hooked upon the warm social rewards of popularity, approval, and love which the churches have traditionally imposed upon their people-orientated 'pastors'. The pastors of tomorrow must lead

their sheep across raging torrents – and they must go through the waters first, or else the flock will not follow. Niceness is not enough. (*ibid*.: 159)

How such a change in approach and attitude was to be realised, Adair then addresses in a subsequent chapter on 'Further Training: A Change Agent'. He examined the growth of professional continuing-education in all professions, and explored the response of the Church of England to this movement and momentum. He encouraged Diocesan responsibility in this respect and explored opportunities for Diocesan collaboration in ways which preempted the 'Hind Report' by nearly 30 years.[4] Turning to the national scene, he returned to his vision for a 'staff college for the Church of England', and reviewed both his original 1962 article and the subsequent developments at St George's House. He advanced this thinking to the supranational level, and argued for a central college for the Anglican Communion which would emphasise training not consultation. This, he concluded, should be seen not as a solitary star on top of the Anglican Christmas tree, but as one among a small galaxy of ecumenical centres or institutes which have an official existence and a proper purpose within the context of the world Church.

While the book as a whole received mixed reviews, the central chapters on church organisation and leadership clearly embody and exemplify John Adair's concern for, and concept of, Church Leadership. Over the coming decades, these views and these principles about leadership would be brought to the service of the Church of England in a number of ways, and would maintain the ferment of concern and consideration in the Church about leadership which has resulted in what is happening today.

In 1968 John Adair had already been commissioned to undertake a review of the administrative structures and communications of the Diocese of York and to make recommendations in the light of the forthcoming synodical government for the Church. The object of the review was to enable the Church in that Diocese better to fulfil its pastoral, evangelistic, social and ecumenical vision. This was followed in the early '70s by a report for the Diocese of Chichester which had similar terms of reference. In both cases, the Dioceses were concerned to: develop better support and pastoral care for those engaged in ministry; make more effective use of the time and talents of those who work voluntarily for the Church; promote better communications within the diocese; and simplify the committee structures. In response to these concerns about organisation, John Adair recommended that the two dioceses in question should remain a unity, but work more in three episcopal areas, each under the leadership of a suffragan bishop. This would create units sufficiently small for episcopal leadership to be a reality, whilst being large enough to prevent the suffragan bishop from trying to do the job of his rural deans and incumbents. At the same time, giving the suffragan bishop clear responsibility, within clearly defined areas, meant that the diocesan bishop could exercise supervision and personal encouragement for the three area bishops, whilst his central staff could provide services and administrative support for a sufficiently large segment of the Church to make this cost-effective in financial terms.

In these reports Adair applied his theory of overlapping needs to the particular circumstances of the Church and the Diocese, and he brought together in the person of the bishop the requirement for both visionary and administrative leadership. Both the diocesan and suffragan bishops should exercise episcopal leadership, as well as helping the clergy and laity to plan together in terms of their common purpose: '...the office of a bishop commits him to contributing to the task, team maintenance and individual needs of the whole Church, as a universal phenomenon' (Adair 1977: 147).

Of course, neither Diocese accepted the Reports in toto nor implemented them as a complete package. In particular, they accepted those aspects which could strengthen interdependence and break down isolation, whilst rejecting any too rigid system of line and staff responsibility, and any proposals for increasing the size of the 'establishment'. However, the Diocese of York did take on board his most controversial proposal that the roles of the three archdeacons should be clearly defined as 'staff' rather than 'line', and that they should be given distinct areas of special responsibility – Mission, Ministry and Finance. But nevertheless, these reports, for the first time, forced dioceses to think about their organisational needs and the way in which leadership could best be effected within the structure of the Church. As the Diocese of Chichester later recognised, the concept of 'ministry by objectives', advocated by Adair, brought operational common sense and a good framework to the development of the diocese. And in 1991 Archbishop John Habgood recalled that the Adair Report for York 'worked surprisingly well for a long time', and clergy appraisal had assumed central importance.[5]

These timely initiatives for reviewing leadership in the Church Adair took forward in terms of the 'think-tank' which he set up as the 'Institute for Ecclesiastical Studies', reflecting the Institute for Strategic Studies in the military field. At a more operational level, in the 1980s he returned to St George's House in order to run consultations designed to develop senior diocesan teams. They covered 26 English dioceses and the Church in Wales, and the teams included diocesan bishops, suffragan bishops, archdeacons and diocesan secretaries.

This work continued in different ways at St George's House with the foundation of the Windsor Leadership Trust. Developing out of the earlier work at the House initiated by Charles Handy when he was Warden from 1977 to 1981, the Trust was formed in 1995 with the aim of developing and inspiring leaders for society by assisting and encouraging people from across society to explore and increase their leadership abilities. John Adair spoke on the first of Charles Handy's programmes, and was thus involved with what was to become the Trust from the outset. He ensured its specific focus on leadership as distinct from a broader concern for the changing face of British society which was characteristic of the early 'Windsor Meeting' programmes. He was also concerned that the Trust crossed the sectoral boundaries of public and private enterprise, and in that process he ensured that clergy of the Church of England and others became involved as participants, firstly in the Initial Windsor Meetings for potential leaders, and then, more particularly, in the meetings for Newly Appointed Strategic Leaders. The latter regularly involve newly appointed Bishops, and through these consultations they are enabled to focus on the importance of strategic leadership, as well as the personal and the professional qualities needed for its effective exercise. But, unlike other such education and training for senior clergy, the Trust provides the opportunity of exploring the subject with a broad cross-section of leaders from very different fields, which is an essential ingredient in the educating for leadership process. It is a tribute to John Adair's pursuit and promotion of Church Leadership that (some) Bishops now recognise, not only their needs in terms of leadership training, but also that their leadership is not unique. It may have many differences from that in the commercial world, but it has more in common than the Church could ever have realised. It is clear from the response to the earlier series of consultations at St George's House, and now to the work of the Windsor Leadership Trust, that the Church has come to recognise its own need for training and development in terms of senior leadership, which Adair had identified four decades ago.

In 1985 this change of mood resulted in the House of Bishops agreeing to establish a Working Party on the Induction and Continuing Ministerial Education of Bishops. And seven years later (such are labyrinthine ways of the Church of England), this gave birth to 'The House of Bishops Training Committee'. However, this long period of gestation reflected the continuing opposition of some bishops to any notion that they needed training in order to be leaders of their dioceses. Yet, by the time its first chairman, Bishop Hewlett Thompson of Exeter (who had participated in the first Long Clergy Course at St George's in 1969), retired in 1999, he felt confident that 'new bishops *and their families* are now much better trained and supported than in his early days'.[6]

The Church of England was slowly, but steadily, realising its requirements in terms of leadership, and John Adair's rightful role in this was recognised in an invitation in 1994 to join the Archbishops' Commission to review the machinery of central policy and resource direction in the Church of England, with its focus on 'the nature, the constitution and the management of church affairs'. So, five years on, John Adair was appointed as a consultant to the newly formed Archbishops' Council, with the object of providing some reflection on its first nine months of operation. He acted as an 'observer and enabler' so that 'the opportunity for strategic leadership which the formation of the Council represents' should not be wasted.[7] And in his Reflection, Adair emphasised the need for vision and for strategy in addressing the three interdependent demands on the Church of Finance, Ministry and Laity. Though, when the Council had been established, it was seen by some as the standing committee for the 'central business of the Church of England', it will not be surprising that Adair sought to emphasise the fact that it had been set up explicitly to provide strategic leadership: 'Will the urgent or the pressing drive out the important?'[8] The Archbishops and members of the Council responded to this probing and began to shift the emphasis of their work. As the then Archbishop of York, David Hope, put it: 'My own feeling is that we are still far too much weighed down with a number of things which need not come before the Council, and we ought at times to be more adventurous in thinking the unthinkable and certainly looking at different ways of doing things'.[9]

John Adair had contributed to that changing conception of leadership priorities within the Church. On the way, he had taken his message in the early '90s to the World Council of Churches; but his primary sphere of influence was always the Church of England. And in the Church of England attitudes towards leadership and management had changed dramatically. It cannot be the remit of this Chapter to consider whether the increasing emphasis on management and leadership in the Church has been beneficial and supportive of its spiritual mission, or whether it has been a distraction from its primary purpose. However, the fact is that, over the 40 years that this Chapter has sought to survey, attitudes have altered, and, for good or ill, 'leadership' has become the buzzword in the Church today. That this is so is, in no small measure, due to the initial ideas and subsequent sustained commitment of John Adair.

This commitment to management and leadership in the Church had been recognised in 1993 with the creation of a society called 'Modem', with its mission to promote dialogue between management and ministry. It believed that the Church had singularly failed to understand and accept that organisations, including the Church, needed better leadership and management. Given this remit, it is not surprising that it should have awarded one of its first three Honorary Emeritus Memberships to John Adair, recognising that it probably would not have been there without his drive and commitment to what they believed in. John supported Modem, and in 2001 contributed to its response to the Hurd Report on the organisation of the staff at Lambeth Palace entitled, 'To Lead and to Serve'. In 2004 he collaborated with John Nelson (Modem's National Secretary and Publications Editor) in the editing of a volume of essays under the title *Creative Church Leadership* (Adair and Nelson 2004). This concentrated on the questions of what kind of leaders the Church needs today and how might the Church begin to look if imaginative, risk-taking leadership was fostered at every level of its life?

Between them the editors were able to persuade an impressive and diverse array of eminent writers and practitioners to contribute, and the result was described in *The Church Times* as 'essential reading for anyone in, or aspiring to, any kind of leadership role in any church'.[10] For, as John Adair made clear in his conclusion, creative leadership was a direct challenge to those in the Church who were stuck in the 'tramlines of tradition':

> This book is an exercise in trailblazing. Like it or not, the churches are moving into new and unfamiliar territory. Though not lost, there is certainly some creative bewilderment around already.
>
> What emerges from this book for me is a simple but central question: *What is the gospel?* Among our 14 contributors I sense a shared conviction that it has essentially to do with God's creative purpose in and for the world. This has to be our starting point. It is also, they believe, a necessary condition of creative leadership. (Adair and Nelson 2004: 214)

Therein, perhaps, John Adair encapsulates his concept of Church Leadership: a conjunction of the theories and practices of leadership with the beliefs and purposes of the Church. Both contribute to each other, both enrich each other, and both together support a new symbiosis. Forty years on from John Adair's original article, church leadership was not only being promoted, but was being discussed and debated, and its practical realisation was being addressed in a variety of ways and through a variety of approaches.

It was not perhaps coincidental that the publication of 'Creative Church Leadership' took place at the same time as the launch of 'The Foundation for Church Leadership', which recognised that the Church was not immune from changes and cultural shifts in society, which had resulted in the growing emphasis on leadership in that society. To that end, the Foundation established as its priorities: identifying the theology of leadership; developing the potential for leadership in individuals and teams; supporting continuing education at every level of Church life; encouraging wider use of the opportunities available; promoting good practice. The formal launch of the Foundation in 2005, in the presence of the Archbishop of Canterbury, signalled the acceptance of the importance of leadership within the establishment of the Church of England.

At the same time, training for leadership within the Church was being promoted in various ways and through various organisations. Specific work with senior clergy includes: Continuing Ministerial Education for Bishops; The Leadership Institute; Archdeacons Conferences. Individual dioceses are pursuing their own initiatives: Personal Leadership Programme (Guildford); Chester Leadership Development Programme (Chester); Ministerial Development Programme (London); Developing Servant Leaders (Oxford). And St George's House continues to offer its own established approach to ministerial leadership through its clergy courses, as, in a different way, does the Grubb Institute.

There is much on offer. But in-service training in the Church of England remains voluntary, and there still remains the need for a cultural shift before clergy routinely look for, and accept, training and development. Nevertheless, the growth in provision since the 1960s is impressive and indicative of the importance currently accorded to leadership within the Church.

The provision, however, remains fragmented, often overlapping and uncoordinated. So, in the summer of 2005, John Adair, as ever active in this field, conceived the idea for a 'summit meeting' of all interested parties, which reviewed current provision, assessed the changing needs of the Church – its clergy and laity – in terms of leadership, and addressed developments for the future. Held at St George's House, it did not come up with a common model or a shared template; it did not produce a national plan of action, which at different times John Adair has advanced. But it certainly highlighted the richness and variety of provision, and signalled the possibility of very different approaches and philosophies co-habiting the world of Church Leadership. In turn, the Church can recognise that there is no one 'right' approach to leadership training, but knows that it has to address the need in diverse and different ways that reflect the local, and national needs, of the Church of England.

To have reached that position in 40 years is a measure of John Adair's achievement, of his initial drive and continued commitment, and of his dogged dedication to his cause. As I have already indicated, the question of whether all this action and activity has resulted in a better Church, whatever that means, is not the remit of this Chapter. That is much more focused and constrained, in terms of the emergence of leadership as an issue in the Church of England, the development of education and training with respect to leadership, and the role and recognition of John Adair in that process. And perhaps the most remarkable feature about the process has been the extent to which he remained constant to his original idea and his pursuit of a clearly focused mission. From the 'big idea' to the local initiative, his aim has been consistent, though his objectives have modified with changing times and circumstances. In the process, we must not forget that Church Leadership has, at different times and by different people, been conflated and confused with management, strategic planning, personnel organisation and financial control; and there is no doubt that some of those involved in the leadership cause in the Church today may see leadership in some of such terms. But John Adair has not, however much he has been misquoted, and however much his work has taken him into giving management guidance to the Church. His concern has always been about leadership in the Church in order to enable it to better realise the Kingdom of God on Earth. It provided a unique area in which his theories on leadership and his personal belief could coalesce. As a result: 'John Adair has put the Church greatly in his debt'. (Adair 1977)

Notes

1 Letter from His Royal Highness The Duke of Edinburgh to the Honorary Administrator, St George's House, 18 September 1991. Reproduced by kind permission of His Royal Highness.
2 *St George's House Annual Review 1973–74*, Statement of Purpose, p.2.
3 'The Royal Foundation of St George's, Windsor Castle and the Establishment of St George's House, 1965–1966' (Appeal Brochure).
4 *Formation for Ministry within a Learning Church*. A report to the Synod of the Church of England, 2003, from a working group chaired by John Hind, Bishop of Chichester.
5 Letter from Archbishop John Habgood to Dr John Adair, 20 November 1991.
6 *Church Times*, 22 January 1999.
7 'Reflections on the first nine months of the Archbishops' Council'. Confidential paper from John Adair to the Archbishops' Council, 28 September 1999.
8 *Ibid.*
9 Letter from Archbishop David Hope to Professor John Adair, 12 October 1999.
10 *Church Times*, 29 October 2004.

References

Adair, J. (1962) 'A Staff College for the Church of England', *Theology*, May.
Adair, J. (1977) *The Becoming Church*, London: SPCK.
Adair, J. and Nelson, J. (eds) (2004) *Creative Church Leadership*, Norwich: Canterbury Press.
Moore, H.W. (1972) *Evaluation of the First Five Mid-Service Clergy Courses at St George's House, Windsor Castle*, MA Thesis, University of Leeds.

Part III

Action-Centred Leadership (ACL) in International Contexts

10
Functional Leadership in Australia – The Story

Greg McMahon

The story

Chapters to the story

The story of Functional Leadership in Australia has largely paralleled the story of management in Australia.

That is, there is a chapter to the story of Functional Leadership in Australia corresponding to each wave of management philosophy that swept through each decade of business in Australia. Those waves and decades were:

- Management by Objectives [MBO] in the sixties, when Functional Leadership was introduced to Australia;
- Project Management [PM] in the seventies, which was found as a management movement to be ignoring the needs of project team members;
- Total Quality Management [TQM] in the eighties, which was found to be vulnerable to major failures without the addition of effective change management – for effective change management, leadership was recognised as the key;
- Strategic Management [SM] in the nineties, a contribution from MBA schools which often failed integration with the people factors alive within organisation; and,
- Management for Outcomes [MFO] in the 'noughties', a second MBA school derivative included a heading for people-related outcomes, but many of its practitioners found more energy for the KPIs about the business and the operations than for KPIs about the people.

There is a sense of déjà vu about many aspects of the first and last of these waves of ideas, for those of us who were there for all of them. 'Objectives' and 'Outcomes', for example are synonyms. The first wave, however, was managed by professionals who learned leadership during World War II. The last wave, too, carries the burdens and opportunities of a now 'globalised' world.

The summary headings from all waves do remind us of the developments that have occurred with Functional Leadership through these decades.

The story could also be broken up into chapters organised on the various sourcing of education in management that has occurred, or been available, in Australia during these same times. This break-up might be described by

- **Organisational sourcing**, where organisations take on the task of training managers to meet their own specific operational requirements
- **Vocational sourcing**, where Registered Training Organisations provide nationally accredited management competencies, incorporating as much as possible the operational needs of organisations,
- **Tertiary sourcing**, from universities, focused on management theory and academic requirements but incorporating as much as possible the practical aspects of applying such theoretical concepts.

Introduction of Functional Leadership

Functional Leadership was introduced to Australia by the Defence Department in the mid-sixties, principally by the Australian Army and the Royal Australian Air Force. The Army in particular had a requirement to prepare in quick time young national servicemen for the duties of corporal (section leader) and lieutenant (platoon leader) in Vietnam. Experimental approaches to preparing, in six months at the Officer Training Unit at Scheyville, 20-year olds for leadership of 30 men in military operations became focused on Functional Leadership. The Army published its leadership doctrine in 1973, and it was based on the three circles Functional Leadership model (Australian Army 1973).

Dissemination into industry

Downsizing of the military forces, and the return of national service officers and non-commissioned officers to their civilian careers, propagated the Functional Leadership concepts into the practices of business. Former military officers found ready employment in project management, logistics and human resource management roles (including training development officers for organisations). Some went into business as corporate trainers. This movement was reinforced by the importation of Functional Leadership practices that accompanied the growth of overseas corporations, such as Shell, ICI, Hilton and Kellogs into Australia. The head-hunting of management professionals and consultants from overseas, many of whom had had exposure to Functional Leadership, added to the establishment of Functional Leadership in Australian business.

The growth of Functional Leadership in the practice of management in Australia was demonstrated by the decision of the Australian Institute of Management in the eighties to bring Dr Adair out to Australia. Adair was also brought to Australia in the early 1990s by the Royal Australian Air Force and by a corporate training company, Mountaincraft.

In these ways, Functional Leadership became well established in the training programmes and library shelves of organisational and vocational training units. Functional Leadership was thus well established in the business practices that introduced and implemented MBO, PM, TQM, SM and MFO in Australia.

Universities

Functional Leadership was not taken up within the bulk of Universities in Australia. When the author began a Functional Leadership programme at one of the big six universities in Australia, there was not one Adair book in the University. Down the road, by comparison, at the Australian Institute of Management, and over the hill at the Defence library, the shelves were full of Adair's works.

The Functional Leadership programme begun at the University of Queensland by the author followed the bad reaction of final year undergraduates and first year graduates to a lecture series from the sister School of Management (McMahon and Apelt 1994). Functional Leadership programmes, mirroring the University of Surrey UK programme, have performed consistently well for over a decade at this university. This prosperity has occurred, however, within a context of continuing professional education and hard science faculties rather than within the neighbouring School of Management.

The latter Schools have been influenced by (mainly) American MBA postgraduates. MBA programmes flourished within universities in Australia during the 1980s, and now are offered by several member-based organisations in joint ventures with universities, from lecture series to e-learning formats.

The busy practitioners of Functional Leadership, it seems, have not sought to enter academia (with a few notable exceptions), nor to publish papers outside of the organisational and vocational regimes in which they operate. Given the successes of the Functional Leadership concepts in business practice, it seems a contradiction that the methodology is not more appreciated in academia.

Why academia has not taken up Functional Leadership as much as has industry

Prior to the seventies, management training for professionals at universities in Australia was achieved through a second degree, usually a Commerce, Economics or Arts Degree. The Masters of Business Administration programmes provided the first degree to be seen as a 'Management Degree'. The new schools established in 'Management' differentiated themselves from the traditional commerce and economics departments by delivering MBAs and, later, Bachelor Degrees in 'Business Management' and such.

Generally, these MBA programmes were delivered by lecturers with MBAs obtained from American Universities. The sabbaticals taken by these lecturers returned them to the influence of their former professors, their doctorates typically went to American reviewers, and they sought to achieve publication through distinguished American journals and conferences. In these ways, the initiatives for management training at universities were heavily influenced by the American MBA Schools.

Little is black and white, and generalisations will always be unfair to most, but there were certain features to MBA programmes brought to Australia that separated management training in Australia from the ideas of Adair. Firstly, being masters in 'Business Administration', the thrust of the programmes were strong on management processes – strategic planning, continuous improvement, performance management, and such like. Leadership was secondary, even peripheral to many programmes at a time when situational leadership was the popular American approach to the topic. Functional Leadership practitioners, by contrast, would see the interest in leadership as central rather than secondary.

MBAs largely took an approach that leadership was part of management. Functional Leadership practitioners might see it the other way round. Leadership was the word used in MBA content descriptions to gather the 'people' topics, and these 'people' topics were only a part of the curriculum. Some may have treated such 'people' topics as separated from the other parts of the curriculum, in the way that any item on a list is separated from the other items on the same list. Functional Leadership practitioners would see the overlap in the circles on Adair's model as a constant reminder of the interdependency of the people needs (both 'team' and 'individual') and 'task' issues.

When it came to leadership thinking, the American approach was more psychological than rational, and this was applied to both the leaders and the led. Leaders were profiled, and categorisation of leader styles was the research interest – the primary focus was placed on the leader in enabling a better leadership outcome. Transformational leaders (Bass 1997), earlier referred to as 'persuasive' leaders (Bass 1960), were the goal.

With the psychological approach to people topics, the behaviours of the led were also treated as largely predetermined, in accordance with their profiles. The approach thus to influencing people problems was 'remedial' – a leader-to-fix requirement was inferred, in which the leader might be seen to own the situation. The leader persuaded those who resisted change; the leader gave those with myopia vision, motivating the self-interested to value the common goal. The predetermined behaviours of the led brought increased emphasis to issues like selection of people, and alignment strategies for the workforce – hence the need for remedial specialists to be introduced into the leadership equation, for example, human resource specialists, who tended to displace managers from part of their traditional people management role.

The Functional Leadership concepts, by comparison, are rational in approach – a workforce group responds to the needs of their task, their team and the individuals within the team, and this is normal. The group is motivated to the task before the leader arrives, and the group wants necessary changes to be implemented. The focus is on 'the group', of whom the leader is one (albeit an important functional) member.

The group acts as if it 'owns' all problems, and will follow whichever of their members act to meet the current priority needs of the group. It is important to the standing of the leader that the leader be active in meeting these needs of their group, either by their own actions or through others. The Functional Leadership model asserts that the leader is responsible for needs being met, but the leader does not have to meet the needs themselves. The Functional Leadership practitioner seeks to involve others in the response to the group's situation, because the Functional Leadership model asserts that leadership is an activity that is shared within the group. The leader adjusts their approach to the current priority needs of the group – the leader who sees that there are no, say, 'completer finishers' or 'devil's advocates' in the management team, may take on that role themselves, because that is what their team is lacking and what is the group's priority task need.

Team members too can act to fill any gap or need. The behaviour of the leader and the led is not predetermined by their psychological profile, their dominant Belbin teamwork categorisation, or by their internal leader motivation.

These differences between the general MBA approach taken in Australia in the seventies and eighties, and the Functional Leadership model, were fundamental. In the latter model, there are only two categories of leaders, those that take responsibility for meeting all three types of needs for their group, and those who do not. This is so whatever is the leader's style, gender, internal leader motivation, nationality, skills level or Myers-Briggs profile.

By the mid-1990s, significant failures in the implementation of Total Quality Management within corporations and public authorities in Australia had brought new attention to effective change management. The interest shown by MBA programmes in effective change management brought more focus on leadership strategies for achieving changes within the workplace. Systems and processes alone could not deliver the benefits foreseen from the waves of new management ideas. A national inquiry into ways for improving the performance of industry – the Karpin Report – (Karpin 1995) gave rise to a primary initiative for leadership training of operational leaders, termed the frontline leadership programme. This initiative has been implemented through the vocational educational system within Australia, as is delivered by establishments such as the Australian Institute of Management, rather than through the universities. In these frontline leadership programmes, the leadership concepts of Adair are much in use.

A report on management education at universities in the early 1990s, provided with initiatives for a specialist MBA (Masters in Technology Management) at the University of Queensland, may have seen the problem and the solution for MBA programmes (Faculty of Engineering 1992):

> The 'how to' is vital for success. Having the skills is one thing, getting it all together is another ... otherwise the program becomes like so many MBAs; a group of bits and pieces which hopefully will match the students' needs.
>
> Arguably one of the most important skills of a manager is the ability to draw a common thread out of many differing subject areas ... This connecting of the subjects gives the student the feeling that he [sic] has partaken of a course and not simply studied a variety of subjects.

In this instance, the effort was being made to 'pull the threads together' by establishing a specialist MBA. Other academic management education initiatives have tried to use the topics of 'quality', 'customer service', 'strategic management', and 'best practice' to achieve the common thread. These initiatives, however, appear to have returned to a 'list' approach to the integration of management topics.

The use of the parameter, 'needs', and the Functional Leadership model, has not been taken up by academia to achieve this common thread.

Public sector management authorities in Australia, for example, have been high consumers of well credentialed American and Australian MBAs. Their in-house management development programmes for their executive level and senior level managers have typically followed the 'list' approach.

Failures in the management of changes within the public service have eroded the standing of such degrees in the new century. The Queensland Public Service, for example, has worn scandals from commissions of inquiry into environmental management, mining, child welfare, criminal justice, roads, power, the magistracy, and health and hospitals. The common concern arising from these inquiries has been the apparent inability of executive and senior leaders to develop a beneficial workplace culture and to control management bullying. The apparent inability to achieve outcomes has caused many administrations to engage in strings of new management initiatives, each new initiative timed to disguise the lack of outcome from the last initiatives. The inquiries and commentators have consistently recommended a leadership strategy for reforming a failing public service.

Products from mainstream organisational behaviour models and from TQM demonstrate just how close to, and how far away from, the concepts of Functional Leadership are these waves of management ideas.

Figure 10.1 is copied from a textbook on organisational behaviour [OB] used in Australian university courses (Milton *et al.* 1984). The many arrow linkages have been grouped into three boxes

- A bottom tier box which, with all its detail, is about the **individual** at work, including their needs, e.g., for satisfaction, effectiveness;
- A middle tier box, which is about the **group** – group needs gets an inclusion; and,
- A top tier box, which is labelled as 'organisational climate' but which is strong in **task** needs at the business level – environmental scanning, change management, organisational development and communications.

Leadership, too, is linked to both group behaviour and to individuals (through communications).

Similarly, TQM is widely known for its 'Five Pillars', namely

- Customer Service – a **task need** in Adair's Functional Leadership model
- Improvement through change – a **task need**
- Management by reference to the facts – a power factor, positively affecting task, team and individuals directly
- Teamwork – a **team need**, and
- Respect for Individuals – an **individual need** in Adair's model

With respect then to both OB and TQM bodies of knowledge, the strength of notions about task, team and individuals, and about the needs associated with each of these aspects of a workplace group, has been incorporated into the 'wisdom' offered from these management waves. These management movements, popular in university courses, are close in content to what the Functional Leadership model offers.

The structure of these contents is what separates the Functional Leadership model from waves of management ideas like OB and TQM. In practice, leaders found that, for example:

- Leadership, not management, is the total scope of abilities that the manager must be able to apply, as in the Functional Leadership model – leadership is not just a part of one box, however strong the linkages are drawn to the other boxes;
- Success in the task is dependent on success with both the people as a team and people as individuals, as in the Functional Leadership model – success is not just 'linked' to these people factors; and
- The needs listed in the Five Pillars can be the priority needs in many workplace situations. It is best, however, to judge each workgroup situation on a first principles basis, by analysing the needs at any time for all three areas, task, team and individual, for that same workgroup. This is

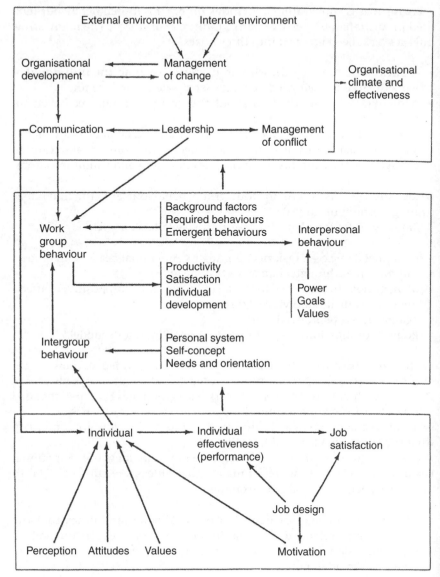

Figure 10.1   A 'three box' model for organisational behaviour

particularly so in fast moving management situations, such as in project management and in managing change (McMahon 1986, 1995, 2005; Rutherford 2004).

The take-up in Adair's concepts of leadership follows the realisation that leadership is central to effectiveness in the workplace. In Australia, this is occurring within vocational education, but has yet to be taken up within academia.

'Form-storm-norm-perform'

Right now, in Australia, the two avenues of education in leadership and management, the vocational-cum-organisational stream and the tertiary stream, are mixing.

Doctrine on leadership in the Australian Army, for example, was recently rewritten by an officer completing an MBA on leadership (Australian Army 2002). That effort was steered by a wide ranging committee of military commanders and chief instructors largely with a Functional Leadership rather than an MBA background.

Vocational training organisations are building up their packages and trainer qualifications in preparations for 'lifting' the content of their training and development packages to the delivery of MBA programmes. The author has experienced the choices to be made in 'lifting' from the vocational Diploma to the tertiary MBA (McMahon 2004) – it can be attempted either by

- A displacement from the Functional Leadership *Group* perspective of how operations are led and managed, to the MBA *Organisational* perspective of how organisations achieve success (if it is allowable to so crudely stereotype the differences between the levels of understanding accruing from the two streams), or by
- A 'mixing' of Group and Organisational perspectives

Adair's recent book, *Effective Strategic Leadership*, (Adair 2002) was very timely to assisting a 'mixing' approach to the 'lifting' challenge. Adair's focus on the simplicity of the three-circles model has generated a perception that Functional Leadership is intended for young leaders. Adair had largely left it to Functional Leadership practitioners to describe its application at the organisational level.

Because Functional Leadership practitioners seldom publish, the field on leadership application at the chief executive level was left unattended by Functional Leadership ideas in Australian tertiary leadership education. MBA percepts filled the field. For example, Bass' frontline leadership descriptions (e.g., a persuasive style), presented in the sixties (Bass 1960) have 'lifted' in the language used to describe these notions (to 'transformational' in the example) (Bass 1997): this language is higher level because it relates to organisational or cultural change, the ultimate in persuasive leadership. Until recently, Dr Adair has not matched this reinvention of his work that the ideas of Bass have achieved. Adair's ideas were not competing with those of the organisational theorists at the level of the total organisation. More is hoped to come from Adair at this level in the near future.

A principal example of how these developments have acted to displace Adair's ideas has been with one of Adair's most fervent clients, the well credentialed leadership schools of the Australian Army.

Australian Army leadership model

The Australian Army was provided with a 'pure' Functional Leadership alternative for serving the development needs of its senior leaders (McMahon 1999). The alternative was an elaboration of the 'Power Factors in Functional Leadership' concept set out later in this chapter at Figure 10.5.

In lieu of a continuation of a pure Functional Leadership approach, however, the Australian Army adopted a mixture of Adair 'Group' and

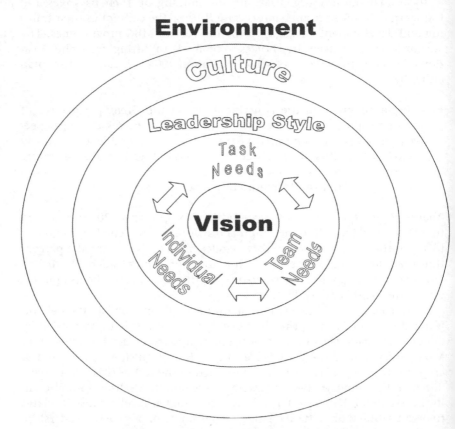

Figure 10.2 The Australian Army leadership model for senior officers
Source: Australian Army (2002).

mainstream 'organisational' ideas in order to meet the doctrinal needs regarding leadership for its most senior leaders.

What happened with the rewrite of leadership doctrine in this organisational training programme may be instructive of what will be the outcome in Australia as the group and organisational perspectives come together in leader development programmes in this country.

Firstly, the need to train armies and other organisations in leadership and management, in very quick time, in East Timor, in Afghanistan and in Iraq, kept the three-circles model in Army leadership doctrine. What the Australian Army did do was to include an additional model into doctrine for use by senior army officers. It is set out in Figure 10.2.

Functional Leadership remains at the core, but the importance of 'Vision' is placed at the intersection of the three circles of Adair's model. 'Vision' has long been identified by Functional Leadership practitioners in Australia as one of at least five factors that impact on all three circles at once and directly – the others are integrity, communications, idea generation and success (McMahon 1993). These power factors are discussed later. (Power factors such as 'Vision' are to be contrasted with, say, team building, career guidance or task definition factors, that impact directly on one of the circles only – team, individual and task circles respectively).

'Vision' is at the core of transformational leadership concepts as well. The point is that this element of the Army Model, taken from the transformational leadership literature, has not distanced the Model from Functional Leadership ideas.

Similarly, this additional Army Leadership Model has surrounded Adair's three circles at the outer perimeter by the organisational perspectives of culture and environment. Adair has stated that this is the most often recommended amendment to his model, and he has welcomed others adjusting the model to suit their needs.

What is not Functional Leadership in the model is the circle on Style, and the loss, in the graphics, of the overlap in the three circles.

The choice of 'Style' included into the Army doctrine is also close to the notions of Adair. Adair's distinction between 'Style' and 'Decision-making' was described in the text of the first publications of the new Army Model, but its explanation is disappearing from presentations of the Model in Army schools. Adair argues that Style is a combination of 'Personality' and 'Decision-making', and that practitioners of the style approach to leadership err when they try to adjust their style by changing their personality. Adair advises that leaders need only to adjust the way decisions are made.

The use of 'Style' instead of 'Decision-making' in the graphics was an attempt to be inclusive of a popular strain of leadership ideas in Australia. As fortune would have it, the most popular 'Style' model in Australia, that derived by Hersey and Blanchard, uses *decision-making* terminology to guide its practitioners to leader action anyway. Thus while the designer of the additional Army Leadership Model mixed to the Adair Model the trans-formational ideas of 'Vision', 'Culture' and 'Environment', and added the popular model on Commander 'Style', the mixed approach did not move very far from accepted Functional Leadership concepts. This need not have been the case, however.

It was the loss in the additional Model of the overlap in the three circles in the continuing Adair Model that caused 'the storm' in negotiating the acceptance of the new Army Model (McMahon 1999). The continuing presence of the three-circles model on the next page of the doctrine publication, *Leadership*, ensures that the significance of the overlap is understood, and that the 'Task' word and circle is kept on top of the other two circles when the task-team-individual analysis is used with either Model.

On balance, the total package of leadership modelling might be close to what Adair might have expected when he left it to practitioners to construct their own versions. The critique of the Adair Model is that the applications of the model for the Executive Managers of large organisations, which Adair addresses in his famous workshops for Chief Executives, need to be placed into his texts if his essential ideas are not to be subsumed by less instructive leadership models that do have the advantage of descriptions that cover all levels of leadership.

The advantages of Functional Leadership in practice

Functional Leadership is task oriented

The realisation that Functional Leadership is task oriented has been important in practical applications of the Functional Leadership concepts to business in Australia. This realisation, when accepted by the manager, becomes a force for integration of efforts at all levels to bring success to the organisation.

The task circle is on top of the three circles, but not by accident. This is not to say that people, both as individuals and as teams, are not essential to success in the task, but

- In Functional Leadership, teams are defined by the task, the objective, the goal, the purpose, or the mission that they share. Which word is used, 'task', 'goal' or 'mission', depends on the level of the organisation at which the team under attention operates;
- In Functional Leadership, McGregor's Theory Y dominates – leaders believe that people actively seek work and success in their work. The group, not just the leader or the organisation, are naturally motivated towards achieving success in the 'task', 'goal' or 'mission';
- In Functional Leadership, the perceptions of individuals and teams regarding what are the priority needs in the task, team and individual circles is all directed at achieving success in the task;

- In Functional Leadership, leaders gain followers and goodwill through achieving the task – the interdependence of success in the three overlapping circles simply explains that this achievement in the task circle will not be maximised without maximum success in the team and individual circles as well.

These notions rendered Functional Leadership well suited to supporting managers under the MBO regime which was popular in Australia in the sixties and seventies. MFO is a revisit to the core of the MBO approach.

Functional Leadership readies professionals for leadership quickly

A second advantage with Functional Leadership is that it provides guidance that a practitioner can start to use 'next Monday'.

Step back, make observations of needs in all three circles, prioritise those needs and conduct actions – plans, briefs, controls, support, communications and reviews – is a set of leader actions that can be started now. These are also readily amenable to effective training methods. This set of leader actions can be undertaken by a manager irrespective of the qualities, style, internal leader motivation, Myers-Briggs profiling, gender, cultural background, etc., of the manager. It is action centred – the leader needs only to act.

The simplicity of the Functional Leadership concept and the associated leadership training regime has proven particularly useful in the project management environment. Here, tasks are new and evolving, teams are formed and reformed progressively and quickly. The expert professional typically obtains her or his first leader task as a project leader, before any organisational position as a frontline manager arises.

Functional Leadership in fact proved complementary to normal project management training, which tended to focus on task and team issues and largely ignored individual needs. Project Management Forum, formed in Australia in the early 1970s, devoted its first years to overcoming the individual needs deficiencies with the implementation of project management structures within organisations. Functional Leadership, when applied with Project Management training packages, met the need by giving Project Managers a model that focused them on people as teams and people as individuals.

The Functional Leadership culture

Functional Leadership includes a leadership culture for its adherents that enables them to accommodate the various waves of management ideas without becoming immersed in those ideas. This is a third advantage to the Functional Leadership practitioner in evaluating new management paradigms and in working within such paradigms in ways that remain successful.

While the 'visibility' of a Functional Leadership practitioner is essentially action, the rationale behind the actions taken includes some strong beliefs, norms, attitudes and assumptions about the leader role.

For instance:

Intent: The Functional Leadership practitioner is intent on meeting priority needs from all three circles, irrespective of the management wave of ideas at hand – this intent helps the successful implementation of the latest 'wave'.

Norms: Leadership is a shared activity – the Functional Leader is responsible for the task, team and individuals, but doesn't have to meet the associated needs herself or himself – so maximum inputs are gathered from all participants capable of contributing to the needs of any of the three circles in efforts to succeed under the management culture in place.

Beliefs: The group and the individuals want to be successful at the task – they will exhibit Theory Y behaviour if given this opportunity – so the Functional Leadership practitioner supports such opportunities. As a result, more often than not, Functional Leadership managers themselves become inspired by what their team members achieve in implementing an organisational strategy, system, programme or plan.

Attitudes: The Functional Leadership adherent has a continuing interest in identifying needs and making observations. This demonstration of interest in the work becomes infectious amongst his or her followers and these positive behaviours drive the incorporation of innovations into existing management systems with greater effect.

Assumptions: The Functional Leadership professional continually acts as though success in the three circles of needs is interdependent – the implications of failure in any one circle is understood for the effect on the other two circles. Any deficiencies in this regard in a new management wave sweeping through an industry of organisation is overcome by the Functional Leader's overriding vision as to what **in total** has to be done.

The separation of the people factor into team and individual circles

This fourth advantage brings depth and breadth to the way Functional Leadership practitioners scope their management roles.

The management of the significant changes that have occurred in Australian private and public sector organisations has demonstrated how differently people respond to change. There can be a difficulty in defining a team position at any moment during the grieving and denial that accompany significant change.

For example, vital to effecting change is the communication plan that is implemented at each level of the organisation. Design and timing of communications are crucial facets of leadership. Critical to this design and timing is the choice of one-on-one communications versus group communications. The Functional Leadership circles impose a practical discipline upon its practitioners forever to observe and consider both the individual and also the team needs for receiving and discussing information from the organisation and for providing feelings, reactions, views, ideas and feedback back to the organisation.

TQM was a wave through Australian industry and organisations that was met with both success and failure in the eighties. The determinant of that success, it was quickly recognised, was the change management programme that accompanied the implementation of TQM. Leadership strategies dominated these efforts. Functional Leadership, with its two 'people' perspectives, as the team and as the individual, had a particular advantage for managers in responding to the 'people' needs.

The focus on needs

When the tide turned in the nineties to Strategic Management ideas in Australia, the category most commonly used in analysing customers, users, stakeholders, regulators, and other target groups for strategic assessment was their 'needs'. Needs, for Functional Leaders or managers, became the parameter for analysis of both the external environment and also the internal situation to which they were expected to respond.

This orientation had been established a decade earlier with the emphasis on customer needs that accompanied TQM and even Project Management, including the useful concept of internal and external customers. With Strategic Management, however, the universal application of the needs parameter was established. Figure 10.3 was a useful picture for organisations in understanding the roles of needs analyses in the management of their total environment.

Needs, the identification of them, the prioritisation of those needs, balancing needs, distinguishing needs from wants, the hierarchy of needs (within organisations rather than within individuals), the separation of causes and symptoms – these Functional Leadership notions were now extended from leadership of organisations to leadership of markets and industries and community programmes.

Needs became a central part of a common language within an organisation, with which supervisors, managers, executives and directors could communicate about both internal and external organisational requirements with great advantage. In this environment, the Functional Leadership adherents were legitimate in thinking that the world had caught up with them.

The development of tools for observation and prioritisation of needs

Practice of Functional Leadership in Australia has developed its own and adapted and adopted the ideas of others so as to improve abilities in the observation and prioritisation of group needs.

Regarding observation techniques:

- Instruments have been developed for the identification by survey of needs in groups and organisations during times of significant change [case studies of the results of such instruments are given later in this text – see also McMahon (1994)].

- Instruments have also been developed for identifying the natural preferences or tendencies of individual managers for operating in the task, team and/or individual needs circles (e.g., McMahon 2002).
- Grief cycles (such as shock-withdrawal-reaction-acceptance-exploration-adoption) have been widely used in mapping progress through needs cycles during the processes of change (see Figure 10.4).

Regarding techniques for the prioritisation of needs:

- The power of those factors capable of impacting directly on all three circles of needs, namely the factors of vision, integrity, communication, idea generation and success, has been acknowledged (see Figure 10.5).
- The hierarchy of needs for the organisation, namely of Survival before Stability before Growth before Significance, (a kind of Organisational

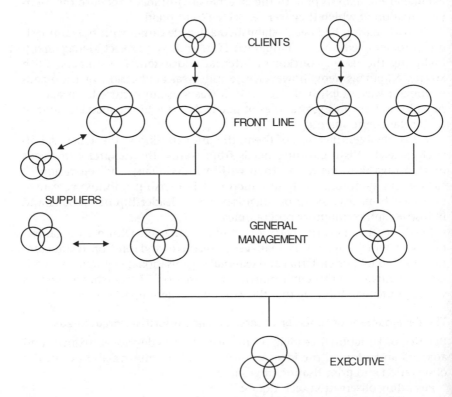

Figure 10.3 A needs analysis for an organisation and its external stakeholders
Source: McMahon, 1996.

version of Maslow's Hierarchy) has also assisted in needs analyses for organisations (see Figure 10.6).

- The priority of cause over effect, as with, say,
  ○ objectives over roles, systems and relationships, then of
  ○ roles over systems and relationships, then of
  ○ systems over relationships has also been used extensively (see Figure 10.7).

Thus when the leader scans their task, team and individuals for what is needed to improve outcomes, the leader is guided by notions such as those

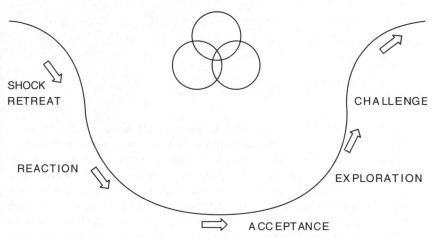

Figure 10.4 The grief cycle during change
Source: McMahon (1995), drawing on CTri (1995).

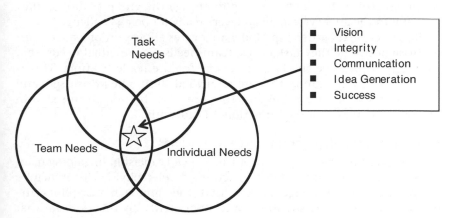

Figure 10.5 Power factors in Adair's leadership model
Source: McMahon 1993.

A HIERARCHY OF ORGANISATIONAL NEEDS

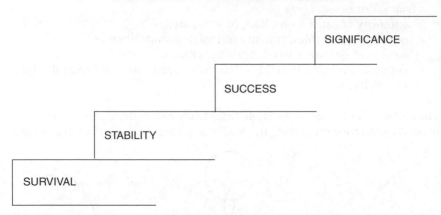

Figure 10.6   A hierarchy of organisational needs
Source: G. McMahon 1993 [Adapted from MBC Rosalie 1991].

in Figures 10.4, 10.5, 10.6 and 10.7 to identify those needs deserving of priority of effort. If the needs identified arise from lack of career structure, poor communications and poor task planning, communications is the power factor and should be given priority attention by the leader. If a group is facing issues of survival, a survival strategy will take precedence over efforts to introduce a new Recognition of Excellence scheme. If roles of a new team are unclear, priority of focus on defining and clarifying roles will solve more conflict than engaging in conflict resolution exercises with the loudest of the office disputes. If the bulk of a group are still *reacting* to a major change in the workplace, then the need now is to progress them to *acceptance*; this is better than trying to engage the group as though they were not in the grief cycle at all and were ready for being challenged.

The Functional Leadership Model advocates allocation of leader effort to those needs, be they task needs, team needs or individual needs, that are likely to provide the largest benefit for the leader's effort. This is why the needs in a group that are identified should be prioritised, and why Figures 10.4, 10.5, 10.6 and 10.7 are most helpful to this step in the practical application of Functional Leadership.

Functional Leadership works from First Principles

As a last point on the practicality of Functional Leadership in guiding managers to successful leader actions, Functional Leadership is a First Principles technique. The advantage here is that the approach disciplines the manager to treat every situation on its own merits. By this is meant that the method comes up with an action plan for the leader specially derived for the unique situation faced by each leader of each team at each moment

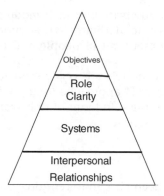

The Relative Populations of Issues within Teams

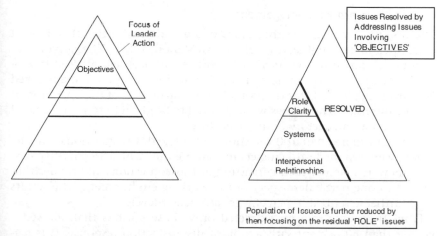

Figure 10.7 The priorities for leader action in dealing with team needs
Source: McMahon (1993), drawing from Reserve Command and Staff College LWD-02 (1991).

in time. The three circles needs analysis, flowing to a planning, initiating, controlling, supporting, informing, and evaluating action plan, offers the manager this approach reflecting closely the circumstances demanding the leader's attention.

Another popular approach in Australia, the Hersey & Blanchard model (Hersey and Blanchard 1996), shares this 'first principles' advantage based on a 'readiness' parameter (at least as it is commonly applied in Australia).

Other models in practice tend to be 'wisdom' models. Wisdom models of leadership are derived from laudable solutions to an impressive number of historic circumstances faced by other leaders and teams – it is very wise to give the example, possess the quality, and/or demonstrate the discipline or habit advocated by such models, and it would be very unwise not to reflect these attributes. These models, though, have not been honed for the present set of people and purposes faced by each particular practitioner.

Nonetheless, wisdom models are very useful for developing a deeper understanding of the needs approach. Asking why any leader has succeeded, and then explaining it in terms of task, team and individual needs, can be a very profitable exercise.

Case studies

Two case studies have been chosen to reinforce observations made in this chapter about the direction that can be gained from analysis of situations using the Functional Leadership model.

Case study in project management

The case history concerns the results of a questionnaire completed by all personnel in an engineering office (McMahon 1986). The survey was conducted some three years after the office had been reorganised from a discipline oriented to a project oriented structure. The questionnaire asked employees at all levels for their opinions on all aspects of the operation of the organisation. The replies were required to be given in terms that rated each aspect as satisfactory or unsatisfactory.

Although more than 100 questions were asked, the questions and the replies were grouped into clusters in framing the results. Twenty-five (25) clusters were formed, each consisting of those questions and replies that related to one particular aspect of the working environment. The results were further described in percentage satisfaction levels.

From these results were extracted only those clusters that showed a greater than 60 percent satisfaction or dissatisfaction response. It is reasoned that 60 percent or higher is a significant majority opinion. The high response clusters are listed in Table 10.1. The significant clusters are given a unique identifier, e.g., a number, before plotting.

Applying Adair's model and its definitions to the results of the survey, each of the clusters obtaining a significant response was assessed as to which area of the functional model the response highlighted.

Figure 10.8 is a plot, on Adair's three-circle model, of those responses demonstrating a significant level of satisfaction in the minds of the staff. The location of each plot is only significant as to within which circle or circles it has been drawn.

Figure 10.9 repeats this exercise for the responses which showed that the staff was decidedly dissatisfied.

In rifle shooting parlance, the points in Figure 10.9 have a good grouping. Clearly the results of this analysis suggest that the thinking of man-

Table 10.1 Clusters scoring significant levels of response

60% Satisfaction	60% Dissatisfaction
2. Cohesion and Conflict (within the team)	1. Career Guidance and Planning
3. Goals (of the office and the team)	6. Job Variety
4. Information and Communication re technical matters	7. Management Concern for Staff
5. Involvement (of the members of the team in their work)	8. Supervisors Positive Feedback (recognition of good work)
9. Supervision (the supervisors willingness and ability to help)	11. The Promotion System and Incentives
10. Supervisors Concern (for the task and for people)	14. Training and Professional Development
12. Supervisors Support and Empathy	
13. Work Relations (among members of the team)	

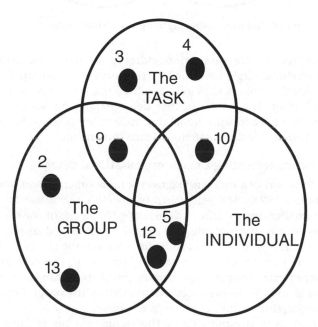

Figure 10.8 Plot of clusters enjoying high satisfaction levels

agers of the office surveyed are not sufficiently directed to satisfying individual needs. In this case we can see that the tools and skills encouraged by the Project Management Technique can serve to reinforce an emphasis on the task and group oriented aspects of the total management function. The

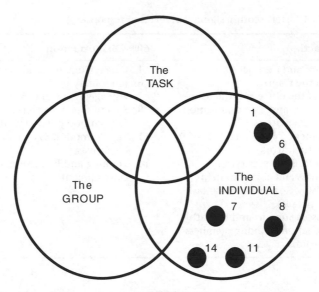

Figure 10.9   Plot of clusters showing high dissatisfaction levels

results prompted the organisation to address and review not just the items from the individual circle identified by the survey, but all aspects of managing individuals – that is the circle in which the leadership of the organisation was failing. The results further demonstrate the power of analysis that comes from a leadership model that treats the people factor with both a team dimension and a separate individual dimension.

Case study in implementing a major organisational change

This case study was of a merger (takeover) of one organisation into a larger one (McMahon 1994). The leadership perspective taken was for that of a part of the smaller organisation. In this case, the needs of the organisation under analysis were assessed one year after the merger and, again, two years after the merger. Figure 10.10 sets out the results of the needs analysis after 12 months of operations in the new environment. In this case the pattern is not evident from a simple inspection of the plots within the three circles of the Adair model. So it was necessary to identify the natures of the issues that were registering a significant needs response.

The pattern from the plotting of the significant needs indicated that there were strengths and weaknesses across all three circles. There were, however, twice as many low satisfaction needs as high satisfaction needs. Closer inspection of the nature of the issues revealed that half of the low satisfaction needs were to do with some aspect of planning within the new merged organisation.

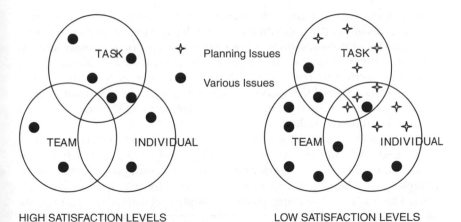

HIGH SATISFACTION LEVELS   LOW SATISFACTION LEVELS

Figure 10.10   The results of the needs analysis after one year into the merger

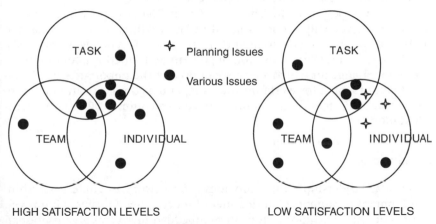

HIGH SATISFACTION LEVELS   LOW SATISFACTION LEVELS

Figure 10.11   The results of the needs analysis after two years into the merger

While frontline managers were supported in dealing with the particular issues impacting on the successful leadership of their teams and groups, issues relating to planning were identified as the priority need for action by the executive of the affected units. Figure 10.11 represents the results of the needs analysis undertaken on the next annual leadership assessment.

The priority of action by the executive management team for improving planning issues has seen a 70 percent reduction in the number of low satisfaction needs concerning planning issues. Overall, there has been a halving of total low satisfaction plots, reflecting the efforts of both the executive at their level and frontline (and senior) managers at their levels to focus on the low satisfaction needs identified by the previous needs analysis.

The pattern of needs after two years shows that 75 percent of low satisfaction needs are in the individual needs circle. The executive management team, for the next year, switched their priority attention to a more general focus on individual needs, supporting leader actions by the line managers rather than actioning their own initiatives. This decision to support the line managers reflected the success of line managers in achieving high satisfaction outcomes in the important overlap area between the task needs and the individual needs circles.

The case study demonstrates the ways in which the leadership instrument based on Adair's Functional Leadership model can guide each level of management within an organisation to priority action programmes or initiatives appropriate to the responsibilities held by that level of management. The leadership instrument can be applied at different stages during the progression of the change, identifying, say, where different groups are at in the grief cycle. This can signal the time for a change in response by the leader so as to move the group further along the progression of states of group morale that accompanies all changes.

Further, the power of the Theory of Group Needs upon which Adair's Functional Leadership model is based (Adair 1970) is the ability that an analysis of needs can have to predict, in advance of a change, what needs are likely to occur. Corporatisation of government functions, for example, is a major change for which a leader can predict the importance of a business plan, of a plan for workforce training, and a communication plan to leading such a group from a public service to a commercial environment (McMahon 1992).

Conclusions

Functional Leadership clearly provides a framework to guide leadership development in support of all manner of more general business improvement processes. The approach is now embedded in several organisational contexts in Australia.

Training institutions in Australia running Functional Leadership-based training and development programmes, to the author's knowledge, include the University of Queensland, the Australian Institute of Management, The Cyber Institute and the Leadership Academy.

Organisations with in-house training and development programmes that are strong in their attention to Functional Leadership include Customs, the Defence Forces, the Games Workshop and Roche. Recent programmes for companies with over 100 participants include Western Mining Corporation, the University of Queensland's workshop for Chief Executive Officers, and Centrelink in Australia, and PT Freeport, Kelian Equatorial Mining and PT Telkom in Indonesia.

Of special interest are the performances of the Functional Leadership Model as a basis for developing leaders and for training people to leadership abilities. One aspect of the separate training workshops for Senior Managers and for First Line Managers conducted by the University of Queensland has been its success in attracting women to the programme. When the programme started in 1993, the University gave away two free places to ensure that women were represented on the programme. In 2004, women made up 60 percent of the participants. Other training successes have been in preparing civil engineering undergraduates for their rapid elevation to supervisory roles after graduation, and in the rapid development of leaders for new armed services and police forces in countries for which the Australian Army is providing assistance in nation-building.

References

Adair, J. (1970) *Training for Leadership – A Tutor's Manual*, London: BACIE.

Adair, J. (2002) *Effective Strategic Leadership*, London: Macmillan.

Australian Army (1973) *Leadership Theory and Practice*, Canberra: Department of Defence.

Australian Army (2002) *Leadership*, Land Warfare Doctrine LWD 0-2, Canberra: Department of Defence.

Bass, B.M. (1960) *Leadership, Psychology and Organisational Behaviour*, New York: Harper & Row.

Bass, B.M. (1997) 'Does the Transactional-Transformational Leadership Paradigm Transcend Organisational and National Boundaries?', *American Psychologist*, 52(2), 130–9.

CTri (1995) *Management of Change*, Workshop delivered to Queensland Department of Primary Industries, Brisbane.

Faculty of Engineering (1992) *Master of Technology Management*, Internal Paper: University of Queensland.

Hersey P. and Blanchard, K.H. (1996) *Management of Organisational Behaviour: Utilizing Human Resources*, 7th edn, New Jersey: Prentice Hall.

Karpin, D.S. (1995) *Enterprising Nation*, Industry Task Force on Leadership and Management Skills, Canberra.

MBC Rosalie (1991) *Leadership Training*, Presentation to Parents, Brisbane.

McMahon, G.M. (1986) *Project Management and the Total Management Function*, Engineering Conference, I.E. Aust., Adelaide.

McMahon, G.M. (1992) Chair: *Report of the Task Force on Commercialisation*, Institution of Engineers Australia, Brisbane.

McMahon, G.M. (1993) *The Transition to Manager*, Functional Leadership Workshop for First Time and First Line Managers, University of Queensland.

McMahon, G.M. (1994) *Leadership Shown in Organisations Undergoing Significant Change*, International Conference on Engineering Management, SEMA/IEAust Melbourne.

McMahon, G.M. (1995) *General Management and the Management of Change*: Functional Leadership Workshop for Senior and Middle Managers, University of Queensland.

McMahon, G.M. (1996) *Developing Leaders in your Organisation*, Functional Leadership Workshop for CEOs, Directors, Chairpersons, University of Queensland.

McMahon, G.M. (1999) *Comments and Feedback: The Army Leadership Model*, Land Warfare Centre, Canungra.

McMahon, G.M. (2002) *Leader Action Preferences for Chief Executives and Executive Managers*, Instrument, GM McMahon Consultants.

McMahon, G.M. (2004) *Corporate Strategy*, e-Learning training package, Australian Institute of Management, Brisbane.

McMahon, G.M. (2005) *The Experienced Project Manager*, Brisbane: Australian Institute of Management.

McMahon, G.M. and Apelt, C.J. (1994) *Training Programs in Engineering Management Based on the Functional Leadership Concept*, ENGCON 94, IEAust Melbourne.

Milton, C.R. Entrekin, L. and Stening, B.W. (1984) *Organizational Behaviour in Australia*, London: Prentice-Hall.

Reserve Command and Staff College (1991) *Conflict Resolution*, Presentation to Intermediate Operations Course, Brisbane.

Rutherford, P. (2004) 'Leadership for the 21st Century', *Australian Project Manager*, 24(2), June.

11
The Application of Action-Centred Leadership (ACL) in Hong Kong

Wai-ming Mak

Introduction

In this chapter, I would like to report how I apply Action-Centred Leadership (ACL) in Hong Kong and take this opportunity to thank Dr John Adair for his practical and useful concepts on leadership. I shall make use of Checkland's (1985) Framework, Methodology and Application (FMA) Model to link theory and practice together. In the framework section, I shall explain the development of ACL, The Three-Circle Model, The Leader's Checklist, The Fifty/Fifty Rule, The Hour-Glass Model, Needs and Motivation, Use of Time, Creativity at Work and The Short Course on Leadership. I shall describe how I present the ideas to the course participants in Hong Kong. This is followed by a methodology section, in which I explain the training methods used in ACL. I shall compare it with action learning and the Chinese philosophy on leadership. The use of cue cards and Leadership Observation Sheet, the role of observer and course tutor and the reflection on cards game, magazines, the jigsaw puzzle, the letterpoint, the mast contract, campus orienteering and Toxic. In the application section, I shall discuss how I use ACL with both university students and business executives. In addition, I shall describe how I put the framework into practice, among private, public and non-profit organisations through consultancy services. I shall also make use of the Course Evaluation Form to report the feedback from the participants.

In the conclusion, I would like to explain The Hour-Glass Model, with special reference to the concepts of learning skills and time management. I shall explain how to integrate the Chinese philosophy on leadership in ACL. I shall also explain how the World Scout Bureau introduce ACL in the Asia Pacific Region. Finally, I shall propose and discuss a way forward for leadership development.

John Adair

John Adair was educated at St Paul's School, London, and studied at Trinity Hall, Cambridge. He holds the degrees of MA from Cambridge, MLitt from Oxford, and PhD from London. He is also a Fellow of the Royal Historical Society.

He did his national service in the Scots Guards, and served as adjutant in a Bedouin Regiment of the Arab Legion at the age of 20. He worked as a deckhand on an Arctic trawler and as an orderly in a hospital operating theatre. After Cambridge in 1961, he became Senior Lecturer in Military History and Leadership Training Adviser (1963 to 1968) at the Royal Military Academy, Sandhurst; then Director of Studies at St George's House, Windsor Castle; and an Associate Director of The Industrial Society. He has also been a Visiting Fellow at the Oxford Centre for Management Studies (now Templeton College, Oxford). Later, he became the world's first Professor in Leadership Studies at the University of Surrey (1979 to 1983). He also helped to establish Europe's first Centre for Leadership Studies at the University of Exeter. He now works as an international management consultant in leadership and management development. Kennedy (1991) praises John Adair as a pioneering British thinker in the theory and practice of leadership. And van Maurik (2001) comments, 'In the UK, his [John Adair's] reputation has largely been carved out through his works on leadership'.

My experience with ACL

I came across John Adair's Action-Centred Leadership in the early eighties. I bought the book *Effective Leadership* (Adair 1983) published by Pan Books and was attracted by the cartoon of the black sheep and the white sheep on the cover. At the time I was a member of the Regional Training Team of the Hong Kong Island Region, one of the five Regions of the Scout Association of Hong Kong. The then Regional Training Commissioner, Mr S.K. Wong, decided to improve the quality of training in the Region. With the assistance of the Training Adviser, Mr T.C. Lai, the then Training Manager of the Royal Hong Kong Jockey Club, developed 'The Tree Model' on the skills of effective trainers. Mak (1991) presents the Tree Model, including transactional analysis as the root, Action-Centred Leadership (ACL) and team building as the trunk, and effective chairmanship, time management, planning and control as well as problem solving and decision-making as the branches. I had the opportunities to attend or assist all of the above training courses.

In November 1985, the Hong Kong Island Region conducted the first Action-Centred Leadership Course and I assisted as Course Tutor. Mr J. Hui, the Course Leader and the then Vice-Principal of the Police Training School in Hong Kong, introduced the ACL Course in Hong

Kong, after he spent one year on secondment to The Police Staff College at Bramshill in UK. He attended the train-the-trainer workshop conducted by John Adair and our Course Team modified *Training for Leadership: A Tutor's Manual* (Adair 1984a) to suit its application in Hong Kong. Subsequently, the Hong Kong Island Region conducted four more ACL Courses in April 1986, July 1990, March 1991 and December 1991. I was involved in all of them as Course Staff and developed my knowledge in ACL through practice.

From 1988 to 1989, I studied management learning at Lancaster University. In the class discussion, I mentioned my interest in ACL. My classmate, Mr Clive Peacock, a former colleague of John Adair, suggested that I conduct an interview with John. Before I returned to Hong Kong in 1989, I visited John and had a lunch meeting with him at his home in Pewley Hill, Guildford.

During the meeting, I asked John why he did not join the three overlapping circles together and form one large circle. He said he did not think of it in that way because he wanted people to remember the three circles and not just one large circle. He explained the Hour-Glass Model to me and said that he might add two more skills to it. In addition to Communication Skills, Problem Solving and Decision-Making Skills and Leadership Skills, he said he might add Time Management and Learning Skills. He asked me about the Chinese concept of time management and I replied that it was similar to relativity. If you live seven days in the mountain, several thousand years might already have passed in the world. I described how the Scout Association of Hong Kong used his ACL model. Moreover, I asked him whether I could conduct ACL in Hong Kong and receive recognition from him. He said, 'You just follow the instruction in the training manual (Adair 1984a) and there is no need to have my recognition.'[1] I was empowered by his encouragement and decided to conduct ACL courses in Hong Kong. In view of my keen interest in ACL, John invited me to attend a half-day workshop on 'Developing Effective Leaders' that he was going to conduct in Churchill College, Cambridge. I was most happy to accept because I could experience how he facilitated the learning of senior managers on leadership development.

On 20 October 1989, I attended John's workshop at Churchill College, Cambridge. He challenged the participants to define management. It was a simple question, but the answer was not easy. And then, John wrote down GTDTOP on the whiteboard and he defined management as 'Getting Things Done Through Other People'. To take it a step further, he defined leadership as 'Getting Things Done Through Other People, Willingly'. Subsequently, he explained the Three-Circle Model and discussed its application in the business world. After the workshop, I returned to Hong Kong and joined the Hong Kong Polytechnic, now The Hong Kong Polytechnic University, on 23 October 1989.

The FMA model

Adair (1968) states that theory and practice should mutually interact with each other and there should be a dialogue between what is learnt as theory and what is undergone as practical experience. The two principles are: the relation of theory to practice should begin during the formal syllabus and the methods of education employed should be appropriate to the aims of the course.

In the same vein, Checkland (1985) argues that neither theory nor practice is primary in management science because theory leads to practice, which subsequently generates new theory. Checkland advances the FMA Model thus, 'We have some linked ideas in a Framework (F), a way of applying these ideas in the Methodology (M) and an Application area (A)'. In this chapter, the Framework is the Three-Circle Model, the Application is in Hong Kong and the Methodology is the training method used in Action-Centred Leadership. According to Checkland, through the reflection of the Methodology, we could improve the Framework, the Application as well as the Methodology. As Kurt Lewin said, 'There is nothing quite so practical as a good theory'. In fact, only bad theory is not practical. Instead of searching for useful knowledge, we should also look for usable knowledge, that is, knowledge that is applicable in the real world. Argyris (1993) defines it as actionable knowledge or knowledge in action.

The framework

According to Checkland (1985), a framework is 'a basic set of ideas'. In this chapter, the framework is leadership, with special reference to ACL advances by John Adair. Potter and Hooper (2005) conclude, 'Leadership is one of the most researched yet least understood aspects of human behavior'. Back in the nineties, Kets de Vries (1995) said, 'In the area of leadership, it seems that more and more has been studied about less and less'. There are numerous researches in leadership but most of them are too academic or too theoretical to be applied in the real world. Adair (1968) describes the drawback and the positive contribution of the qualities and situational approaches and advances the functional approach. While the qualities approach focuses on 'What a leader is?' and the situational approach concentrates on 'What a leader knows?' the functional approach concentrates on 'What a leader does?'. The psychologists would focus on personalities of leaders but it is difficult, if not impossible, to change the personalities of participants within a short time given the duration of a training course. Even if we can teach participants what they should do as leaders, how to put theory into practice would be another difficulty. The functional approach just reminds participants to model their behaviours as effective leaders, for example, check resources, prepare time budget, appoint a deputy and say thank you. It is easy to understand and simple to use.

The Three-Circle Model

Adair (1973b) describes 'The Three-Circle Model': task needs, group maintenance needs and individual needs. The three areas of need influence each
other for better or worse. In order for the needs in these areas to be met in
any group or organisation certain functions, that is, the responsibility of
leadership, have to be performed. The difference between 'task' and 'team
maintenance' is always in danger of falling into a dichotomy. The value of
the three overlapping circles is that they emphasise the essential unity
of leadership: a single action can be multi-functional in that it touches all
three areas. Adair (1997) states that 'leadership is essentially an other-
centred activity – not a self-centred one'. Instead of focusing on what a
leader should do to achieve the task, John Adair suggests focusing on how
a leader should satisfy the needs of the team members and the team, with a
view to achieving the task.

If one of the three circles is neglected, it would affect the performance of
the other two. In fact, all three circles should be closely linked together.
And it is the function of leadership to satisfy the three different needs. In
addition to the three circles, Adair (1997) describes the eight functions,
namely, defining the task, planning, briefing, controlling, evaluating, motivating, organising and providing an example. The success of a leader
depends on how he or she put the three circles and eight functions into
action.

The Leader's Checklist

At the end of the session on the Leader's Checklist, the Course Tutor
would give participants two cue cards and say, 'These two cue cards are
the symbols that you have attended an ACL Course. Like the American
Express Card, do not leave home without them. You can use them
during the course and after you return to your workplace'. The first card
is The Three-Circle Model and The Leader's Checklist; the second one is
The Three-Circle Model and The Ten Points for Leadership Action. The
participants can use the two cue cards as memory aids for a behavioural
checklist as effective leaders. The cards create a huge impact on the participants and some of them do not believe that they can keep the cards
for references. They are encouraged to use them during and after the
training course. The Leader's Checklist describes the five actions of a
leader: define objectives, plan, brief, support/monitor and evaluate. And
when leaders take each action, they are reminded to link the three
circles: the task, the team and the individual together. The assigned
observer can also use them when they observe the leader's behaviours.
The Leader's Checklist we adopted from John Adair is listed in
Table 11.1.

Table 11.1   The Leader's Checklist

	Task	Team	Individual
Define Objectives	Specify task Identify constraints	Involve team Share commitment	Clarify objectives Gain acceptance
Plan	Consider options Establish priorities Check resources Set standards Decide	Consult Invite action Develop suggestions Structure	Encourage ideas Assess skills Set targets Allocate jobs Delegate
Brief	Describe plan Check understanding	Explain decisions Obtain feedback Answer questions	Listen Enthuse
Support/Monitor	Report progress Maintain standards	Coordinate Resolve conflicts Recognise efforts	Advise Assist/reassure Counsel/ discipline
Evaluate	Summarise progress Review objectives Replan if necessary	Learn from mistakes Give praises	Review performance Offer guidance Provide training

Needs and motivation

There is a precourse assignment for the participants. They have to complete a 'Needs and Motivation' form. They are required to rank the importance of various motivational factors for both themselves and one of their subordinates. In this assignment, most participants respond that leaders need 'Recognition' while members need 'Salary'. As a result, it seems that salary is the only means to motivate people. But it is not the case. The important message is that whether one is a leader or a member, one is a human being. The needs should be similar, if not the same. If a leader needs 'Recognition', a member should need 'Recognition' too. Besides the 15 factors on the list, I add 'Personal Autonomy', making a total of 16 factors. It is because when Herzberg conducted his research in the early sixties, personal autonomy was not considered an important factor. However, in the year 2000, personal autonomy ranked high on the list.

The function of the leader is to motivate his team members to achieve the common task. The ACL Course explains McGregor's theory X and theory Y, Maslow's hierarchy of needs and Herzberg's hygiene-motivator theory. These three models are prevalent in many management textbooks. However, John explains the models with reference to applications.

Although there are other models on motivation, these three models are relatively easy to understand and apply.

Subsequently, Adair (1990) expounded 'The Fifty-Fifty Rule' in which he contended that half an individual's motivation comes from within himself or herself, the other half from external factors, including the leadership of his or her superior. Managers often complain of the poor performance of their subordinates; however, effective leaders realise they themselves are important motivational factors too.

Use of time

There is a 30-minute session on 'Use of Time' in the ACL Course. Instead of asking participants to complete a time log for the past two weeks, the course encourages participants to prepare a time budget and reserve some contingency time before the deadline. Moreover, it encourages participants to delegate some of their job to their subordinates by 'Appointing a Deputy'. In the Police Training School, Hong Kong, the tasks in the training might involve a dangerous operation. If the leader does not brief the members about the details, no one would know what to do if the leader was 'injured or killed'. Moreover, by appointing a deputy, the leader can step-back and have a better picture of the situation.

Creativity at work

Another 30-minute session in ACL is entitled 'Creativity at Work'. It starts with the nine-dot problem and brainstorming. After that, it carries on with two more creativity exercises. The main purpose is to encourage participants to think outside of the box. They should have the courage to ask the questions: 'Why?' and 'Why Not?', and they should not just take things for granted, doing whatever their predecessors were doing in the past. The reason is that what worked in the past might not work in the present, not to say the future.

The Hour-Glass Model

Adair (1983) devised an Hour-Glass Model to explain general management competences. In a recent personal communication, Adair pointed out to me that in Australia, this is regarded as his second most important model after The Three-Circle Model. From secondary education to senior management, a functional manager must possess analytical skills as a technical expert in order to go through a narrow neck of specialisation. After that, they must possess synthesis skills to be a general manager. They require leadership skills (Adair 1968), decision-making skills (Adair 1971) and communication skills (Adair 1973a).[2] From the perspective of Chinese philosophy, Liu (1984) questions whether leaders must act either as generalists or specialists. They must act, he argues, as the specialised-generalists; that is, their specialisation is that they are generalists.

During our meeting in 1989, John suggested that learning skills and time management are also important to the generalists too. Adair (1987) explains how to manage one's time. However, normally the Hour-Glass Model is not included in ACL. In Hong Kong, I explain it through a short session of 30 minutes.

A Short Course on Leadership

Adair (1983) introduces 'A Short Course on Leadership':

Six Most Important Words	'I admit I made a mistake'.
Five Most Important Words	'I am proud of you'.
Four Most Important Words	'What is your opinion?'
Three Most Important Words	'If you please ...'
Two Most Important Words	'Thank you'.
One Most Important Word	'We'.
One Least Most Important Word	'I'.

The words and phrases are simple but they have a huge impact on human relations. Adair (1997) reminds us of a Zulu proverb: 'I cannot hear what you are saying to me because you are shouting at me. As a leader, it is not just what you do to achieve the task. It is how one does it, including some friendly and encouraging sentences, that make the differences'. A few years ago, I explained this concept to a professor on the Chinese mainland and he subsequently, developed a similar model in Chinese. Recently, I add 'The Shortest Course on Leadership': the manager would say to their subordinates, 'Go!'; while the leader would say, 'Let's Go!' The former manages by word while the latter leads by action. We all know that 'action speaks louder than words'.

The methodology

Checkland (1985) explains methodology as, 'a process for applying those ideas in an organized way'. In this chapter, methodology is the training methods and activities used in ACL. In addition, the role of the course tutor and observer is also an essential feature of the ACL Course.

Action-Centred Leadership

To evaluate the training effectiveness of ACL, Adair (1973b) reports 'The ACL Course concentrates on the actions and awareness necessary to improve leadership performance'. ACL took shape at the Royal Military Academy, Sandhurst, between 1962 and 1964 as a part of an overall programme for developing the potential in officer cadets whose average age was 18 to 20 years. In 1964, when adopting it as their basic approach, the Royal Air Force called it Functional Leadership. Four years later, the Industrial Society entitled this approach Action-Centred Leadership. While Functional Leadership (FL) is used in the military services, Action-Centred Leadership (ACL) is widely used in business. According to John Adair, both terms are interchangeable.

In 1969 Edwin Smith in collaboration with John Adair wrote *The Action-Centred Leader Course Tutor's Manual*. It was translated from its military setting into a form which could be understood and used by industrial training managers in Britain and overseas. He joined The Industrial Society management advisory staff in 1967, specialising in management by objectives and leadership development. He was also the author of *The Manager as an Action-Centred Leader*, an Industrial Society booklet, published in 1971.

In October 1969, John Adair accepted an invitation to join the Industrial Society for one year in order to establish a small leadership department so that ACL training could be made much more widely available. By the end of 1970, over 5,000 managers and supervisors had already attended ACL in-company courses led by training managers who had been on the Society's one- or two-day 'Training for Action-Centred Leadership' courses.

Adair (1984a) explains that the ACL Course method emphasises observing and participating in practical leadership tasks. Formal lectures are kept to the minimum and all members of the course take part in the exercises, group discussion and case studies. At the same time, the handouts distributed to participants are also kept to a minimum.

Casey and Pearce (1977) report how Professor Reg Revans used 'action learning' sets to develop senior managers in the General Electric Company Limited, from March 1974 to May 1975. Kolb (1983) describes the Action-Observation-Reflection (A-O-R) Model, where Action is achieving the task, Observation is the feedback of observer, and Reflection is the role of the course tutor. In fact, back in the sixties, John Adair had already applied the action learning approach in leadership training.

Krouwel and Goodwill (1994) explain the emergence of outdoor management development and praise John Adair's use of a variety of exercises that contribute to this approach. John Adair's influence grew when his ideas were enthusiastically adopted and disseminated by the Industrial Society. In the use of the outdoors, John Adair's work was further developed in the early 1970s by many others, including programmes run at Brathay Hall for HP Bulmer & Co., a large producer of cider.

The role of course tutor

Adair (1984a) explains the role of course tutor as follows: 'To promote understanding of the concept of functional leadership and the practical implications of functional leadership within the member's own practical situation; To ensure that everyone participates and that tasks are fairly distributed and the lessons learnt at each session are relevant to the stated purpose of the session and that vital ones are not overlooked by stating the aim of each session at the start, and finally checking how well this has been achieved'. The course tutor is not only responsible for assessing the performance of the leader accurately, but also for ensuring that each observer is capable of recognising leadership functions in action. In ACL, the course tutors are reminded to encourage participants with positive reinforcement.

The observer

The Observer's Code stated in ACL is: be objective/specific; no long-winded stories; no sweeping statements; report what the leader did; if critical, suggest an alternative. The observers are required to observe the behaviours of the leader in satisfying the three needs: achieving the task, building the team and developing individuals. Based on the Leadership Observation Sheet provided by Adair (1968), observers report what the leader actually said and did during the process of achieving the task. For example, 'He did tell the team exactly what they were supposed to do,' is acceptable phrasing. However, 'he communicated well,' or, 'he is a good leader' are not. The observers are required to produce evidence and 'speak to the data'.

> Some of the questions suggested by the Course Manual are:
> Was the task achieved? If not, why not?
> Which of the functions should have applied here?
> Which were done? How well? Which omitted?
> Were the needs of each of the three areas served adequately?
> Were the needs of one area allowed to dominate to the detriment of the task?
>
> Some questions for members:
> Did you feel you were taking part as a team?
> Who was dominating the situation?

Some questions for the leaders:
What have you learnt from the experience?
Repeating the exercise, what would you do differently, and why?

Practical Leadership Tasks

The Practical Leadership Tasks play an important role in ACL. According to John Adair, although these sorts of practical exercise are sometimes referred to as 'Management Games', he tries to avoid calling these games if possible, as it gives some people the wrong idea. The tasks help participants to learn by doing. It is easy to say what a leader should do, or 'what I would do' as a leader in abstract. However, when it comes to the real life situation, leaders often forget everything. This training approach using practical exercises, such as 'The Mast Contract' and 'The Letterpoint' was new in the sixties and early seventies. The method stimulates participants to learn leadership skills. Moreover, such practical exercises allow the participants to see the results or performance of their team, unlike some management case studies, where participants may talk about it and make recommendations, but they can never see the results of their recommendations.

Some of the Practical Leadership Tasks in ACL are as follows: 'The Jigsaw Puzzle', which requires leader and members to develop mutual trust; 'The Letterpoint', which reminds the team that there are certain conditions required to achieve the task; 'The Indivisible Load', which encourages the team to share information to achieve the task; and 'The Mast Contract', which requires the team to make a trade-off to complete the task. These tasks are exciting and the team can see the results of their efforts.

The original ACL Course included the movie 'Twelve O' Clock High'. It may be a good film for its purpose, but participants in Hong Kong found that the English dialogue in the movie was difficult to understand. As a result, we have tried some alternatives, such as *Apollo 13*, a Japanese Cartoon movie, and even a Cantonese Jacky Chan movie. The participants learnt how to observe effective leadership actions in real life situations through such movies.

At the PolyU, I introduce 'Campus Orienteering' to students. The purpose is to help participants to become familiar with the university by locating certain buildings and lecture theatres and finding out some important dates and persons in the university's history. It is a very popular exercise because it gets students out of the classroom. In Hong Kong, we also add a task called 'Toxic'. It was started in the Police Training School, and subsequently, used in scout training. The team is required to search for a bucket of poisonous liquid within a certain area and, once found, send it to a safe place. Any member who touches or stays within one meter of the bucket will be 'killed'. Moreover, the course tutor is reminded to 'kill' the leader once the leader sees the bucket. Often the team does not know what to do after the leader is 'killed'. It teaches a very good lesson: that leaders must fully explain the task to the team and appoint a deputy right from the start, especially in a dangerous operation.

Medium of instruction

At the university, the medium of instruction and the training materials are in English. However, some Chinese students find it difficult to express themselves in a second language. In private organisations, the medium of instruction and the training materials are either in English or Chinese. However, in the Scout Association of Hong Kong the medium of instruction is normally Cantonese and the training materials could be either in English or Chinese. But in the Asia Pacific Region the medium of instruction and the training materials are in English.

Following the tradition of ACL, the course tutors are reminded to collect back all the instructions after each task. We explain to the participants that the task is not difficult if participants are given more time to think and plan. It is only within that short period of time that leadership skill is essential for the success of achieving the task. Participants are very cooperative in returning the instructions to us because the learning process is more important than the task outcome.

The application

Based on the definition provided by Checkland (1985), an application is 'a human activity' that puts theory into practice. In this chapter, the emphasis is put on the implementation of the ACL model in Hong Kong, both in the academic institution and business organisations. It also explains how the ACL model has been introduced in the scout movement, especially in the Asia Pacific Region of the World Scout Bureau.

Application in the Hong Kong Polytechnic University

In 1989 I introduced ACL at PolyU under the theme of 'Training and Development'. The focus was on the course method, such as the use of cue cards and the role of course tutor. In 1998, I designed a new subject called 'People Management Skills'. I managed to introduce the contents of ACL through the exercises of Card Games, Magazines, The Jigsaw Puzzle, The Letterpoint, and The Mast Contract. I also added a new Practical Leadership Task on 'Campus Orienteering' for the students to familiarise with the PolyU Campus. The Leader's Checklist was introduced and the students liked it very much. Subsequently, the subject was renamed 'Developing Management Skills' and again I managed to keep the ACL elements in it. In the past two years, those students who proved that they had attended the last seven sessions of the subject would be awarded an ACL Certificate signed by me. The sessions on 'Use of Time' and 'Creativity at Work' were introduced earlier in the subject. The ACL timetable for 'Developing Management Skills' is listed in Table 11.2.

Besides students in Hong Kong, I have some exchange students from the Chinese mainland, the United States and Europe. They found ACL very useful and reflected on what they had learnt throughout the semester in personal journals. Moreover, I also introduced ACL in a postgraduate course called 'Human Resource Development'. This time, students were professional trainers or human resource practitioners and they gave positive feedback about the ACL experience. I also used the ACL model in the PolyU MBA programme, offered both in Hong Kong and the Chinese mainland. However, because of the time constraints, I could only introduce the three-circle model and one practical leadership task in the residential training.

Adair (1988) contends that, 'At university, the prime aim should be to sow the seeds of leadership and team work'. He adds, 'All university

Table 11.2 The ACL sessions in developing management skills

Session	Lecture (60 mins) or Tutorial (120 mins)	Details
1	Lecture	John Adair and Action-Centred Leadership Motivation: Why People Work? Questionnaire: Needs and Motivation Maslow, McGregor and Herzberg Adair's The Fifty-Fifty Rule
2	Tutorial	The Observer's Code The Observation Sheet Practical Leadership Task 1: Magazines and The Jigsaw Puzzle
3	Lecture	The Nature of Leadership: The Qualities Approach The Situational Approach The Functional Approach
4	Tutorial	Practical Leadership Task 2: The Letterpoint
5	Lecture	The Leader's Action Cycle: Define Objectives, Plan, Brief, Monitor and Evaluate The Leader's Checklist
6	Tutorial	Practical Leadership Task 3: Campus Orienteering
7	Lecture	The Hour-Glass Model Chinese Philosophy on Leadership A Short Course on Leadership

students should have the opportunity for such a course in leadership, communication skills and creative or innovative thinking'. At the PolyU, we are proud to have the opportunity to introduce John Adair's ACL to our students, both undergraduates and postgraduates.

Table 11.3 Organisations that use the ACL model

Private Sector	New World First Ferry Services Limited
	Hong Kong School of Motoring Limited
	Broadway Photo Supplies Limited
	Le Saunders Limited
	Toshiba Electronics Asia Limited
	MC Founders Limited
	Lee Kee Metal Group
	Chu Kong Optical Manufacturing Company Limited
Public Sector	Hong Kong Security and Futures Commission
	Hong Kong SAR Government
Non-profit Sector	Scout Association of Hong Kong

Table 11.4 Timetable for one-day ACL Course

Time	Duration	Details
0900 hrs	15'	Welcome and Purpose
0915	90'	Session One: What is Leadership?
		Practical Leadership Task 1: The Jigsaw Puzzle
1045	15'	Session Two: The Leader's Checklist
		Practical Leadership Task 2: The Letterpoint
1230	60'	Lunch
1330	60'	Session Three: Needs and Motivation
1430	30'	Session Four: Use of Time
1500	15'	Break
1515	45'	Session Five: Leadership Challenge
		Practical Leadership Task 3: Campus Orienteering
1600	30'	Session Six: The Hour-Glass Model
1630	15'	Action Plan
1645	15'	Course Review
1700		End of Course

Application in consultancy projects

Besides introducing ACL on academic courses, I also introduce the model to the business world as a training consultant. Over the past ten years, I have organised ACL Courses for different types of companies and organisations. The names of the organisations that applied the ACL model in their training courses are listed in Table 11.3.

Based on the concepts of ACL, supervisory, leadership and team building workshops are organised to satisfy the needs of companies in different sectors. The timetable for a one-day ACL Course is shown in Table 11.4.

Application in Scout Association of Hong Kong

Adair (1988) recalls his involvement in leadership training in The Scout Association in the UK. He reflects on how he designed and led his first leadership course for patrol leaders in 1955. We now have a 'Patrol Leaders' Training Course' in Hong Kong based on his work. John mentioned to me his working relationship with one of our former Chief Scouts, Michael Walsh, who was an instructor at Sandhurst when functional leadership training was being developed. In The Scout Association, the leadership training syllabus for both the scout leaders (the adult leaders) and patrol leaders (the youth members) is based upon the three-circle model. John Adair also served as a member of the Surrey Scout Association's Council. He is currently acting as adviser on leadership development to the World Organization of the Scout Movement as well as to the Scout Association, a role he has also occupied in relation to the World Girl Guides.

As reported earlier, from 1985 to 1991, The Hong Kong Island Region of the Scout Association of Hong Kong conducted five ACL Courses in Hong Kong. However, it was not adopted as a recognised skill course in our Adult Leader Wood Badge Training Pattern. Not until more than ten years later in October 2004, did the Training Committee of the Scout Association of Hong Kong make ACL a recognised skill course. Thereafter, we organised ACL Courses for both volunteers and professional scout executives. Volunteers are adult leaders while professional scout executives are paid staff of the Scout Movement. Since then, four ACL Courses have been organised. We now need to develop more trainers to be course tutors in ACL Course. Mr J. Hui, who introduced ACL to Hong Kong was appointed as Chief Commissioner of the Scout Association of Hong Kong from 1997 to 2003. He is also a member of the Hong Kong Training Team, and we have already trained up more course tutors in the past few years. A timetable for ACL Course offered by the Scout Association of Hong Kong is depicted in Table 11.5.

The fourth ACL Course, organised by the Scout Association of Hong Kong, was held in June 2005. There were 21 participants in the course and

Table 11.5 Timetable for ACL Course of the Scout Association of Hong Kong

Day One

Time	Duration	Details
1900	10'	Reporting
1910	20'	Opening Remarks & Introduction
1930	60'	Session (1): Define Leadership
2030	15'	Break
2045	60'	Session (2): Practical Leadership Tasks I & II – Cards & The Jigsaw Puzzle
2145	15'	Debriefing/Briefing
2200		Dismiss

Day Two

Time	Duration	Details
1900	10'	Reporting
1910	30'	Session (3): The Leader's Checklist
1940	60'	Session (4): Practical Leadership Task III – The Letterpoint
2040	10'	Break
2050	30'	Session (5): Use of Time
2120	30'	Session (6): Creativity at Work
2150	10'	Debriefing/Briefing
2200		Dismiss

Day Three

Time	Duration	Details
1900	10'	Reporting
1910	90'	Session (7): Practical Leadership Task IV – The Indivisible Load
2040	10'	Break
2050	60'	Session (8): Motivation
2150	10'	Debriefing/Briefing
2200		Dismiss

Day Four

Time	Duration	Details
0900	10'	Reporting
0910	120'	Session (9): Practical leadership Task V – The Excursion
1110	30'	Debriefing/Briefing
1150	60'	Session (10): Practical Leadership Task VI – Site Survey
1250	70'	Lunch
1400	60'	Session (11): Practical Leadership Task VII – The Mast Contract
1500	60'	Session (12): Practical Leadership Task VIII – Toxic
1600	60'	Session (13): Practical Leadership Task IX – Bulk Transport
1700	30'	Session (14): Final Challenge
1730	30'	Course Evaluation
1800		Dismiss

17 of them returned the Course Evaluation Form. They reported that they had improved their behaviours in communication, checking resources, delegation and time management. They would like to have had more case

studies on successful leaders. One suggested that we have different teams working together to achieve an integrated challenging task. They would like to have had Chinese handouts and training materials. Fifteen out of 17 said they would recommend this course to their friends. In general, 53 percent and 35 percent rated the course as 'Excellent' and 'Very Good', respectively. The results were very positive and is indicative of ACL reception in Hong Kong.

Since the introduction of ACL in the UK, the concepts have been transplanted to different parts of the world, including Hong Kong, Canada and Australia. In December 2004, I was elected as Vice Chairman of the Adult Resources Sub-Committee of the Asia Pacific Region (APR) of the World Scout Bureau. In December 2005, I received an email from the Regional Director, Mr Abdullah Rasheed. He told me that the World Scout Bureau invited John Adair to conduct a One-Day Seminar on ACL for all Regional Directors and senior staff at the Geneva Head Office. All scout regions are encouraged to cascade down the ACL model to each national scout organisations. In February 2006, I was invited to introduce the ACL model to the participants of the 46th Asia Pacific Regional Basic Management Course for Professional Scout Executives, hosted by the Thailand Scout Association. There were 46 participants, coming from Thailand, The Philippines, India, Vietnam and Hong Kong.

Contributions of John Adair

Adair (1983) introduces ACL as a self-development leadership programme in which the idea that leadership can be learnt is centrally important. It is difficult to change one's personality in a short training course but it is possible to learn and apply the behaviours of effective leaders. In the same vein, Parks (2005) argues that leadership can be taught and she explains the methods used at the John Kennedy School of Government at Harvard University.

Sadler (1997) comments, 'The ACL program tends to be used primarily for executives in junior or junior to middle level appointments'. But in the same year, Adair (1997) describes three levels of leadership: team leadership (about five to 20 people), operational leadership (a unit in an organisation) and strategic leadership (the whole organisation). Adair (1997) argues that the three circles and eight functions apply at all these levels, albeit in different ways. Adair (2002) introduces the concept of strategic leadership. I agree with John that there can be different levels of leadership. However, to satisfy the needs of leaders at the strategic level, we may have to design some new activities for them. In 2005, I attended an executive programme on 'The Art and Practice of Leadership Development' organised by the John Kennedy School of Government at Harvard University. The programme was led by Marty Linsky and Ronald Heifetz and there were 50 senior executives from different parts of the world attending the programme. We experienced the Case-in-Point Method and found that it was very powerful in developing strategic leaders (see Parks 2005).

Hooper and Potter (2000) highlight two aspects of Adair's contribution: 'first, it led thinking towards the idea of leadership development; and second, it split the "people" aspect into two parts – the team and the individual'.

Despite his long list of publications, with more than 50 books and articles, now in 25 languages, John Adair did not put a full stop in his publication list. His latest book, *How to Grow Leaders* (Adair 2005) has recently been published by Kogan Page. He sets an excellent example as one of the world's leading authorities on leadership. As a Chinese, I am grateful that he accepted an appointment as the first Honorary Professor of Leadership at the China Executive Leadership Academy in Shanghai in 2005. I look forward to having more Chinese translations of his books so that people in that region can learn about leadership in a useful and practical way.

The way forward

Since the sixties, the body of knowledge about leadership has changed a lot. Senge (1990) describes the five core disciplines – that is, personal mastery, mental models, shared vision, team learning and systems thinking – that a leader must master in order to build a learning organisation. Heifetz (1994) differentiates between the concepts of adaptive challenge and technical problems faced by leaders. Subsequently, Heifetz and Linsky (2002) argue that leadership is a dangerous job. In order to survive, leaders must maintain a good relationship with their colleagues and other stakeholders.

Wheatley (1999) explains the relationship between leadership and the new science. Leaders must discover order in a chaotic world. Mintzberg (2004) argues that we should take a hard look at the soft practice of managing and management development. The MBA graduates receive too many theories in management but may not have the skills to put them into practice. ACL can provide a simple and useful tool to management. In the UK, Pedler *et al.* (2004) explain how managers can learn leadership. At the same time, Storey (2004) outlines different ways of introducing leadership development in the real world.

Adair contends that one can be appointed a manager, but one is not a leader until one's appointment is ratified in the hearts and minds of one's subordinates. In Hong Kong, I explain to students that effective leadership is 'getting things done with other people'. There is a distance between the leader and members if it is '*through* other people'; while the working relationship is much closer among leader and members in 'working *with* other people'. In a first aid scouting competition, a judge commented, 'I can spot the leader in the St. John's Ambulance Brigade Team because the leader shouts the instruction to his team members. However, it is more difficult to guess the leader in the Scout Association of Hong Kong Team because they are all working together quietly'.

In contrast to the western style of leadership, the Chinese philosopher Lao Tzu (600 BC) asserted that a leader is best when people barely know that he exists, not so good when people obey and acclaim him, worst when they despise him. As he said, 'Fail to honor people, they fail to honor you,' and of a good leader, who talks little, when his work is done people will say, 'We did it ourselves'.

Back in the eighties, Hodgkinson (1983) argued for the importance of exploring the philosophy of leadership. However, there was not much response to his call. Mak (2000) outlines three elements of Chinese philosophy on leadership. First, make your members feel happy. If not, they might go elsewhere. Second, your members can support you or overthrow you, just like water can float a boat and it can also capsize a boat. And third, lead members with virtue and they will support you, just like the Polar Star in the sky, surrounded by all other stars. Unlike the western idea that the leader must possess technical knowledge in a specific context, the Chinese expect leaders to accomplish things through virtue.

Adair (1973b) admits that, 'Certainly ACL is not a panacea, a cure-all or a substitute for high standards in other aspects of the practice of management. Yet if both ACL theory and methods are thoroughly understood and interpreted imaginatively in terms of a particular organizational setting, this kind of leadership training has a valuable contribution to make to management development'. It is worth bearing in mind Adair's fundamental point, 'one cannot teach leadership – it can only be learnt' (Adair 1968).

Notes

1   In a recent personal communication regarding accreditation, John explained, 'True then, but in order to prevent distortions in my work and misuse of my intellectual property, I do now expect ACL trainers to be accredited by the Adair Leadership Foundation'.
2   These three dimensions were later synthesised by Adair (1984b).

References

Adair, J. (1968) *Training for Leadership*, London: Macdonald.
Adair, J. (1971) *Training for Decisions*, London: Macdonald.
Adair, J. (1973a) *Training for Communication*, London: Macdonald.
Adair, J. (1973b) *Action-Centred Leadership*, Maidenhead: McGraw-Hill.
Adair, J. (1983) *Effective Leadership: A Self-Development Manual*, London: Pan.
Adair, J. (1984a) *Training for Leadership: A Tutor's Manual*, London: BACIE.
Adair, J. (1984b) *The Skills of Leadership*, Aldershot: Gower.
Adair, J. (1987) *How to Manage Your Time*, Guildford: Talbot Adair.
Adair, J. (1988) *Developing Leaders*, Guildford: Talbot Adair.

Adair, J. (1990) *Understanding Motivation*, Guildford: Talbot Adair.

Adair, J. (1997) *Leadership Skills*, London: CIPD.

Adair, J. (2002) *Effective Strategic Leadership*, London: Macmillan.

Adair, J. (2005) *How to Grow Leaders*, London: Kogan Page.

Argyris, C. (1993) *Knowledge for Action*, San Francisco: Jossey-Bass.

Casey, D. and Pearce, D. (eds) (1977) *More than Management Development: Action Learning at GEC*, Farnborough: Gower.

Checkland, P.B. (1985) 'From optimizing to learning: A development of systems thinking for the 1990s', *Journal of Operational Research Society*, 36(9), 757–67.

Heifetz, R.A. (1994) *Leadership Without Easy Answers*, Cambridge: Harvard University Press.

Heifetz, R.A. and Linsky, M. (2002) *Leadership on the Line: Staying Alive through the Dangers of Leading*, Boston: Harvard Business School Press.

Hodgkinson, C. (1983) *The Philosophy of Leadership*, Oxford: Basil Blackwell.

Hooper, A. and Potter, J. (2000) *Intelligent Leadership: Creating a Passion for Change*, London: Random House.

Kennedy, C. (1991) *Instant Management: The Best Ideas from the People who have made a Difference in How We Manage*, New York: William Morrow.

Kets de Vries, M. (1995) *Life and Death in the Executive Fast Lane*, San Francisco: Jossey-Bass.

Kolb, D. (1983) *Experiential Learning: Experience as the Source of Learning and Development*, Englewood Cliff: Prentice Hall.

Krouwel, B. and Goodwill, S. (1994) *Management Development Outdoors: A Practical Guide to Getting the Best Results*, London: Kogan Page.

Liu, S.H. (1984) 'A view from the past', *South China Morning Post*, 20 July 1984.

Mak, W.M. (1991) Developing voluntary trainers for quality training, paper presented to the *IDPM International Conference*, organised by the Institute for Development Policy and Management at the University of Manchester, Manchester, 25 to 28 June 1991.

Mak, W.M. (2000) 'The Tao of people-based management', *Total Quality Management*, 11(4/5&6), 537–43.

Mintzberg, H. (2004) *Managers and MBAs: A Hard Look at the Soft Practice of Managing and Management Development*, London: Prentice Hall/Financial Times.

Parks, S.D. (2005) *Leadership Can Be Taught: A Bold Approach for a Complex World*, Boston: Harvard Business School Press.

Pedler, M., Burgoyne, J. and Boydell, T. (2004) *A Manager's Guide to Leadership*, London: McGraw-Hill.

Potter, J. and Hooper, A. (2005) *Developing Strategic Leadership Skills*, London: CIPD.

Sadler, P. (1997) *Leadership*, London: Kogan Page.

Senge, P.M. (1990) *The Fifth Discipline: The Art and Practice of the Learning Organization*, New York: Doubleday/Currency.

Storey, J. (ed.) (2004) *Leadership in Organizations: Current Issues and Key Trends*, London: Routledge.

van Maurik, J. (2001) *Writers on Leadership*, London: Penguin.

Wheatley, M.J. (1999) *Leadership and the New Science: Discovering Order in a Chaotic World*, 2nd edn, San Francisco: Berrett-Koehler.

Part IV
Summing Up

12
The Forward View

John Adair

> *Full lasting is the song; though he*
> *The singer passes; lasting too, be*
> *For souls not lent in usury,*
> *The rapture of the forward view.*
> Meredith

The provenance and purpose of this book are academic ones. It is a 'recon-naissance in strength' into the contributions – such as they are – that I have made to the field of Leadership Studies. As one of my principal concerns has been to establish Leadership Studies as a form of scholarship, I should like to round off this enjoyable and thought-provoking book by offering you some reflections and pointers for the future of Leadership Studies as an academic pursuit.

First, to define the terms. The original 'academy', of course, was the garden, grove or gymnasium near Athens where Plato taught and founded a school in the 4th century BC. He named it after a legendary military leader of the Trojan war, *Akademos*. Later *academy* became a general name for a society or institution for the advancement of literature, art or science. The academy in question could be a place of study or training in a special field, such as an academy of dance. The Royal Military Academy Sandhurst, the China Executive Leadership Academy and the Tesco Academy are examples of such places and their staffs, strictly speaking, are academics. You can see why I prefer the wider term *specialist* to *academic*.

The noun *academic* in English today, however always refers to a teacher or scholar in a university or institute of higher education. As well as obviously referring to an academy, the adjectival form *academic* has acquired the overtones of theoretical, scholarly, abstract and unpractical. In the most pejorative sense of the word an *academic* is perceived to be someone who may be knowledgeable in their subject but they are inexperienced and out of touch with the world of practical reality. To say 'that is academic' means that is theoretical but without any immediate or practical bearing or useful significance.

Academe, the poetic word used by Shakespeare and Milton to refer to the university environment has now become the rather more prosaic *academia*. It's a useful term. It reminds us that every profession has its sociology; those who live and work together in the environment of academia, tend to acquire the same professional traits, ethos, values and methods. Doubtless an occupational sociologist would also be able to trace subcultures in the particular academic disciplines, like Chemistry, History, Psychology or Sociology itself.

Turning now to Leadership Studies – a phrase I coined in 1979 when I created the world's first Professorship at Surrey University. At that time Leadership Studies was not much more than a convenient phrase, a blank canvas in my mind. I was not asked to define it or to teach it. The received wisdom of the time at Surrey was that academically speaking leadership was merely a chapter-heading in the textbook of Psychology. Thus I was placed in the Department of Psychology, where I spent the next five years.

While I was at Surrey my main occupation was thinking, writing books and working experimentally – notably in my pioneering of a leadership development strategy in ICI with Sir John Harvey Jones. But I did initiate leadership training for engineering students, and later for university heads of departments and vice-chancellors (see Chapter 8, Leading the Way in Higher Education, pp.124–45). And I continued to lead and support this work for a further six years as Visiting Professor in Leadership Studies.

The idea of founding Leadership Studies at a university initially, in the form of a postgraduate degree, must have been forming in my depth mind. For in September 1990 I mentioned the idea to a friend whose path I crossed in Birmingham where I was presenting the prizes at the National Quality Standards Conference. Howard Betts suggested that Exeter University might be interested, and – cutting the story short – that led to my meeting and subsequent partnership with Alan Hooper and his team – including Howard – in first developing and then delivering over ten years the world's first Diploma/Master postgraduate degree in Leadership Studies. The 12 outstanding people on the first course and their response to our programme convinced me that Leadership Studies had a future in academia.

The next step was already in my mind: to establish an institute or centre for advanced Leadership Studies. In 1991 the editor of *The Times Higher Educational Supplement* invited me to review an important book by a New Zealander called Gary McCulloch, entitled *Philosophers and Kings: Education for leadership in modern England* (1991). It was based on his doctoral dissertation and demonstrated the contribution that scholarly historical research could make to my field. The editor invited me to use the review to make my wider case for Leadership Studies in the context of the university. In an article (26 September 1991) which was headed 'John Adair on the need for an Institute of Leadership Studies', I concluded:

> The time is now ripe for a new initiative in the field of Leadership Studies in Britain. We need an Institute of Leadership. It would provide a focus for the research already being conducted at such Universities as Aston, Surrey and Cranfield, as well as at some of the more forward-looking management centres, notably Ashridge College. At present, in disciplinary fields and in different sectors of higher education, this research seems to be uncoordinated; it does not as yet represent a major thrust in the area of leadership. Industry and other major fields of human enterprise also need a 'centre of excellence' in the leadership development field: a place to find resources of knowledge, advanced programmes for specialists and help from independent consultants.
>
> Perhaps above all such an institute would both stimulate and contribute to the mounting debates in industry, the public services, the National Health Service, secondary school education and higher education itself, debates concerning the nature of leadership appropriate in such environments and how such effective and appropriate leadership can be best developed.
>
> As a nation we do need to think deeply and clearly about the nature of leadership at its different levels and 'education for leadership' – its content and its methods, the relation of principles or ideas to practical experience, and the interwoven parts to be played by school, further and higher education. In wise societies this is a matter not left to chance. We must give more attention to how to develop good leaders – and leaders for good.

In 1996 the University of Exeter on my prompting decided to establish such a Centre for Leadership Studies. The Vice-Chancellor Sir Geoffrey Holland, Alan Hooper as Founding Director and myself, working as a team, then set about planning and raising funds for the project. During that gestation period I gave an open lecture to the University, chaired by Sir Geoffrey, in which I explained why Leadership Studies merited acceptance as a subject worthy of a University. By its very nature, I argued, it could not properly be studied in the confines of a Business School.

By this date the name Leadership Studies had been picked up and used in America. In 1993, for example, the Jepson Centre for Leadership Studies at the University of Richmond was founded with an endowment of some 20 million dollars and a staff which included eight professors. Unlike Exeter its focus was on teaching undergraduates.

Today Leadership Studies is established like a bridgehead in academia on both sides of the Atlantic and elsewhere – there is, for example, a

Centre for Leadership Studies in New Zealand and one in South Africa. In Britain there are several university centres, leadership MBAs, research conferences, an academic journal, several professors with 'leadership' in their designations, and a growing number of younger academics who see it as their principal field.

Leadership Studies is still a young and relatively immature subject: no-one can wave a magic wand and create a new academic subject just like that. It has to find its own way and establish its own identity, which will be distinct from the various academic disciplines – Psychology, Social Psychology, History, Philosophy, Sociology and Pedagogy – which have contributed to it. Not easy as Psychology in particular still claims all or part of the territory as its own.

The struggle for independence, identity and direction – especially in the area of research – will be a long and hard one. Nor is it going to be easy to develop 'scholar-practitioners' – to borrow an American term – who are not academic in the pejorative sense. For you cannot do Leadership Studies – which is a branch of Practical Philosophy – if you are interested only in theory and not at all in practice. It would be like trying to study pharma-cology – the study of drugs and medicines – but leaving out any knowledge to whether or not the drugs worked, or in what conditions they were efficacious, or what might constitute misuse. You need to know if the white pill in the gift-wrapped box is an aspirin or a placebo. Does it work and if so why?

With globalisation and the advent of the internet, Leadership Studies is ceasing to be a parochial subject, mainly pursued – albeit very differently – in Britain and the United States, and hardly anywhere else. It is about to become global and this factor will eventually transform it into what it should have been from the beginning. A common history and a shared knowledge, rooted in the world's rich traditions, gives it unity and harmony.

This world badly needs 'good leaders and leaders for good' – at all levels – in communities, organisations, nations and in supranational organisations. In this context Leadership Studies as I have pioneered it has a key role to play in that story. But will it ever fulfil that role? Will it discover its vocation? Can we evolve and sustain a global leadership development strategy? Will we see a hundred Xenophons in 15 years time – leader-teachers who can take forward this intensely practical and relevant subject?

I can only bequeath my vision to you. Will it ever begin to be realised? I can only answer in Arabic, *Insha'llah*, God willing. But you and I have to do our part. For we do not read the Future from some prewritten script – we are called to create it. 'As for the Future' wrote Saint-Exupery in *The Wisdom of the Sands* (1948), 'your task is not to foresee, but to enable it'.

References

McCulloch, Gary (1991) *Philosophers and Kings: Education for Leadership in Modern England,* Cambridge: Cambridge UP.

Saint-Exupery, Antoine Jean Baptiste Roger de (1952) *The Wisdom of the Sands,* trans. Stuart Gilbert, London: Hollis and Carter.

Index